Desolation Sound

The frost-shattered peak of Mount Denman dominates Desolation Sound.

Desolation Sound

A HISTORY

Heather Harbord

HARBOUR PUBLISHING

Harbour Publishing Co. Ltd.
P.O. Box 219
Madeira Park, BC V0N 2H0
www.harbourpublishing.com

Cover painting, *I Name This Place Desolation Sound*, by John M. Horton (detail).
All photographs by the author unless otherwise indicated.
Maps by Roger Handling, Terra Firma Digital Arts.
Printed and bound in Canada.

Harbour Publishing acknowledges financial support from the Government of Canada through the Book Publishing Industry Development Program and the Canada Council for the Arts, and from the Province of British Columbia through the BC Arts Council and the Book Publishing Tax Credit.

THE CANADA COUNCIL | LE CONSEIL DES ARTS
FOR THE ARTS | DU CANADA
SINCE 1957 | DEPUIS 1957

BRITISH
COLUMBIA
ARTS COUNCIL
Supported by the Province of British Columbia

Library and Archives Canada Cataloguing in Publication

Harbord, Heather, 1939–
    Desolation Sound : a history / Heather Harbord.

Includes bibliographical references and index.
ISBN 978-1-55017-407-6

    1. Desolation Sound Region (B.C.)—History. 2. Desolation Sound Region (B.C.)—Biography. I. Title.

FC3845.D47H37 2007   971.1'31   C2007-900092-4

To Maria Zaikow,
who started the whole process

CONTENTS

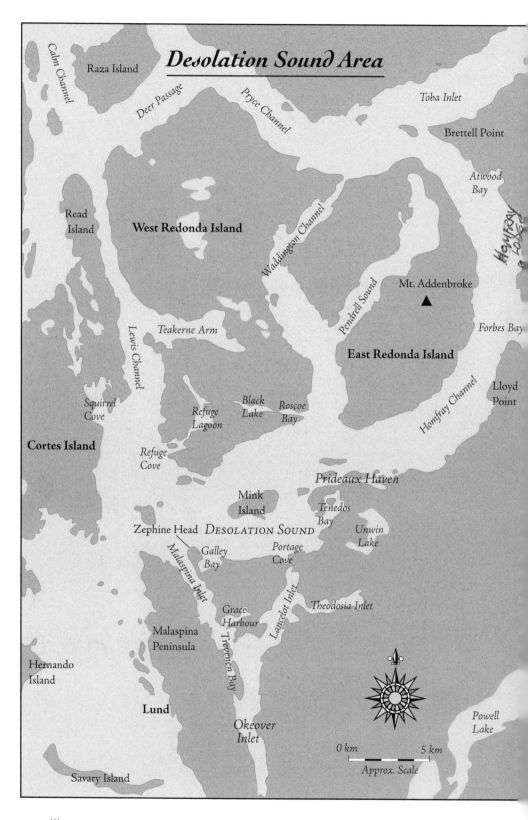

Desolation Sound Area

Calm Channel

Raza Island

Deer Passage

Pryce Channel

Toba Inlet

Brettell Point

Atwood Bay

Read Island

West Redonda Island

Waddington Channel

Pendrell Sound

Mt. Addenbroke

▲

Forbes Bay

Homfray Channel

East Redonda Island

Teakerne Arm

Lewis Channel

Squirrel Cove

Refuge Lagoon

Black Lake

Roscoe Bay

Lloyd Point

Cortes Island

Refuge Cove

Prideaux Haven

Mink Island

Tenedos Bay

Unwin Lake

Zephine Head DESOLATION SOUND

Galley Bay

Portage Cove

Malaspina Inlet

Grace Harbour

Lancelot Inlet

Theodosia Inlet

Malaspina Peninsula

Treven Bay

Hernando Island

Lund

Okeover Inlet

Powell Lake

0 km   5 km
Approx. Scale

Savary Island

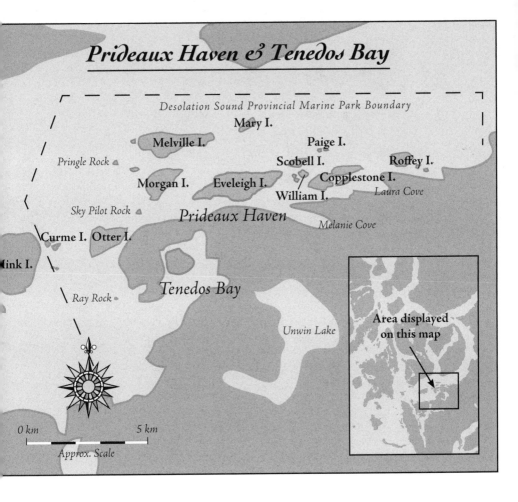

Prideaux Haven & Tenedos Bay

Desolation Sound Provincial Marine Park Boundary

Mary I.

Melville I.

Paige I.

Pringle Rock

Scobell I.

Roffey I.

Morgan I.

Eveleigh I.

Copplestone I.

William I.

Laura Cove

Sky Pilot Rock

Prideaux Haven

Melanie Cove

Curme I. Otter I.

Mink I.

Ray Rock

Tenedos Bay

Unwin Lake

Area displayed on this map

0 km   5 km

Approx. Scale

DESOLATION SOUND
SETTLEMENTS LEGEND

1. McCauleys
2. Heatleys, 1915 pre-emption
3. Heatley homestead, 1920–32
4. Jensens
5. Ahpookwum Village
6. Archie Stewart
7. Lindberg Brothers
8. Squirrel Cove Village
9. McGuffies
10. Blacks & Stanifords
11. Christensens
12. Tredcroft Brothers
13. John Bunyan Scott
14. Thompsons
15. Smiths, Tindalls, Hopes &
    Refuge Cove Coop
16. Saulter & Pritchard
17. Phil Lavigne,
18. Mike Shuttler
19. Will Palmer family
20. Hansons & Galley Bay School
21. Heatleys homestead, 1932–44
22. Copeland, Bristers, Finches, Day
23. Bishops & Parkers
24. Toquana Village
25. James Palmer family
26. Kahkaykay Village
27. Jones
28. Ed Berglund
29. Crowthers
30. Tux'wnech Village
31. Roos
32. D'Angios
33. Vaughns
34. Chambers

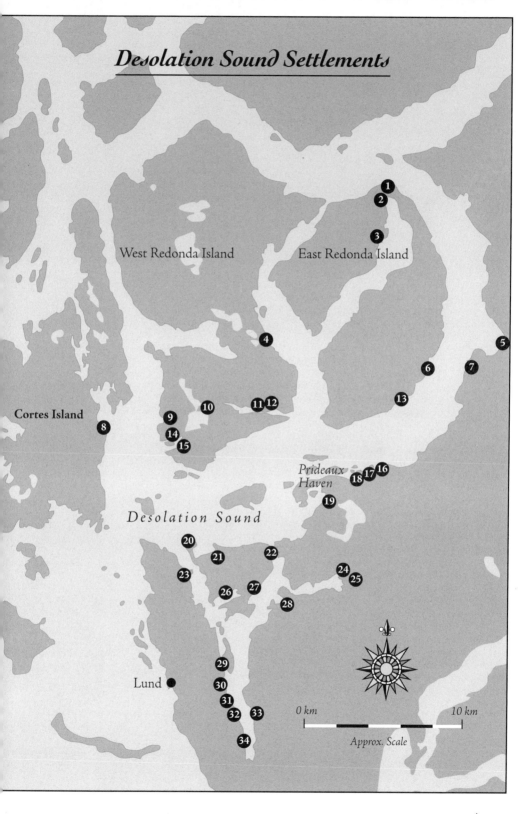

Desolation Sound Settlements

West Redonda Island

East Redonda Island

Cortes Island

Prideaux
Haven

Desolation Sound

Lund

0 km   10 km

Approx. Scale

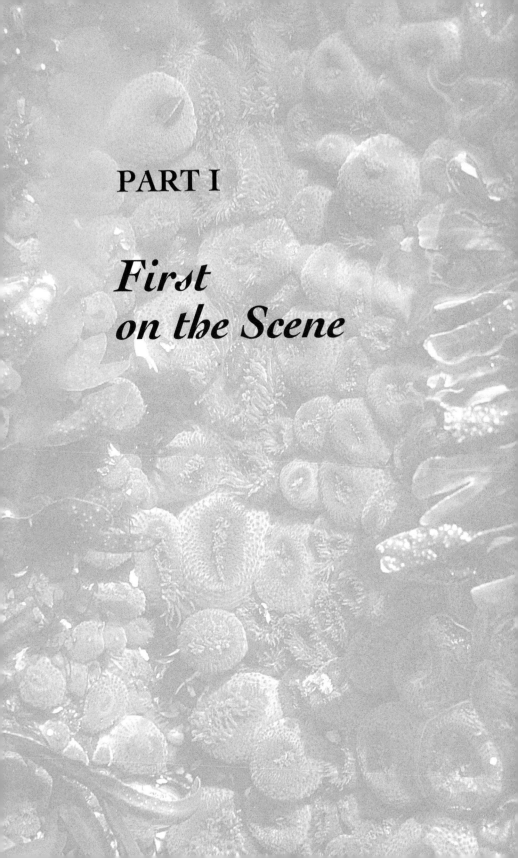

PART I

First on the Scene

1

DESOLATION SOUND

A Sense of the Place

Desolation Sound is famed far and wide as one of the must-see destinations along the Inside Passage, but more people hear of it than actually get to visit. It is 160 kilometres (100 miles) northwest of Vancouver, British Columbia, and few roads penetrate its rugged physical beauty. Only by boat can you explore most of its winding inlets or travel into Prideaux Haven, the central jewel of hidden coves and tiny islets. Much of the area is park or ecological reserve. Except for the residents of Okeover Arm, very few people live here all year round.

Captain George Vancouver, the British explorer, is responsible for giving Desolation Sound its unflattering name. In his defence, it was "dark and rainy" the night he arrived, June 25, 1792.[1] During the two weeks he was in the area, he complained, even his second anchorage in Teakerne Arm "afforded not a single prospect that was pleasing to the eye, the smallest recreation on shore, nor animal nor vegetable food . . ." Ironic words to describe a place that would become the most popular recreational boating destination on the BC coast, and which in those days teemed with shellfish and salmon, but Captain Vancouver was a typical European of the eighteenth century. He preferred the gentler terrain along the eastern shore of Vancouver Island, which more closely resembled the civilized landscape of the Old Country. Some of the women whose stories are told in the following chapters also thought the place desolate, but it was a paradise for eccentric bachelors. The people of the Sliammon First Nation, who lived here for millennia, viewed their territory as a land of plenty. Its abundant cedar trees supplied them with housing, transportation and clothing, while tasty clams and salmon provided food.

George Vancouver's Desolation Sound included all of the area between Sarah Point and the mouth of Bute Inlet, but on today's marine chart, Desolation Sound encompasses the water between Sarah Point and Horace Head on East Redonda Island. In this book, I include both Redonda Islands, Homfray Channel, Desolation Sound and the three inlets that flow into Malaspina Inlet. I chose these boundaries because they reflect the community that existed during the heyday of white settlement in the first half of the twentieth century, when all of the people who lived within these limits collected their mail at the Refuge Cove Store on West Redonda Island.

On sunny days the pink centres of green aggregating anemones provide a splash of colour across the warm rocks.

Most visitors approach from the south. As you round Sarah Point, Desolation Sound opens up in front of you, ending in a wall of high, rounded mountains that are part of the Coast Range running all the way to Alaska. Tens of thousands of years ago, mighty glaciers smoothed their rough peaks—except for the summit of Mount Denman, which stood alone above the ice. Again and again it was shattered by frost till only the present horn was left.

As the glaciers retreated, they left traces still visible today. High up in the mountains above Lloyd Point, a round-bottomed valley once held a glacier. The valley looks as if it has been cut in half, leaving one half in place and nothing of the other. This is known as a hanging valley.

Glaciers flowing over exposed rock outcrops either scraped or polished them. The big boulder at the end of Copplestone Island, facing into Laura Cove, is an example. It features in the story of Phil Lavigne's goat, to come later.

The meltwater from the glaciers drowned the maze of valleys they had carved, creating a labyrinth of waterways edged by steep-sided mountains. Mount Addenbroke on East Redonda Island rises to 1,590 metres (5,247 feet), but within 7.6 kilometres (4.5 miles), the seabed has dropped 726 metres (2,396 feet) to the depths of Homfray Channel. There are not many places on the British Columbia coast where this happens in quite such a short distance. Beaches are few and rocky.

Where the sea ends, the trees begin. The most common are red cedar, Douglas fir and western hemlock, as well as scattered alder and arbutus. The latter is near its northern limit.[2] There are few hiking opportunities except for short trails at a handful of anchorages, where you see the rainforest up close. Over a hundred species of moss blanket trail, trees and rock. Watch you don't step on a Pacific banana slug emerging from a fern frond. These ubiquitous creatures come in assorted shades of green, with and without black spots, and can grow to twenty-six centimetres (10.5 inches) long. Listen for a drum roll high up in the forest canopy. That's the pileated woodpecker, a large black bird with a spectacular scarlet beret.

Back on the water, pairs of tiny birds, brown in summer and black and white in winter, will dive as soon as you get too close for their comfort. These are the famous marbled murrelets, whose nests are so well hidden high up in the nearby Bunster Hills that they were not discovered until the 1970s.[3] They lay their eggs and raise their young in slight depressions on the wide, mossy branches of old-growth trees. Spending most of their lives at sea, they are poor at coming in to land, so the nest branch has to be easily accessible from their flight path and wide enough for them to crash-land on it. In addition, it must be sheltered from rain by the upper branches of the forest canopy. The murrelets' behaviour is under constant study.

Bald eagles sit on snags at regular intervals, their white heads shining against the dark forest. Listen for their high-pitched "weep, weep" call. Fish are their favourite food, but now that stocks have been depleted, the birds have turned to other prey such as gulls, ducks and small land animals. Consequently, you rarely see mink running along the shore any more, and fishery regulations severely limit your own catch of ling or rock cod and salmon.

In the water, harbour seals are common. They haul out in large numbers on Pringle Rock at the mouth of Prideaux Haven and on Ray Rock near Tenedos Bay. If you're lucky, you'll see a small pod of orca or killer whales surfacing, or even a rare humpback whale or pod of Pacific white-sided dolphins. In April, you may see thousands of surf scoters gathering in Waddington Channel before they fly north to their

The engaging antics of generations of river otters have entertained everyone from First Nations warriors to modern vacationers.

*Steller's sea lions are often seen passing through Desolation Sound. Long ago, First Nations
warriors preparing for feasts cooked them in buried ovens lined with seaweed.*

7

breeding grounds in Alaska, the Yukon and the Northwest Territories. Their wings make a lovely whirring sound as they rise in clouds when you get too close.

Although most rain falls in winter, savvy boaters recalling George Vancouver's experience bring clothes for cool, wet weather as well as sunny and hot at any time of year. Temperatures average 18°C to 23°C (59°F to 73°F) in summer and range from 0°C to 5°C (32°F to 41°F) in winter.

Especially in summer, the sun heats the land, causing air to blow up the inlets during the day and down them at night. The hotter the temperature, the stronger the winds. The same thing happens in winter, with the added hazard that cold air from the interior of the province comes rushing out, especially down Bute Inlet and over the Redonda Islands.

Once I spent three hours paddling the eight nautical miles from Tenedos Bay to Galley Bay against an inflow wind. The water was so warm that I wasn't uncomfortable, but I was bored. If the tide had been low and the waves less rambunctious, I'd have been able to amuse myself by staying close to the rocks to search the seaweed for the telltale scarlet of a blood or vermilion sea star.

If you're sailing, you'll want to take advantage of these inflow and outflow winds to speed your passage. In these relatively sheltered waters so far from the open ocean, they will often affect you more than the prevailing northwesterly winds of summer or the southeasters of winter.

Depending on the type of boat you are in, tides may also affect your ability to travel. The strong tide races are all north of here, so they are not a problem. The two great tidal streams of the coast meet just south of Desolation Sound. One flows round the northern tip of Vancouver Island and down Johnstone Strait, and the other flows round the south and up the Strait of Georgia. This means that the waters in and near Desolation Sound tend to stay around instead of flowing away. Consequently, in summer the water heats up to about 23°C (73°F) in sheltered places like Pendrell Sound, which is good for swimmers and oyster growers.

As you visit Desolation Sound in the twenty-first century, imagine the people who were here before you. For millennia, First Nations lived in the area. The European explorers Vancouver, Galiano and Valdés came in 1792. Settlers started arriving in the 1890s to harvest the trees or fish, search for minerals or escape the madding crowd, and throughout the twentieth century there were travellers who became famous for written accounts of their visits.

Perhaps the best remembered of these is M. Wylie Blanchet, author of *The Curve of Time*. In 1891 she was born Muriel Liffiton to a wealthy Quebec family of High Anglican principles. As a child, Blanchet horrified the retired clergyman who tutored her and her two sisters by carrying live squirrels and mice in her pockets. When she was eighteen, she married Geoffrey Blanchet, a banker from Ottawa. He retired early because of poor health, and he moved his wife and four children to Vancouver Island. There he bought an old house on seven acres at Curteis Point near Swartz Bay. One more child was born here.

Tragedy struck in 1927 when Geoffrey's boat was found off Knapp

After her husband drowned, Capi Blanchet rented out the house and took her children sailing from May to October. They spent many summers in Desolation Sound during the 1920s and 1930s. L to R: Francis, Peter, Betty, David, Joan and Capi. COURTESY RICHARD BLANCHET

L to R: *David, Capi, Peter and Joan (in shorts) aboard* Caprice *during one of their summer trips.* COURTESY RICHARD BLANCHET

Amy and Francis Barrow were married in 1906 and started cruising in their newly built power boat, Toketie, *around that time. They continued till 1941. They played crib with the locals, bought vegetables and meat from them, looked for Indian artifacts and pictographs. Francis kept a diary but only 1926–41 survived a garbage fire.* HARBOUR PUBLISHING ARCHIVES

Island and he was presumed drowned. His widow's small income was insufficient for the family's needs, so for fifteen years she rented out the house from June to October and took the family cruising in the Strait of Georgia and up into Johnstone Strait. Desolation Sound was one of their favourite places. Their summer home was *Caprice*, an eight-metre (twenty-five-foot) powerboat.

By this time, Capi, as she preferred to be called, was a competent mariner and mechanic. For twenty years she regularly took *Caprice's* four-cylinder Kermath engine apart, repainted it and re-ground the valves. She may have learned this skill from a Scottish engineer who was a mechanic at the Canoe Cove boat works, near their home on Vancouver Island. He also taught math, chemistry and physics to her three youngest children, whom she home-schooled.

Long before shorts were fashionable for women, Blanchet wore them along with a khaki shirt, a Cowichan sweater[4] and old running shoes, often with holes in the toes. Her eldest daughter said that "she could do almost anything that men did and still be feminine . . . She used to get a bit tense if we were taking green water over the bow or wallowing about in a following sea or running the Yuculta Rapids. Otherwise she took everything in her stride."[5]

While on the water, Blanchet continued the children's education by reading Vancouver's journals aloud to them. She then wrote about their reactions to the places described and the adventures they had. *The Curve of Time*, her dreamlike account of their voyages, has become a Canadian classic.

A quarter century older than Blanchet, Amy and Francis Barrow started cruising after their marriage in 1906, but their 1926–1941 journals are all that were salvaged from a garbage fire by one of Francis's employees. Their boat, *Toketie*, was built in 1903 or 1904 at the Dafoe Machine Works in Vancouver. It was eight metres (twenty-six feet) long, 2.2 metres (seven feet, three inches) wide and drew 1.1 metres (three feet two inches).[6] By the 1930s it was powered by a four-cylinder Universal gasoline screw engine. *Toketie* was still cruising in 1985 under the name *Merlin*.

As they cruised, the Barrows recorded descriptions and locations of the mysterious petroglyphs and pictographs that predate contemporary First Nations' legends. They would also jot down snippets about the area and its inhabitants that, along with Blanchet's vignettes, add to our knowledge of the characters who lived in Desolation Sound. Their journals have been published in the book *Upcoast Summers*, edited by Beth Hill, who wrote about her own journeys in the Sound in the 1960s.

The colourful characters who flocked to settle in Desolation Sound chose it for its remoteness and because they could live off the land. Andrew (Mike) Shuttler, James Palmer, Joe Copeland and their contemporaries all yearned to get away from the evils of civilization. Later arrivals, like the Christensen, Crowther and Parker families, needed to eke out a living during the Great Depression of the 1930s. Although they grew their own vegetables and meat, they were cash poor, so if there was a logging show close by, they would take whatever work they could get. Sometimes the men went away to work in more distant logging camps or even in Vancouver, and sometimes they worked on their own handlogging licences away from their homesteads, as Axel Hanson did.

The population peaked in the 1930s and 1940s, and Refuge Cove became a thriving supply centre. The decline began in 1958, when the destruction of dreaded Ripple Rock, a treacherous marine hazard, made Discovery Channel safer for shipping. Instead of chugging up Lewis Channel and calling in for supplies at the Refuge Cove store, marine traffic now preferred to follow the Vancouver Island coast to Campbell River and Johnstone Strait. At the same time, large logging companies began to supplant the small gyppo loggers who had been the backbone of the local economy. The companies provided transportation for their own workers, and the federal government withdrew its subsidy of the Union Steamships and other shipping companies that had supplied the area, bringing an end to regular freight and passenger service.

Generating cash was an ongoing problem affecting the settlers. Land taxes increased, and people like the D'Angios and the Chamberses lost their Crown-granted lots. The sixties brought a brief influx of back-to-the-landers, including two hippie colonies that did not last. Homesteads in many coves fell silent as the rainforest reclaimed them.

In 1973, the government of BC established Desolation Sound Marine Park. Several satellite parks, along with the ecological reserve on East Redonda, now occupy much of the remaining land. Human settlement has been relegated largely to the Okeover and Refuge Cove areas, while First Nations people have retreated to Squirrel Cove on Cortes Island and Sliammon Village near Lund. Today, Desolation Sound comes alive mainly in the summer, as vacationers return again and again. In July and August the anchorages in Prideaux Haven, Tenedos Bay, Galley Bay and Grace Harbour are packed with sailboats, powerboats, kayaks and canoes. Everyone wants to experience the legendary sheltered coves and warm waters at first hand.

2

FIRST NATIONS
Getting Along with Nature
and Each Other

*L*ong ago, in the far mists of time, anarchy reigned in Desolation Sound. Fierce winds whipped the water into a white froth, rugged cliffs repelled those seeking to enter the mountain strongholds, and cannibal monsters roamed the forests, preying on people from the villages. Unlike the human beings of today, the villagers often had animal names and animal characteristics. They fought bravely against their oppressors, transforming them into rocks and trees, which are still visible today, as well as insects, birds, fish and animals. Little by little the villagers created an orderly land in which human beings could live.

Three people introduced me to this ancient Salish world. The late Chief Joe Mitchell was a short, stocky man who emanated a wonderful air of kindly authority. He was deeply respected in the community and beyond. In September 1999, when I profiled him for the "Powell River People" column that I wrote for the *Powell River News*, he was a traditional advisor to the Sliammon First Nation.

Three months earlier, I had featured Joe's sister, the late Sue Pielle, in the same column, and her story had added to my knowledge of Sliammon culture and heritage. A beloved grandmother to more than just her own family, she was also a popular teacher in the public school system and on the reserve. Many people, both Native and non-Native, learned basket weaving and other Native crafts from her. All enjoyed her traditional stories.

Joe's nephew, Murray Mitchell, is knowledgeable and enthusiastic about his heritage. As the twenty-first century dawned, he was running eco-tours from Lund to Desolation Sound, using a replica of a traditional Nootka canoe to transport tourists into his ancient homeland. (In the old days, Nuh-chah-nulth builders traded such canoes to the Salish in exchange for eulachon grease and other items. Salish canoes were smaller and lacked the high bow and stern that enabled the Nootka craft to handle rougher waters.) In addition to taking his guests for a paddle and treating them to a traditional salmon bake, Mitchell showed them some of the medicinal plants his people used.

All three of these people drew heavily on their memories of their parents and grandparents, Chief Billy and Rose Mitchell of Squirrel Cove. By their own example and through endless stories, the elder Mitchells carefully passed down the traditions of their people as they themselves had received them.

Although modern anthropologists recognize that such traditional teaching can preserve knowledge of events that occurred many centuries

Chief Julius and his wife display a fine catch of coho. With no roads the canoe was a practical means of transportation. UBC. RARE BOOKS AND SPECIAL COLLECTIONS/JIM SPILSBURY FONTS/ALBUM BCI938/3

*Murray Mitchell used this replica Nootka canoe to give tourists a flavour of Desolation
Sound. Here they haul the canoe ashore before setting up a salmon BBQ.*

ago, Desolation Sound contains artifacts that predate even these memories. In a few places, passing boaters may notice ochre-coloured pictographs (rock paintings) and petroglyphs (drawings incised in the rock).
No one is sure of their significance, but Murray Mitchell thinks the por-
poise pictograph in Thulin Passage may have marked a fishing boundary.[7] Almost all pictographs are at the same height above sea level—as
if they were all done by a person standing in a canoe at high tide. Some
show stick men, others are just smudges.

While uncertainty shrouds the pictographs and petroglyphs, many
Sliammon legends are linked to clearly visible physical features. For example, in some places on the coast there are striations that were produced
when stones on the underside of glaciers scraped across the surface of
the rocks. In other places, including the Redonda Islands and in Lancelot Inlet, there are irregularly shaped black spots, called xenoliths. These
are small pieces of lower, older layers of rock that liquid magma from
the earth's mantle carried to the surface when it intruded into cracks and
cavities of the overlying rock.

Chief Joe Mitchell told me the Sliammon explanation for these
phenomena, which is contained in the story of the battle between the

This pictograph in Homfray Channel has faded since it was photographed by Jim
Spilsbury. Some say pictographs mark good fishing spots but they are so old that no one
really knows. UBC. RARE BOOKS AND SPECIAL COLLECTIONS/JIM SPILSBURY FONTS/ALBUM
BC1938/4

17

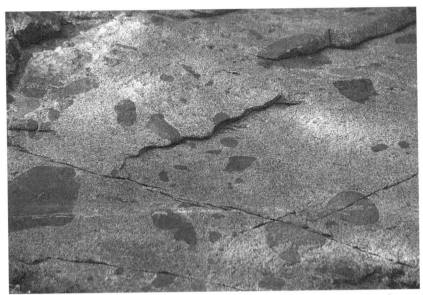

First Nations people explain these xenoliths as the slugs, snails, mice and frogs that the mountain goat and the deer threw at each other during their war.

mountain goat and the deer. "The mountain goat and the deer couldn't make up their minds which of them should live on the mainland and which on East Redonda Island," said Chief Joe.[8] "They went to war over it, and as the deer pulled the goat off the island, the goat's hooves left grooves on the rocks. That's why the mountain goat only lives on the mainland. If you look carefully, you will see black dots on the rocks all along the coast. These are the slugs, snails, mice and frogs that the mountain goat and the deer threw at each other during the war."

The Sliammon were one of many loosely related groups of Salish-speaking people who lived around the Strait of Georgia. In summer, the different groups ranged beyond Desolation Sound. The Homalco travelled up Bute Inlet, while the Klahoose went up Toba Inlet and to Cortes Island. The Island Comox moved to Quadra and Vancouver islands, and the Sliammon established seasonal villages from Lund to Grief Point, as well as on Texada Island. Archaeologists who have excavated their middens say settlement goes back eight thousand years.

However, when autumn storms began to rage, many Sliammon, Klahoose and Homalco people retreated to Kahkaykay, the snug winter

This island provided a stage for winter entertainment. Sliammon villagers, who had travelled together during the summer, walked out there at low tide. They had until the next low tide to relate their doings to the rest of the village seated on the foreshore.

village in tiny Grace Harbour off Okeover Inlet. "The winter village there had six longhouses averaging seventy-five feet in length," Chief Joe told me. "The largest one was two hundred feet. Several families lived in each, with grandchildren looking after grandparents." There may have been hundreds or even thousands of people living in the longhouses and smaller satellite houses surrounding them.

That three otherwise proudly independent nations would choose to live together was unusual on the Northwest Coast, and that they chose to do it in such confined quarters as Grace Harbour is puzzling when so many more commodious sites—like Theodosia Inlet—offered themselves nearby. One possible explanation has to do with security. Coast Salish tribes lived in fear of attack by the Lekwiltok and Haida raiders from the north, and narrow Grace Harbour offered good defences. The large winter gathering might also have to do with consolidation. A series of smallpox epidemics moved up the continent from Spanish Mexico in the late 1800s and devastated the Coast Salish, killing as many as 95 percent of them. Survivors might have found it useful to band together. In any case, Kahkaykay bore witness to close and friendly relations between the three groups, a feature that holds true to this day.

Below the site of Kahkaykay, a small island shelters a big, shallow tide pool full of oysters, clams and mussels. This pool is an example of the First Nations mariculture that Judith Williams has documented in her book *Clam Gardens*.[9] Elders supervised not only the harvesting of shellfish, especially butter clams, but also the removal of rocks from the diggings. These rocks were piled below the high-tide level, thus expanding the area in which the clams liked to grow and encouraging bigger harvests.

Salmon were another important source of food. After eating the fish, the people always respectfully returned the bones to the sea so that the salmon people would swim back to their villages and return many times to give their flesh to humans.

Seals, sea lions and porpoises were eaten along with deer, goat, bear and various kinds of sea ducks and geese. Pit ovens were a favourite method of cooking. The pit was lined with rocks that wouldn't split in the heat. A fire burned in the pit for two to three hours. It was then removed or extinguished, and the cavity was lined with green hemlock boughs to create steam. When the wood began to crackle and split, the meat was put in and covered with more boughs, and the pit was sealed with hides. Camas bulbs, fern roots or, in later years, potatoes were added after two hours. In another two hours, everyone gathered to eat.

"The island in front of Kahkaykay was used as a stage," said Murray Mitchell. "Each family had their turn when the tide separated them. They would tell stories of everything that had happened since they left the village in the spring: which children had been born, who had died, that sort of thing."

One of the stories tells of the coming of the Europeans during the winter of 1792. "The people were out fishing in their canoes when they saw a couple of floating islands with sticks on them," said Murray. "As these approached, they were surprised to hear someone ask them how they were doing in their own language. It turned out that when Captain Vancouver and the Spanish captains Galiano and Valdés had passed through the Sliammon/Texada area, they had taken a local man on board who was showing them around and telling them the Native names for things. He was also learning English."

The Sliammon people and BC Parks are joint custodians of Tux'wnench Provincial Park. They celebrated its opening with a traditional salmon BBQ.

Murray added, "When the white men came, they wanted to know where our cemeteries were, but we didn't have any. When someone died, the body was washed by a specially designated group of people. They dressed it, put it in the fetal position with the hands under the feet and then laid it in a bentwood box. They took the box to the rock just south of Station Island, where they put it in a tree. At the end of a year, they took it down and cremated it with a ceremony. The living were responsible for providing the dead with what they needed in the next world. To get the food translated there, they burnt it while respectfully looking away."

Guardian spirits assisted the living in their daily lives. During their puberty rituals, young men fasted for three days, then climbed the peak on East Redonda Island. They sat there for up to a week until they had a vision of an animal, bird, tree or rock. This became their guardian spirit. Later, a song about the spirit would come to them in a dream, and the elders would help them develop it into a performance for the winter dances. Sometimes the visions came to them in other places. Murray's came to him in a canoe. He sang the song about his vision to his tourists in a pleasant tenor voice.

Come spring, people left Grace Harbour for their summer villages. En route, those going to Prideaux Haven, Squirrel Cove, Forbes Bay or Toba and Bute inlets took the shortcut, dragging their boats across from Wootton Bay to Portage Cove. However, they were careful not to land on the island in Tenedos Bay. "A dog-like animal, *cheen kwah*, dived into the rocks there," explained Sue Pielle. "If you land, you'll get arthritis."[10]

Joe Mitchell told me about other places the Sliammon avoided. "Our people never jig for cod off Horace Head," he said. "There is something bad there. The last person who fished there got something very heavy on his line. He rocked the boat and gradually pulled the line up. Suddenly it came loose. It was a sunny day, and when he looked down into the water he could see a mountain goat with pink hooves and nose and red eyes. Being very scared, he cut the line as big whirlpools tossed his boat. They disappeared with the creature and haven't been seen since."

Today, some of the villages, like the ones at Prideaux Haven and

Forbes Bay, are no longer inhabited. Although Chief Joe knew there had been a village in Prideaux Haven, he had no memories of it, but he remembered both Laura and Melanie coves were popular clam-digging areas. The berm between Eveleigh Island and the mainland shields Prideaux Haven from heavy storm waves. It is another example of First Nations mariculture.

When the men from Captain Vancouver's expedition visited Roffey Island, just past Laura Cove, on June 30, 1792, they mistakenly thought the village there had been abandoned. "My grandfather said our people had the original mobile homes," said Murray. "Planks were lashed to posts and taken with them when they moved." Vancouver's men saw the posts but didn't realize that the people had taken the planks with them for use elsewhere.

As the Europeans poked into piles of "filthy garments and apparel of the late inhabitants," they were attacked by a multitude of fleas. Although they jumped into water "up to their necks," they were unable to get rid of the creatures until they had boiled all their own clothes.

"The people hadn't fled," said Murray. "They had just been transformed into the fleas which Vancouver's men found there. The village was called Machinay—meaning Flea Village. It was not used for long.

"Similarly, the people at the Forbes Bay village, Ahpookwum, further up Homfray Channel, were transformed into maggots. The white marks on the cliff at the north end of the bay are their eggs. Other people became bedbugs, ticks, sand fleas, and those descended from Cannibal Woman became mosquitoes. People only ate other people if they were starving, such as when they got lost in the bush."

At Flea Village, Vancouver's men also noticed that a cantilevered deck in front of the houses made it impossible to scale the cliff. Murray said that when the villagers were in residence, they would have piled rocks and heavy branches on the deck, ready to hurl down on invaders. The small village at Lund had similar defences. Most villages were either fortified or concealed, as raiders were a big problem. Some houses were built back among the trees, and others were sunk in trenches invisible from the water. Haida or Kwak<u>wa</u>k<u>a</u>'wakw warriors paddling fifteen-metre (fifty-foot) war canoes swept down from the north in search of house planks, food prepared for winter, and slaves. It may have been a band of such raiders that briefly captured Robert Homfray at the mouth of Waddington Channel while he was on his way to survey Bute Inlet in 1861 (see Chapter 3). Luckily, the Klahoose chief from the village at the mouth of the Brem River on Toba Inlet was passing by and rescued him.

In the late 1860s, Roman Catholic priests persuaded the people to split up and establish new winter villages at Sliammon, Squirrel Cove and Church House, because they felt the main winter village at Grace Harbour was too remote.[11] Not coincidentally, this had the effect of separating the elders who supervised the winter dance ceremonies, reducing their power and making it easier for the priests to convert people to the new beliefs they wanted to introduce.

Having seen so many of their relatives die in the 1862 smallpox epidemic, the grieving survivors were willing to embrace the new faith. It came at a price. According to the anthropologist Wilson Duff,[12] the converts were required to give up all primitive dances, potlatches, shamanism and gambling. The priests appointed captains to supervise work, Native watchmen to act as truant officers enforcing attendance at mass, arranging marriages and other things, and bell-ringers who rang the church bell. Delinquents were lashed, fined or made to stand for hours with their arms stretched out like Christ on the cross. Wives sold their clothes to pay their husbands' fines. These practices, labelled the Durieu System after its originator, Bishop Paul Durieu, lasted almost forty years, until around 1910.

Nevertheless, in the Squirrel Cove village on Cortes Island (near the popular anchorage of the same name), children, including the Mitchell siblings Joe, Sue and Elizabeth, still listened intently to stories and legends passed down from ancestors through many generations.

"I remember Old Magee, who was 120 years old, used to invite people all winter to come and hear stories of how people got along with each other," said Chief Joe. Some of these stories, as told by Rose Mitchell, are reprinted in Dorothy Kennedy and Randy Bouchard's book

Sliammon Life, Sliammon Lands. The theme of getting along with people is a common one. Hunters and gatherers always shared what they got with everyone, often ending up with little for themselves, knowing that next day they would be on the receiving end. "I felt good when my mother cut up the deer I brought home and gave it away," Chief Joe said. "It meant I was a good provider." He was so well respected, traditionally, academically and spiritually, that he was given five honorary names, one of which was *Hewkin*, meaning swan, as a symbol of his caring for others.[13]

Gradually, new ideas mingled with the old. One of the new ideas was the Chinook language, which was developed by First Nations people and Hudson's Bay Company traders and used throughout the coast.[14] "My grandfather thought human beings should get up at breaking daylight," said Chief Joe. "He would wake us at that time to ask what was for breakfast. He spoke in Chinook so that we would have to learn it too."

Well into the twentieth century, Sliammon people maintained ties with Grace Harbour and Okeover Inlet. Elsie Paul, another revered elder, has memories of Tux'wnech near the Okeover government wharf. "Tux'wnech was a peaceful little place where my grandfather's brother and several others had cabins," said Paul. "We used to go there for the salmon spawning. We'd barbecue the fillets on sticks by the fire or smoke them for the winter. Fish from Tux'wnech tasted different from the bigger ones we caught in Theodosia."[15] The beach at Tux'wnech has the characteristic low-tide rock pile signifying one or more clam gardens. Today, it is almost submerged under Pacific oysters.

The Theodosia village was built on stilts to protect it from the river's floodwaters. Named Toquana, it was abandoned in the 1920s,[16] perhaps when the turmoil of the big railway logging camp arrived in 1922 (see Chapter 12).

In the 1950s, when Elsie Paul, an elder, was a new bride, she lived on the Tokenatch reserve at Freke Anchorage with her mother-in-law.[17] Leaving her two children with their grandmother, she would walk almost seven kilometres (four miles) to the main road between Lund and Powell River to catch a bus to shop. On the way back in the gathering dark, with a heavy bag of groceries, she walked quickly as every shadow seemed to be a bear. She never met one but remembers the feeling. In those days no one imagined that the shy young woman would eventually become a magistrate. She served both Natives and non-Natives in that position from 1989 to 1996. Now retired, she coordinates the elders and officiates at ceremonies where a Sliammon presence is required. In her black and red cloak covered in traditional designs, she is a majestic figure when she rises to say a prayer to the Creator or give a blessing in the Sliammon language. Her people call upon her to perform traditional rites after a death, in addition to conventional church rites. "We believe that the living must let the dead person go with gladness," she said. Sometimes this requires a lot of talking.

The Sliammon, Homalco and Klahoose people felt strong ties of kinship to and respect for the natural world. Before they took anything for their own use, they would give thanks to the Creator for providing it, request permission to use it and ask that it replenish itself and return. Their populations and needs were modest. Customs and taboos ensured that they never took so much that anything became extinct. Thus they preserved the orderly world the Transformer created for their ancestors.

3

EARLY EXPLORERS
Tall Ships and Long Boats

The first European ships to penetrate Desolation Sound were part of a joint expedition led by the English captain George Vancouver and the Spaniards Dionisio Alcalá Galiano and Cayetano Valdés y Flores. Both Spain and England were looking for the Northwest Passage from the Atlantic Ocean to the Pacific, which, had it existed at an ice-free latitude, would have given Europe direct access to the spice trade. Vancouver and the Spanish captains set out separately, but met near the present-day site of Vancouver, British Columbia. Both parties had been instructed to co-operate with each other, but both felt a need to see things for themselves.

Captain George Vancouver (1757–1798) was an experienced mariner who had gone to sea at age fourteen.[18] He was with Captain James Cook in 1778 when Cook landed at Friendly Cove on Nootka Island, becoming the first European to set foot on the coast of what is now British Columbia. The 1792 voyage was Vancouver's first command. His orders were to use his two ships, *Discovery* and *Chatham*, to map the coast and take possession of the Spanish settlement at Friendly Cove. He or later marine surveyors named a number of points of land after members of his crew, including William Robert Broughton (captain of the *Chatham*), James Johnstone, Peter Puget and Joseph Whidbey. The Latin names of plants such as

Douglas fir, *Pseudotsuga menziesii,* commemorate Archibald Menzies, the expedition's botanist.

Dionisio Alcalá Galiano (1762–1805), who was in charge of the Spanish expedition and the brig *Sutil,* and CayetanoValdés y Flores (1767–1835), in command of the schooner *Mexicana,* were to map the coast from San Francisco to 55° north latitude. Both were experienced Spanish naval officers recruited for Alejandro Malaspina's scientific expedition, which visited Nootka in 1791. Galiano spoke English (which was helpful, as none of the Englishmen spoke Spanish), while Valdés's knowledge of the Mowachaht language enabled him to make himself understood in Salish.

The four ships were tiny by today's standards. Half the size of a small BC Ferries vessel, HMS *Discovery* was under thirty metres (ninety-nine feet) long and nine metres (twenty-eight feet) wide. At that time, ships were rated according to their capacity to carry wine casks, called tons or tuns. *Discovery* was 330 tons. The *Chatham* was 130 tons, and *Sutil*

On June 26, 1792, Vancouver and the Spaniards anchored their ships on the north side of Kinghorn Island (on the right).

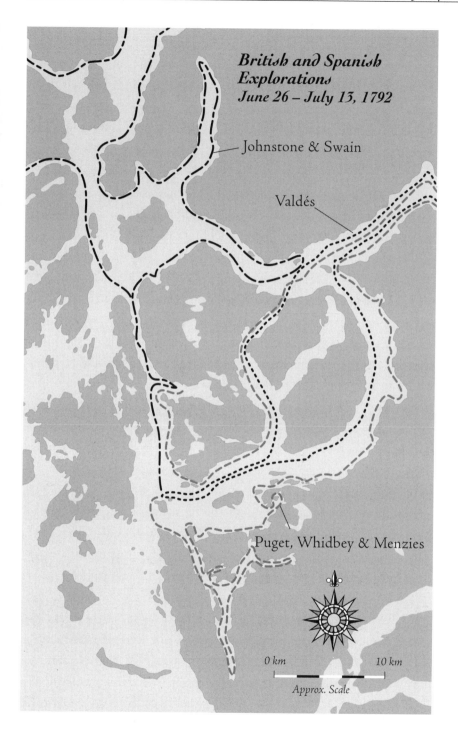

British and Spanish Explorations
June 26 – July 13, 1792

Johnstone & Swain

Valdés

Puget, Whidbey & Menzies

0 km   10 km

Approx. Scale

and *Mexicana* were 46 tons each. All four had several ship's boats for shore work. The most popular was a seven-metre (twenty-three-foot), clinker-built launch wide enough for five pairs of rowers to sit side by side. When the wind was favourable, its two masts could be rigged with lugsails. At night, oars held up a sail to form a tent. There was also a six-metre (twenty-foot) cutter with three rows of oarsmen and a single mast.

Sorting out what really happened in Desolation Sound is like unravelling a mystery story. Even though both Spanish and English admiralties had strict rules requiring that all journals be turned in at the end of the voyage, the crew did not always comply. Thomas Manby wrote letters to a friend;[19] other crew members kept two journals: one to be turned in and one to be kept. Vancouver's official journal, after Admiralty editing, came out in 1798. The Hakluyt Society version, edited by W. Kaye Lamb, cites a page and a half of manuscript logs and journals kept by seventeen members of the crew in addition to Vancouver. Lamb, who was in charge of the National Library of Canada when he edited the account, had access to many of these. His 291-page introduction summarizes a lot of the information in them, and his footnotes to the journal are often more helpful than the text itself in identifying where the exploration parties went. This is partly because many place names were added later.

What we know for sure is that late on the dark and rainy night of June 25, 1792, the *Discovery* and the *Chatham* anchored in thirty-two fathoms off the north side of Kinghorn Island "in company with . . . the Spanish vessels," according to Vancouver's journal. The Spanish account says their ships were much slower than Vancouver's, and they made a side trip to Nanaimo and anchored in Descanso Bay at the north end of Gabriola, where Jose Cordero, a surveyor and draftsman, drew three landscapes. As a result, according to the historian Donald Cutter, they didn't see Vancouver again till June 27, when he came alongside the *Sutil* in a launch.[20] Manby says the Spanish "kept in company with us, followed our motions and anchored with us in the evening." Archibald Menzies, who on other occasions was not afraid to contradict Vancouver, said that "the two Spanish vessels followed our example and came too and the same time close by us."[21] He continues that on the morning of June 26, Galiano came aboard the *Discovery* for a meeting with Vancouver. At this time they decided to send out five exploration parties. [21]

Valdés, in one of the Spanish launches, explored Homfray Channel and Toba Inlet.

William Robert Broughton, in another small boat, went up Lewis Channel in search of a more protected anchorage, which he found in Teakerne Arm. (Vancouver subsequently moved the ships to this spot.)

Vancouver took the yawl to explore "the main channel of the gulf we had quitted on the Monday afternoon," but bad weather drove him back to the ship.

James Johnstone in *Chatham's* cutter and Spelman Swaine in *Chatham's* launch headed northwest. They explored Ramsay Arm and also went up Bute Inlet, where they exchanged some nails for "a Large Supply of Fresh Herring" at a Native village beside the Arran Rapids. The residents of the village also helped them line the boats through the rapids into Cordero Channel. Unfortunately, the weather socked in, making surveying impossible, so they turned back, returning to the ships on July 2. Reprovisioned, they went out again with orders to proceed beyond the Arran and Yuculta rapids to the Pacific Ocean. Once past the rapids, Johnstone and Swain explored Frederick Arm and Phillips Arm, and looked at Nodales Channel. They observed that the tide was four hours earlier in these channels than in the Strait of Georgia. They went up Loughborough Inlet and Chancellor Channel and past the village of Cheslakees to what are now Port Hardy and Pine Island, then back via Johnstone Strait and Nodales Channel. They returned July 12, having discovered the passage to the Pacific. However, they felt it would be hazardous to take the ships through the narrow channels.

The fifth expedition, that of Peter Puget and Joseph Whidbey in the *Discovery's* launch and cutter, started at Sarah Point and followed the shore into Malaspina, Okeover, Theodosia and Lancelot inlets. Vancouver did not want to entrust the important task of mapping the continental shore to anyone other than his own men.

One of the most detailed accounts of these explorations was written by Menzies, who accompanied Whidbey and Puget. These three men were an experienced team who had already charted the islands off Seattle. They landed on points to take compass bearings of significant features. Every day at noon, Whidbey took a sighting of the sun to establish their latitude. In between landings, they sketched the shapes of the mountains and islands and wrote notes of their observations. This information was later amalgamated onto a chart and tied in to their other maps.

From Sarah Point, Whidbey, Puget and Menzies went into Malaspina Inlet and continued their survey to the head of Okeover Inlet, where they spent the night in a small cove "two miles from the head." Penrose Bay is three miles from the head, but there's no other cove.

In the morning they found Lancelot Inlet and went "about 4 miles till it got so narrow and shallow that it was not thought worth while to put off time in following it further." Since the head of Lancelot is a wide bay, perhaps they went through the narrows on the south side and into Theodosia Inlet, which is very shallow for the latter half of its short length. They must have got up early, as Menzies said they breakfasted on Thynne Island, which is back in Lancelot Inlet at the mouth of Thors Cove.

Leaving Malaspina Inlet, they turned northeast past Mink Island. In Tenedos Bay they "saw a great number of fish stages erected from the ground in a slanting manner" for drying fish. They were carefully crafted out of tree roots and occupied such a length of foreshore that the explorers assumed a considerable number of people must have used them when the fish were running.

At the north end of Prideaux Haven, behind Roffey Island, they found "the picturesque ruins of a deserted village." It was on a high rock connected to the mainland by a set of steps accessible by one person at a time. Menzies noted that above the village, the branches of a bigleaf maple provided adequate concealment for a group of defenders. The top of the rock was flat, and the area was extended by "large scaffolds." From the "intolerable stench," they assumed that it had recently been inhabited. "The Narrow lanes between the Houses were full of Filth, Nastiness and swarmed with myriads of *Fleas* which fixed themselves on our Shoes Stockings and cloths." They retreated hastily, undressed and swam, but the fleas pursued them. They tried towing the clothes behind the boats, but nothing got rid of the pests until they boiled the offending garments (see Murray Mitchell's account of this visit in Chapter 2).

Next day they proceeded up Homfray Channel past Forbes and Atwood bays. Just beyond Brettell Point, they met Captain Valdés coming out of Toba Inlet. He shared his survey information but did not show them the sketch he had made of a striking Native design on a wooden plank. He named the inlet Toba, meaning "tablet," to commemorate this find.[22] Valdés told them that the inlet "terminated in shallow water surrounded with low land about eleven miles off." On a windy day, waves up to two metres (six feet) in these shallows create hazardous conditions for approaching vessels. Valdés also told Menzies' party that he had seen Johnstone at the mouth of the inlet the previous day. "As Mr. Puget who

Trees have overgrown the site of Flea Village, which was also the location of Saulter and Frank's cabin in the '20s and '30s.

commanded our party, had no particular orders how to act in case of meeting in this manner with Capt. Valdés," Menzies wrote, "we took our leave of him and continued our examination in the Northern Branch."

In the evening they passed more fish stages, but after their encounter with the fleas they were afraid to land and consequently slept in the boats that night. A strong current that they attributed to the many "waterfalls and torrents" gave them a swift trip back down the inlet. They looked at Ramsay Arm but did not travel up it, assuming—correctly— that Johnstone had surveyed it. Rather than duplicate his efforts, they crossed over to the north side of West Redonda Island and camped, perhaps in Redonda Bay. In case they were close to the other party, they fired a gun, but heard no reply. Next day, July 5, they arrived back at the ships now anchored in Teakerne Arm.

Vancouver promptly sent Puget and Whidbey out again with a week's provisions to explore the main channel. They went to Savary and Harwood islands before crossing to the east coast of Vancouver Island, which they followed north up Discovery Passage to about Campbell River.

Menzies stayed behind with the ships. He enjoyed a ramble up to the summit of Nipple Peak and took a trip with Broughton over to Squirrel Cove. Among the plants he found were four new pyrolas. These are delicate pink or white flowers, often with evergreen leaves.

On July 13, when all the exploration parties had returned to the ships, Vancouver left Teakerne Arm and the Spanish to travel to Nootka on the west coast of Vancouver Island. The Spaniards continued their explorations, going through the Arran Rapids and up both Loughborough and Knight inlets, then returning round the north end of Vancouver Island to Nootka. They arrived three days after Vancouver on August 31.

For the next seventy years, few Europeans had occasion to visit Desolation Sound. It was a long way north of the Hudson's Bay Company's western headquarters at Fort Vancouver in the Oregon Country. Nevertheless, that irascible Scot James Douglas, a trader at the fort (later the chief factor or trader), ranged widely up and down the coast. In 1838, he recorded in his diary that his ship *Beaver* had encountered Sliammon people (from Grace Harbour) at the north end of Texada Island.[23] Two years later, off Cape Mudge, he traded woollen blankets for fifty beaver skins from local Native people. In 1843, the Hudson's Bay Company moved its headquarters to Fort Victoria, a location chosen by Douglas that was far from the encroaching American wagon trains pouring over the Oregon Trail. In 1846, Queen Victoria granted the Company the right to be the "true and absolute lords and Proprietors" of Vancouver Island.

Ten years later, Douglas was governor of the fledgling colony. American gold miners pushing north from the exhausted goldfields of California were beginning to find the precious mineral north of the forty-ninth parallel, which was now the established border between Canada and the United States. In 1858, the year of the North Thompson and Fraser River gold rushes in southern British Columbia, William Downie reported some interesting, possibly gold-bearing, black sands along the Homalco River and veins of pyrites in Bute Inlet.[24] Nearly twenty years later, in 1876, G.M. Dawson, a legendary geologist who later became director of the Geological Survey of Canada, checked out the area on his way north to the Queen Charlotte Islands.[25] Despite his short stature—about 145 centimetres or four foot nine—and hunched back, Dawson was an indefatigable worker. Up with the dawn, he hiked all day and wrote notes far into the evening. An old miner who knew him said, "Wasn't none of us could keep up with him." In 1885 Dawson returned and spent some time in Malaspina Inlet. He was likely looking to see if there were enough indications of precious minerals to warrant a full survey. He didn't find much here.

Coal was discovered at Nanaimo and Fort Rupert on Vancouver Island, though production was somewhat hampered by hostile Natives, so Britain sent a couple of gunboats, HMS *Forward* and HMS *Grappler*, to keep order. In 1860, *Forward* had occasion to attack the fierce Lekwiltok people of Cape Mudge, and a year later the same ship vanquished the dreaded Haida encamped nearby on Vancouver Island.

Vancouver moved his ships to near Cassel Falls for better protection from the wind. Today's maritime explorers enjoy washing their hair in the falls and swimming in the warm lake above.

These ships couldn't be everywhere at once, and in their absence, some Natives continued to attack Europeans. One such attack occurred right in Desolation Sound. In the 1860s, there was no shortage of young men with a taste for adventure. Robert Homfray (1824–1902), an English civil engineer who had studied under Isambard Kingdom Brunel, the noted bridge and railway builder, was one of these. First attracted to the California gold rush, he continued north to Victoria, arriving in 1860 just as Alfred Pendrell Waddington was promoting his scheme for an overland road from the Cariboo goldfields to the head of Bute Inlet. In September 1861, Waddington sailed to the head of Bute and made contact with the local Natives.

Enthused by his report, the Hudson's Bay Company hired Homfray and another man, Harry McNeill, to survey the mountain pass. Equipped with a leaky canoe, Homfray and McNeill, along with "the Hudson Bay Company's three best French-Canadian voyageurs" and two Natives, set out from Victoria in October 1861.[26] Almost swamped by heavy seas while crossing the Strait of Georgia, they rounded Sarah Point and headed for the distant snow peaks. As they drew level with Waddington Channel, a large canoe swept alongside and forced them toward a beach, where they expected to be killed. Before this could happen, a loud war whoop sounded in the distance. Their captors fled as a large Native man in a canoe appeared. Homfray and his companions "stood shoulder to shoulder on the beach, determined to die together," but found themselves rescued instead. The large man turned out to be the Klahoose chief. He took them home to his village at the mouth of the Brem River on Toba Inlet before escorting them up Bute Inlet.

With increasing numbers of Europeans arriving in search of gold and then land, it became necessary to establish law and order, including accurate maps and, before long, a system of land tenure (see Chapter 4). The British Admiralty commissioned Captain George Henry Richards to survey the Strait of Georgia from November 1857 to January 1861.[27] His ship, HMS *Plumper*, was a barque-rigged steam sloop with a speed under steam of six knots. It was armed with twelve guns. Richards visited Desolation Sound in 1861 and 1862 and named Waddington

Channel as well as the Otter, Mink and Martin islands. In the course of this work, he developed a system to transfer survey data quickly and efficiently to new and existing charts.

In 1863, Richards returned to Britain, leaving Staff Commander Daniel Pender in charge of the survey aboard the *Beaver*, which had been leased from the Hudson's Bay Company. During his trip to Desolation Sound in 1863, Pender named Wootton Bay after Henry Wootton (1828–1875), who arrived in Victoria in 1859 as second officer aboard the Hudson's Bay Company's new steamship *Labouchere*. He retired from the sea shortly after his arrival, becoming at various times postmaster general of Victoria and British Columbia and harbour master of Victoria.

Pender came back to Desolation Sound in the *Beaver* in 1864 and 1867. He named Connis Point after his Skye terrier, Homfray Channel after the English engineer who surveyed the route from the head of Bute Inlet, and the Coode Peninsula and Trevenen Bay after Trevenen P. Coode, the colourful captain of HMS *Sutlej*. According to midshipman Lord Charles Beresford, an Irishman who liked to tell a good story, the captain "was tall and thin, hook-nosed and elderly." He had a habit of bending his elbows and folding his hands inside his sleeves. "He was a taut hand and a fine seaman." When Spain and Chile declared war, British and American ships put to sea to avoid the conflict. Beresford writes that they "left Valparaiso about the middle of April 1866, and proceeded to Vancouver Island. On the way the *Sutlej* ran into a French barque, taking the foremast out of her. Captain Coode stood by the rail, his arms crossed, his hands folded inside his sleeves, looking down upon the wreck with a sardonic grin, while the French captain, gesticulating below, shouted: 'Oh, you goddam Englishmen, for you it is all-a-right but for us it is not so nice!' But we repaired all damage so that at the latter, he was better off than when he started."[28]

The website of the BC Geographical Names Information System (BCGNIS) says several Desolation Sound sites were christened by either Captain Richards or Captain Pender.[29] Amongst them are Melanie and Laura coves, which appear on an 1864 chart, along with Copplestone Island and Point, Edward Point, Ellen Point, Eveleigh Island, Lucy Island and Point, Mary Islands, Morgan Island, Paige Islets, Roffey Island, Scobell Island and William Island.

Names in the immediate vicinity of Prideaux Haven appear to have connections to the English counties of Devon and Cornwall. Daniel Pender himself came from Falmouth in Cornwall, so he may have named them. Prideaux Place, a stately home outside Padstow in Cornwall, dates back to Elizabeth I, and the family has been around since the French Normans invaded England in 1066. The Eveleigh family has many members in Devon and Cornwall, and Copplestone is a village in Devon, not far from Padstow. Were Laura, Melanie, Ellen, Edward and William members of the Prideaux family or people known to Daniel Pender or his crew? The search for an answer to this question continues.

By the end of 1864, Pender had completed charting the maze of islands. The area was ripe for an invasion of European settlers.

PART II

European Settlers

4

THE EUROPEAN INFLUX

In Search of Big Timber and Solitude

*T*he first newcomers to try to make a living in Desolation Sound may have been whalers working out of Whaletown on Cortes Island. Although much of the action took place in the open Strait of Georgia, the seamen likely also pursued their quarry into Desolation Sound, around the Redonda Islands and up Bute and Toba inlets. From 1869 to 1870, the Dawson and Douglass Whaling Company used a former sealing schooner, the forty-seven-ton *Kate*, to harpoon mainly humpback whales.[30] The whalers towed the bodies to Whaletown Bay on the west side of Cortes Island, where they removed the liver and blubber, abandoning the rest. By 1871, the big whales were fished out. Only the occasional humpback is seen now.

With the whales gone, the next attraction was the forest. "Most settlers were fishers, loggers or remittance men," said Ingrid Andersen Cowie, who lived at Seaford on Cortes Island as a toddler and visited Desolation Sound frequently during her childhood at Lund.[31] Frank White, who has spent most of his ninety-plus years working on the coast, said, "Many people were looking for adventure. It was like a whirlpool. The adventurous souls were spat out to the wilderness. Now people come looking for easy living."[32]

In the last quarter of the nineteenth century and the early years of the twentieth, those who came were a tough breed who could turn their hand to anything. They lived off the land by hunting, fishing and growing their own vegetables. Cash needs were met by selling logs that were now in demand as European shipbuilders had decided they preferred the straight-grained Douglas fir timber from the Pacific Northwest to Baltic timber for their thirty-metre (hundred-foot) spars.

Initially, timber could only be cut on land owned by the logger, but in 1865 the government permitted those in the logging business to stake timber leases on Crown land without buying the property. After 1888, the government issued leases for limited periods and charged rents of five to ten cents an acre. Nine years later, it began charging a royalty based on the volume of timber cut and removed from the land. Individuals wanting to cut ungranted Crown timber could take out handlogging licences at a cost of ten dollars a year plus the royalty on the timber cut.[33] After 1906, handloggers were not allowed to use machinery that was steam-powered.

Vancouver sawmills used up all the timber close at hand, and the loggers turned their attention farther north, first to Jervis Inlet and then to the maze of islands north of Powell River known as the Jungles.[34] Desolation Sound is at the southern end of this maze. In 1882, Mose Ireland, a legendary BC timber cruiser, surveyed two thousand hectares (five thousand acres) of "the finest bunch of timber man ever saw at Malaspina Inlet." He sold it to "young Mr. Merrill from Michigan," who set up a camp in Okeover for thirty men.[35] It was difficult to obtain supplies, and the men complained bitterly. To make matters worse, the cook frequently got sloshed on moonshine.[36]

Starting in the mid-1880s, both logging companies and individual loggers poured north. Most companies, many of which were from the United States, located beyond Desolation Sound in the Johnstone Strait area, but traces of oxen roads and log chutes attest to the presence of some in the Redonda and Forbes Bay areas.

Gyppo loggers, men who preferred to work by themselves rather than for a large logging company, clawed their way into niches wherever they could find them. Some came to Desolation Sound. Such men sought tall trees growing at the top of steep slopes. After spending considerable time studying where the tree should fall, the faller cut notches above the flare of the trunk to hold springboards that he would stand on. These notches are clearly visible on many old stumps. Using a double-bitted axe, the faller made a cut on the down side. Moving to the upper side, he sawed into the wood, hammering in steel wedges to open the cut and keep the saw from binding. The two-man saw would be about 2.5 to 3 metres (eight to ten feet) long. If a logger was working on his own, he would remove the second handle from the saw, thread some rope through the hole left by the handle, and fasten the far end of the saw to a sapling under two metres (6.5 feet) tall to keep the saw from sagging. He would also bend the top of the sapling down and bury it in the ground so that he could saw back and forth without the saw end opposite him flopping around.[37]

Saws had become readily available by the 1870s and were preferred over axes for felling big trees. In addition to the falling saw, men had falling axes that were narrower than the regular chopping axe. There was also the swamping ax, with a broad head, that was used to limb trees and clear or "swamp out" brush. These axes were all double bitted. An axe with a bit on only one side was called a hatchet.[38]

After the tree fell, the man used heavy jacks and much patience to slide it down to the water, where he bucked it into logs and stored them till there were enough to make a boom. Towboats, usually owned by sawmills, then took the boom south to Vancouver markets. (Steam tugs on their way north, especially those heading for Bute and Toba inlets, put crew members ashore in Desolation Sound to cut wood to fuel the return journey. Later, when the tugs converted to coal or oil, they had no need to do this.)

In Desolation Sound, even today, all traffic goes by water. The shore is made up mostly of alternating stretches of cliffs and steep, forested slopes, and most beaches that do exist are rocky, making landings from small boats difficult. Before about 1885, few towboats operated outside of Vancouver, Victoria and Nanaimo. The lack of regular boat traffic made it expensive for logging companies and canneries to get supplies and men to their worksites. Individuals often hitched rides on boats headed in the general direction of their destination, but after that they were on their own. They'd have to wait for another ride to bring them back.

Sometimes men remained in the area after the logging camps withdrew, content to live off the land in splendid isolation. In 1884 the provincial government passed the BC Land Act, which allowed Canadian citizens to pre-empt sixty-five hectares (160 acres). (Axel Hanson, a Finn, became a Canadian citizen so that he could pre-empt land in Galley Bay.) An individual selected a piece of land, staked it and made a written application for it. After sending out surveyors to verify the location and extent of the land being claimed, the provincial government issued a Certificate of Pre-emption. The holder of this then lived on the land while making improvements to it to a value of $2.50 an acre. These improvements could include clearing the land or cultivating a garden, but had to include building a dwelling place.

Sometimes the pre-emption certificate was issued subject to an exemption of the timber. This happened to Joseph H. Copeland of Portage Cove, whose pre-emption certificate, dated December 29, 1910, states: "This record is granted on the understanding that the Pre-emptor is not entitled to any of the timber on the land covered by this pre-emption record."

Once the improvements were made, the pre-emptor would apply for a Certificate of Improvement. This was signed by witnesses, usually neighbours, attesting to the improvements. On at least two occasions, Forest Ranger Ernest (Ernie) Cowie refused to sign a certificate, claiming the improvements were not completed. The Lindberg brothers of Lloyd Point contested Cowie's decision and won, but Carl Christensen didn't want the hassle and eventually moved away, leaving his Salt Lagoon land behind. With the Certificate of Improvement in hand, a pre-emptor could pay a dollar an acre to purchase the land as a "Crown grant," which gave him clear title to the land.

The residency requirement appears to have been relaxed while the holder was serving with the armed forces during the First World War. Bertram Saulter and George Walker Parker pre-empted land in 1915 and got their Crown grants immediately upon discharge from the army in 1919.

Often it took cash-poor settlers many years to scrape together enough money to buy their land. Phil Lavigne pre-empted his land in 1908 but didn't get his Crown grant until 1930. With little competition for these remote parcels of land, settlers were often lax about following through. Mike Shuttler, who first arrived at Melanie Cove in the early 1890s, made "a declaration" (whatever that was) in 1904, pre-empted in 1916 and got his Certificate of Improvement and his Crown grant in 1924.

Once landowners had paid for their Crown grant, they then had to pay yearly taxes on the property. Axel Hanson's Certificate of Purchase, dated March 12, 1917, notes that he had to pay taxes for 1914–1916. His pre-emption was dated 1912. If the landowner stopped paying taxes for any reason, the land reverted to the Crown. This happened to the D'Angios and Chamberses in Okeover.

It didn't happen to the Thulins, who explored Desolation Sound before settling down to establish the first hotel and store at Lund, just outside the Desolation Sound area. In March 1889, Fred Thulin arrived in Vancouver from Sweden. He had come to join his brother Charles, who was handlogging in Pendrell Sound. Two weeks after his arrival, Fred was on the sidewheeler tug *Mermaid*, which was going north for a tow of logs. The *Mermaid* was steam-driven, so the crew towed a scow laden with slabwood for fuel. Even though it slowed them down, it was more efficient to do this than to go ashore every so often to cut wood.

Charles and Fred logged in Pendrell Sound all that summer, and in December they moved to the site of an old Native village just south of the Copeland Islands, on the west side of the Malaspina Peninsula. The next year they christened the place Lund because the name was easy to spell and easy to remember. Mail and supplies arrived every three to four weeks on tugs belonging to the Hastings Mill. (The mill, which went into production in 1867, was the second to be established in what is now Vancouver. Located on the south shore of Burrard Inlet, it was owned by Edward Stamp, who had previously established sawmills at Port Alberni and Port Neville.) The tugs didn't have room for everything, so the Thulins often had to row to Vancouver for additional supplies, but not for long. Within four years they built a wharf, opened a post office and store, and established the first hotel north of Vancouver.

At this time there were a few ferry services for people and cattle across Burrard Inlet. The Moodyville Ferry Company, which had a three-year contract to deliver mail across the inlet, was owned by the recently formed Burrard Inlet Towing Company. Discussions to expand ferry service to logging camps up the Strait of Georgia resulted in the formation of the Union Steamship Company on July 1, 1889. Its mandate was "to own steam ships, lighters and vessels, for mail, passenger and freight traffic in the waters of British Columbia and elsewhere."[39] The first scheduled passenger service to the Desolation Sound area began with the *Comox* in April 1892. Its weekly route included Lund, Manson's Landing on Cortes, Read Island, Stuart Island and north to Sayward's Camp.

Soon the red-and-black–funnelled ships with their black hulls and white superstructures were a familiar sight. By 1911, the *Cheslakee* serviced Lewis Channel on her way to and from logging camps at Port Neville and Wellbore Channel. However, this did not last long as the boat sank at the Van Anda wharf on January 7, 1913. Refloated and refurbished, it served another twenty-five years as the *Cheakamus*.

Desolation Sound's most popular Union Steamship was the *Chelohsin*, which was in service from 1911 to 1949. The ship, built in Dublin and Belfast, Ireland, was a steel twin-screw passenger-freight vessel, fifty-four metres (175.5 feet) long, with a breadth of eleven metres (35.1 feet), a depth of four metres (14 feet) and a gross weight of 1,134 tons. Its twin triple-expansion engines were built by MacColl and Company, Belfast, and there were two multi-tubular boilers amidships. The *Chelohsin's* average speed was 12.5 knots, with a 14-knot maximum. It was licensed to carry 191 passengers and had cabins for sixty-six, with ninety-five deck settees. Its cargo capacity was 150 tons. The *Chelohsin's* first route was to Prince Rupert, but it later serviced the principal logging route to Port Hardy, and during thirty-eight years of service it called in at almost every port in the Union Steamships' territory. Everyone knew the *Chelohsin's* captains: Bob Wilson, from the Shetland Islands, and Harry Roach, a Cornishman.

The *Chelohsin* brought the mail to Refuge Cove, took turkeys from Lloyd Point to the Hotel Vancouver and brought countless grocery orders from Woodward's department store in Vancouver to housewives in remote spots. After the disastrous fire at Black Lake, it took the Christensen family to Vancouver (see Chapter 7).

In 1937, the *Chelohsin* had an extensive refit. While it was out of service and afterward, the *Lady Cynthia* serviced Desolation Sound. The *Lady Cynthia*, a twin-screw passenger freighter, was in service from 1925 to 1957. It was 72 metres (235 feet) long, 9 metres (28.6 feet) wide and 5 metres (16.3 feet) deep with a gross tonnage of 950. Its triple-expansion engines and Yarrow boilers gave it a maximum speed of

The Union Steamship Chelohsin *carried freight and people to and from civilization.*
BRITISH COLUMBIA ARCHIVES, H-06484

15.5 knots and an average speed of 13.5 knots. Built primarily as a daily excursion vessel, the *Lady Cynthia* could carry eight hundred passengers in summer and five hundred in winter.

On his way to work in logging camps around Desolation Sound and farther north, Frank White boarded the Union Steamships many times. "Travelling was like a loggers' convention," he said.[40] "Leaving Vancouver in the evening was a sobering-up job. Next morning, everyone was trying to scrounge a drink. Then at stops along the way, we'd see friends on the dock and call out 'Come with us, Joe' or 'Come to town,' depending on which direction we were going."

In 1958 the federal government withdrew its subsidy to the Union Steamships line. Logging camps were moving inland as the easily accessible coastal timber had been logged, and the companies found it more convenient to use their own crew boats. Later they flew in workers and supplies. Without the government's help, the Union Steamship company could no longer operate at a profit, and it ceased service, much to the chagrin of many coastal communities.

Even when the Union Steamships were visiting the camps and communities on a regular basis, people living in Desolation Sound and other upcoast areas were isolated. Many of them preferred this isolation, but it

Before the Union Steamships plied these waters, travelling salesmen hitched rides on scows like this one in Lewis Channel. PHOTO COURTESY INGRID COWIE

John Antle moved his family from Newfoundland to British Columbia's west coast where he started the Columbia Coast Mission along the same lines as the Grenfell Mission, which brought health care, social services and the comfort of religion to remote outports. BRITISH COLUMBIA ARCHIVES, D-00401

could be a problem when people were ill or injured. Men who were hurt in logging accidents had a particularly poor survival rate.

The first regular medical service came to the Desolation Sound area when the Columbia Coast Mission began in 1905. John Antle (1865–1949), a maverick Anglican priest from Newfoundland, started the mission. He would go from settlement to settlement in his boat and offer religious services and medical attention. At the age of eighteen, he taught school on the north coast of Newfoundland, where he was exposed to Wilfred Grenfell's mission to the poor. After studying theology, he returned to serve the outport communities as a minister. In 1897 he moved to his wife's home in Washington State.

Two years later, he was appointed to Vancouver's Fairview parish. While he was there, a newspaper account of four nameless, dead loggers arriving in Vancouver on the SS *Cassiar* prompted him to action. With a $100 grant from the church, he bought a gas engine for his home-built five-metre (sixteen-foot) sailboat *Laverock*. In 1904, he and his nine-

Wherever it called, the Columbia Mission Ship was always welcome. Its crew saved the lives of countless accident victims and its captain married many couples and christened their children. In winter the ship and its successors brought Christmas to poor settler families like the Bishops and took the children on picnics with ice cream in summer.
HARBOUR PUBLISHING ARCHIVES

year-old son rowed and sailed eight hundred kilometres (five hundred miles) up the coast of British Columbia to Alert Bay. On the way he saw the same kind of self-reliant people dealing with the same kind of rugged isolation that he had seen in Newfoundland. He quickly recognized the need for pastoral and medical care as well as the social and labour justice so dear to his heart, noting that there were "four thousand men in the camps, working in the most dangerous calling in Canada, and the nearest doctor from fifty to three hundred and fifty miles away."[41] Thanks to fundraising appearances at churches and other speaking engagements across Canada, Antle raised money to start the Columbia Coast Mission and expand it till it comprised seven mission ships and five hospitals. Hospitals servicing Desolation Sound were located at Rock Bay in Discovery Passage (built in 1905), Van Anda on Texada Island (1907) and Garden Bay in Pender Harbour (1930).

Alan and Heber Greene took over when Antle retired in 1936. In addition to transporting patients to hospital, some ships carried doctors or registered nurses as well. The chaplain—skippers lived aboard their ships and held church services whenever they stopped, christening, marrying and burying as required. They visited settlements and individual dwellings between the Sechelt Peninsula in the south and the head of Kingcome Inlet in the north, and from Discovery Passage in the west to the ends of Bute and Jervis inlets in the east. Not all the skippers were good navigators. The names of "Sky Pilot Rock and Pringle Rock in Homfray Channel suggest that some skipper-captains sometimes had their bad days too," Michael Hadley wrote in his book about the Columbia Coast Mission, *God's Little Ships*.[42] Although both these rocks are named after the lesser-known United Church mission ships, which operated at the same time, Anglican captains also ran aground. According to Jim Spilsbury, Alan Greene was notorious for this.

In the 1940s, one of the ships, the *Rendezvous*, followed a four-week schedule that concentrated on the Desolation Sound area. Rev. Rollo Boas captained the ten-metre (thirty-two-foot) powerboat from 1944 to 1955, accompanied by his wife, Kay, a registered nurse, and their two daughters, Louise and Yvonne.

During the Second World War, Jim Spilsbury's radio boat was another familiar sight. The *Five B.R.* was named after its owner's ham radio call sign, VE5BR. After Spilsbury was turned down when he tried to enlist in the armed forces at the beginning of the war, he and his wife, Glenys, ran a floating radio service shop, calling in at every community between Pender Harbour and Seymour Inlet. One of the great characters of that time, Spilsbury knew just about everyone and all their stories—a rich fund of lore that enlivens his books and lives on in the memories of all coastal dwellers.[44]

There were other floating merchants at the time, selling everything from clothing to hardware. Some, like Carl Christensen, used their routes to check out places where they might want to pre-empt land. But there were no floating merchants and few other visitors when the first settler arrived in the late 1880s.

5

PRIDEAUX HAVEN
The First Settler

Prideaux Haven is the hub of Desolation Sound. Its central location, sheltered coves and scenic islands guarantee that it will be jam-packed with yachts in July and August. It is not surprising that the settler who likely had first pick of the whole place should settle there.

Up until his death in 1931, Mike Shuttler's craggy face with the scar running down his nose was well-known to everyone who visited Prideaux Haven. Several authors wrote contemporary accounts of him. The best are by M. Wylie Blanchet and Stewart Edward White. In his novel *Skookum Chuk*, published in 1925, White portrayed Shuttler as Tim, the Transcendental Hand Logger, who meets Roger Marshall, a bored young man who learns about life through a series of adventures on the coast.[45] One of Marshall's adventures takes place in Melanie Cove, where he meets Tim.

Mike, whose Christian name was Andrew, was born in Minnesota in August 1858. He acquired the scar in a brawl when he was young. His opponent left him for dead, and when he recovered consciousness several days later, the blood-soaked mattress on which he had been placed was buzzing with flies. "I decided then," Mike told Blanchet in his deep, slow voice, "that if that was all there was to life, it wasn't worth living, and I was going off somewhere by myself to think it out."[46]

He came north and immigrated to Canada in 1884.[47] How he

arrived at Prideaux Haven is a mystery, but he probably rowed up from Vancouver like many of the other early settlers. Around 1890 he found land at the head of Melanie Cove and homesteaded there. For some reason, perhaps a certain insouciance toward government red tape, he did not formally pre-empt Lot 4354 until 1916. When he finally bought the Crown grant for his property in 1924, Phil Lavigne, Mike's neighbour in the next cove, and Fred Wing, a peripatetic Chinese logger, signed the documents witnessing that he had performed the necessary improvements totalling $2.50 per acre.

A shortage of ready cash may have been the reason Mike did not buy the land until he had been there for thirty-odd years. Many settlers had this problem, and some never got their land. Lack of money may also have been the reason Mike did not buy Lot 4183, which lay between his property and Phil Lavigne's. Some of Mike's terraces overlapped the lot, and no doubt he considered it his.

In his heyday, Mike loved company. Armed with a posy of flowers, he would row out to visit anchored boats. Like many people of that era, he rowed standing up, pushing forward on the oars, with a slight lean to his powerful body. He wore a uniform of black pants, high leather boots, a battered felt hat and the famous unshrinkable, ribbed, grey woollen Stanfield underwear made popular by the Yukon gold miners.

When Capi Blanchet and her family cruised into Prideaux Haven, Mike instructed them to anchor no closer than the copper stain on the cliff. They went ashore after supper to pick windfall apples and discovered he had a cabin on the sheltered side of a small island at the head of the cove. It was engulfed in honeysuckle and "old-fashioned flowers— mignonette and sweet-williams, bleeding-hearts and bachelor's buttons." There were also Shirley poppies and a climbing rose. As he showed the Blanchets the property, Mike pointed out the stone terraces, two metres (six feet) wide and three metres (ten feet) long, that he had laboriously built by hand up the steep slope from the water. Apple and cherry trees grew on them, with more on the hillside above.

The author Stewart Edward White, who visited Mike before the Blanchets, said the apple trees were planted between tree stumps,

Moss cloaks the remains of the fruit trees planted by Mike Shuttler on terraces at the head of Melanie Cove. PHOTO BY JOHN DAFOE

perhaps the remnants of the trees used to build the cabin. Among them, vegetables grew in irregular plots of soil fertilized by seaweed.

White wrote of a split-cedar fence surmounted by stakes festooned in old fishnets to keep the deer out. Blanchet, visiting later, described an eight-foot sapling fence for the same purpose. It encompassed 1.5 hectares (four acres) of orchard. She said that a man came ashore one day and gave Mike an apple. He liked the taste and "heeled in his core beside the steps." It took a while to grow but was mature when she saw it. The terraces are still visible, but alder have overwhelmed most of the fruit trees.

Both White and Blanchet were invited inside the cabin. White thought it a typical bachelor establishment with all the untidiness of a person living alone with few visitors. There were two rooms. The walls were plastered with pictures cut out of magazines. In later years, canvas stretched across the roof rafters sagged with the nests of generations of packrats. In the main room was an old leather chair and a shelf full of books across one end. At the other end was "a muddle of stove, dishpan and pots" and a table. The second room was down three steps so that half was below ground. "Warmer in winter," Mike told Blanchet.

Jens Andersen of Corbie's Point on Cortes Island was a friend of Mike's for twenty years. His daughter, Ingrid, visited Mike when she was a small child and remembered that "his windows were darkened by grape vines with big white spider webs between them. He used to drop flies in their webs saying: 'These are my friends.'"[48] Fleas inhabiting the hides on the floor bit her bare ankles so she hated coming. Alan Morley, a BC writer who took over the cabin after Mike died, said there were deer, bear and cougar hides on top of newspapers dating back to the early 1890s. He spoke of a third room containing a cider press and "a score of large wooden barrels with the aroma of hard cider and black-berry wine." Mike liked to share a glass with visitors.

White probably visited during the First World War and perhaps be-fore it. In *Skookum Chuk* he says Tim "appeared to be about forty years of age." As Mike was born in 1858, this sighting may have taken place in the early 1900s—or White may have used poetic licence in the book. Mike tried to join up but was told he was too old. However, he did his bit by looking after the properties of neighbours young enough to go, including George Walker Parker and Bertram Saulter of Roffey Island. Mike was unable to visit more than once a week and was appalled by the looting: "Even axes weren't safe." He never caught anyone in the act but dismissed the culprits as "poor things, just undeveloped."

Visitors were an excuse for music. Mike had a rule that he never played his record collection unless someone else was there. Several months might go by between such occasions, but he stuck to his decision. White noticed his big hands were deft when it came to setting up the small phonograph. He expected to hear jazz and ragtime but got classical music instead. Mike despised ragtime, saying that "it just makes fun of good music." He put on Wagner's *Tannhauser* and then sat down to enjoy it with his chin resting on his fist and his kindly blue eyes focussed on a point far in the distance.

Although he left school early to go to work, he was intelligent and educated himself by reading voraciously. He owned many books including copies of the classics—Marcus Aurelius, Epictetus, Plato and Emerson—and a Vancouver library lent him books. In turn, he'd lend his books to anyone interested. For a while there was a logging camp in Deep Bay (Tenedos Bay), and the people there borrowed some of the books. He also tried to pass on his ideas to his illiterate neighbour, Phil Lavigne.

Mike told White that he had read "about a hundred books on theosophy." His verdict: "I ain't an educated man, no ways; but there seems to me a lot that's sensible in it. But these ready-made religions don't somehow hit me, though. They're always talking about dying, dying, dying, and how to do it. We want something to teach us how to live. Looks like the dying comes natural enough. That part isn't important."

In conversation, he often stated that he believed in living each day to the fullest and being in harmony with nature. He pencilled his credo on a piece of cardboard and hung it on the wall. It began: "Look well of to-day—for it is the Life of Life," and continued: "To-day well lived makes every Yesterday a dream of happiness, and every To-morrow a vision of hope." Blanchet reprinted the whole thing.

One year Blanchet lent him a popular book by an East Indian mystic. After reading it for hour after hour under an apple tree, Mike gave it back to her, saying, "Just so much dope. All words—not how to think or how to live, but how to get things with no effort!" In subsequent years she saved copies of magazines like *Atlantic Monthly* and *Harper's*. By summer's end he would have read them all. Puffing on his pipe, he'd discuss them with her animatedly. Blanchet loved his high forehead, mild blue eyes and droopy moustache, which she thought made him look like Don Quixote.

In White's novel, the character Tim, based on Mike, expounds at great length that money is of little value to him. Marshall, the main character, a bored young rich man, finds it hard to understand that Tim is simply not interested in making money. Likely echoing Mike, Tim says: "What do I want to get rich for?" and "I work when I want to; I get my grub. I am my own boss. I make a few hundred dollars when I want them."

Mike grew his own vegetables and fruits. He sold the excess to the logging camp at Deep Bay, to the store at Refuge Cove, where he collected his mail, and to other people in the area. Melanie Cove was a traditional First Nations clam beach, so he shared the harvest the Sliammon people continued to gather. Salmon were plentiful too. White described how, several days in a row, Mike encountered a fine buck on the same ledge overlooking his vegetable patch. After the second time, he rowed round to a neighbour, borrowed a couple of cartridges and dispatched the buck. It made fine venison. The hide became a gate to keep other deer out.

Mike also kept goats. White wrote of an old billy goat with murderous eyes. It tried to jump the fence during a visit, but Mike grabbed its beard and punched it in the face till it bleated, explaining that he had "to make him cry or he'll get too big for his pants. It don't look pretty to hit the critter, but when a thing is to be done, a man is foolish not to do it. It's Nature. You must work with Nature."

He could be gentle too. He told Alan Morley that one day when he first arrived at the cabin, he was sitting by the stove eating when he felt something pull at his pant leg. It was a mink. He fed it bacon or cold meat and it became a regular visitor.

Small creatures were important to him. He rejoiced in the bees, coloured flies and hummingbirds attracted by the honeysuckle outside his cabin. "But," he commented, "there's lots of people in here with fancy yachts who walk right under it and never notice it's there at all."

Patience was one of his strengths. He told White he planned his agricultural activities eight years in advance. The same was true of the logging that was his main source of cash. Both White and Blanchet climbed the hill to view the scene of action. He spent a great deal of time planning the trajectory of his logs down to the sea. "Working with Nature," he said. First he felled smaller trees to act as skids; then he went to work on the one he wanted to sell. Two thirty-four-kilogram (seventy-five-pound) Gilchrist jacks helped move logs into position for their final whoosh down into the ocean. Some that he sold were used in a big dry dock in Vancouver.

In 1931 he became ill and was moved to the Powell River hospital, where he died on December 1, at age seventy-three, "after being ill for some time." He is buried in an unmarked grave in the Cranberry Cemetery.

When Blanchet visited the next summer, she found the cabin stripped and empty. Mike's books had found a new home in the cabin of his neighbour, Phil Lavigne, in Laura Cove. Phil was illiterate but wanted a memento of his long-time friend. "All dem words, and 'e 'ad to die like all de rest of us!" Phil told Blanchet.

Alan Morley took over Mike's cabin and claimed to be "the second and last Hermit of Prideaux Haven." Unfortunately, he didn't last long—cabin fever got him. Francis Barrow, visiting in the summer of 1933, wrote in his journal that "the late occupant greeted people with a shotgun and had to be removed."[49]

Maria Christensen Zaikow remembered hearing Phil Lavigne tell the story.[50] One afternoon, Morley arrived at Phil's place brandishing a gun.

"You won't laugh at me, will you?" he asked Phil.

"No, I won't," said Phil. He sat and talked to Morley all afternoon, gave him a cup of coffee or tea and tried to calm him down, but he didn't get any better. Phil got a little worried. Eventually he said, "I have to go and milk the goats."

"Okay," said Morley. "You can't get away because I can see you go down to the float from the house."

Phil had to go round the corner of the house and down to the well in order to milk the goats. But instead of milking the beasts he cut up over the hill and into the woods and ran over to Saulter and Pritchard's place at Roffey Island. It was quite a hike. One of them went by boat to Refuge Cove while Phil waited at their place.

By the time the police arrived at Phil's, Morley had gone home. They went round to Melanie Cove and took him away, presumably to the Columbia Mission boat, as Alan Greene remembered taking him aboard. Later visitors found that a BC Parks outhouse had replaced the cabin.

Phil Lavigne (1863–1946) arrived some time after Mike, likely in the early 1900s, and pre-empted Lot 4184 in Laura Cove in 1908. He built a cabin there but didn't get his Crown grant till 1930. Blanchet, who made it her business to find out where people came from, said he "was supposed to have killed a man back in Quebec." He seems to have been well-established when she first arrived in the mid-1920s. She remarked on his habit of sticking his thumbs in his braces as he stood talking to her. When Francis and Amy Barrow met him in 1933, he told them that he was very happy to be receiving the old-age pension of twenty dollars a month. They

Francis Barrow photographed Phil Lavigne and his beloved pipe in 1938. CAMPBELL RIVER MUSEUM 2011O-53

thought he looked a lot younger than his seventy-one years. (According to the 1911 Canadian census, he was born in May 1863.)

Before the pension, he made a living from his garden and from fishing. In her book *Destination Cortez Island*, June Cameron recorded that he bought a one-dollar fishing licence in 1924, and he probably had licences in other years as well. The Barrows bought lettuces, carrots, gooseberries, goat milk and a couple of table-ready roosters from him. They said his goats followed them around "like dogs." Francis made a movie that shows a slight, graceful man fondling his nannies by their horns.[51] He kept his billy goat pastured on Graveyard (Copplestone) Island.

Blanchet chronicled the billy's untimely end. Sometime after Mike's death, the Blanchets' dog, Pam, spent a fearful night ashore in Melanie Cove. During the dark hours and again in the morning, the family found her whining and up to her neck in water. They thought a bear had frightened her, but Phil was sure it was a cougar. Six weeks later, when the family called in on their way home, he told them the sequel. The next night, at four in the morning, he heard the billy goat making a racket. Armed with his gun, he rowed to the island, where he saw the goat's head and shoulders protruding from behind the big round boulder on the beach. On landing, he discovered a cougar already eating it.

"I got 'im first shot—between de eyes ... den I 'ad to shoot de goat," Phil said. Blanchet saw the cougar skin pinned out on the woodshed wall. It was three metres (nine feet) long.

"Don't you let dos kids of your sleep on shore wid de dog at night—ever. De cougar would be atter de dog, but de kids might get hurt too," Phil said. Sage advice even for today. He replaced this goat with another that he shared with the Christensens of Salt Lagoon. It used to stand on top of the boulder where its predecessor died and gaze longingly at the nannies frolicking round Phil's cabin, unaware that the tide had come up and cut it off from the main part of the island.

Barrow said that Phil Lavigne's "shack was as tidy and neat as could be." Maria Christensen Zaikow's memory is that like many other settlers, he threw his garbage out into the cove. Jars, old pop bottles and other items lay exposed at low tide. No doubt the garbage attracted the mink that ran along the beach every day. Once someone suggested they be killed, but Phil wouldn't hear of it. He liked to watch the animals.

Phil's illiteracy was well known. The Barrows wrote letters for him and so did Maria. "What shall I say?" she would ask him when she was writing to his relatives in Quebec.

"Tell 'em I'm fine," he told her.

Mount Denman was a familiar sight to early settlers like Mike Shuttler and Phil Lavigne as they rowed around their homesteads in Prideaux Haven.

"It was very difficult," she said. "I also read the newspaper to him. He always took the Sunday edition because he liked the funnies."

Her father, Carl, visited him regularly. When Maria accompanied her father, Phil would ask her to cut his hair as he knew she did her father's, but, Maria said, "I didn't like doing it because he always pinched me. He was a dirty old man." In 1943, when Carl Christensen decided to leave Salt Lagoon, he asked Phil to stay with his sixteen-year-old son Joe while Carl and Maria went to Blubber Bay on Texada Island to look for work and a place to live. Phil stayed for about four weeks.

Two other visitors to Phil's home at Laura Cove were Herman and Eric Lindberg, two brothers from Lloyd Point. Herman refused to buy tobacco at the Refuge Cove store for Eric, so Eric would get Phil to buy it. Barrow said Phil also bought tobacco for Bertram Saulter, who lived at Roffey Island. Maria Christensen says that like many people (including her father), Phil grew tobacco for his own use. Pictures show him with a comfortable pipe between his teeth.

Unlike Mike, Phil was not a logger. The Palmers from Tenedos Bay tied their boats up to his dock and logged behind his cabin.

In 1945, Phil got sick and was taken to the Powell River hospital. Maria Christensen, who had moved to Texada by this time, visited him but heard no more. He died at the hospital on August 7, 1946, aged eighty-four, and was buried in an unmarked grave in the Cranberry Cemetery. His name is spelled "Levigne" on his death notice, but Blanchet had it as "Lavine," and Francis Barrow called him "Lavigne." Maria always spelled it Lavigne when she wrote letters to his relatives for him. As he was illiterate, spelling was not one of his priorities.

Roffey Island is less than a kilometre (half a mile) north of Phil Lavigne's Laura Cove homestead. There were two Crown land grants in this immediate area—Lot 4185 and Lot 4186. The latter was definitely pre-empted in 1915, and the former may have been pre-empted at the same time as the two loggers who worked on the lots were friends. Two years later, both men enlisted in the Canadian Overseas Expeditionary Force, as the Canadian army that fought in the First World War was called.

George Walker Parker (1874–1925) was the older and taller of the two. His attestation paper, which he filled out to declare his willingness to enlist, states that he was five foot nine with a "dark" complexion, grey eyes and dark hair streaked with grey. He was forty-two at the time and had already put in three years' service with a regiment in Winnipeg from 1893 to 1895. He was unmarried, and his next of kin was his mother in Toronto.

Bertram Saulter (1878–1961) was five inches shorter, with light brown hair, hazel eyes and a "fresh" complexion. Three years younger than Parker, he was married and had no previous military experience. Both men gave Saulter's address, 3436 West Third Avenue in Vancouver, as their home.

After serving in France, they were demobilized in April 1919 and received their Crown grants the same year. Unfortunately, Parker did not enjoy his for long. He died on December 8, 1925, at the age of fifty-one, and Saulter took over his land.

Francis Barrow mentioned two men living at this location in the 1930s, "Saulter and his chum Frank." He photographed their small cabin, built on the site of Flea Village, which Archibald Menzies, Joseph Whidbey and Peter Puget visited in 1792 (see Chapter 3). Maria Christensen Zaikow gave their names as Saulter and Pritchard and said they were the same age as her father. Carl never let his children go ashore to meet them. Maria thought this was because they ran around in the nude.

Over the years, Barrow enjoyed many games of cribbage with Saulter, and he faithfully chronicled Saulter and Frank's boat-building activities. By July 1933 they had reached the stage of planking a nine-metre (thirty-foot) boat. Barrow described it as a West Coast troller.[52] Three years later they had six more planks to put on their "motor-troller," which they hoped to finish "in a month or two." In fact, Barrow wrote that they talked of caulking it the next week. At that point they were only working on the boat in the afternoons. In the mornings, starting at 5 a.m., they went up the mountain to log until 11 a.m. They were teaching Saulter's son and brother-in-law the trade with the idea of sending them out on their own the following year. Wood prices were high, which pleased everyone.

Two years later, Phil Lavigne told the Barrows that Frank had recently taken Saulter to hospital for a second round of surgery. The Barrows went on from Desolation Sound up Jervis Inlet, where they met Peck Easthope, son of the manufacturer of the first famous Easthope engine.[53] Easthope told them Saulter had just returned to Roffey Island, but the Barrows say no more about him, and Maria Christensen Zaikow does not know what happened after that either.

Although the earliest residents lived some distance from each other, there was a sense of community and caring that was perhaps inspired by the isolation. People knew their neighbours and would help them when they could, and they looked forward to annual visitors like the Blanchets and Barrows, who had become friends and brought news and sometimes treats from the outside world. Today Prideaux Haven is uninhabited as it is part of Desolation Sound Marine Park.

"This looks like the manufacture of hooch, but is nothing worse than a steam box for bending planks for their boat," wrote Francis Barrow who took this 1934 photo of Saulter and Frank. CAMPBELL RIVER MUSEUM 20110-72

6

WEST REDONDA ISLAND
Social Centre of the Sound

*I*n the past, there were two fairly active settlements on West Redonda Island: Refuge Cove, on the southwest side of the island, and Redonda Bay, on the northwest side above Teakerne Arm. Today, even in summer, almost no one lives at Redonda Bay. Refuge Cove, which for several decades was Desolation Sound's main social centre, is almost deserted in winter.

The original settlement at Refuge Cove was in the lagoon behind the present store. George Black (1866–1961), a returned Klondike adventurer, obtained his Crown grant to the sixty-three hectares (155 acres) of Lot 2849 in 1913. He drained three swamps on the lagoon south of Black Lake to make his farm. In the narrow entrance to the lagoon, he constructed a dam and a sluice channel to move logs efficiently out into the ocean.[54] The lagoon became a saltwater lake.[55] As access was less convenient, future settlers remained outside in the cove.

Bob and Margaret McGuffie arrived in 1914 and lived in a bay just north of Refuge Cove.[56] They came to escape the war. Margaret (1882–1954) did not want Bob to enlist, leaving her alone to look after their children, of which there were eventually ten. Bob (1884–1962) had arrived in Canada as a nineteen-year-old in 1903. His parents were among the 2,600 Barr Colonists, led by Isaac Barr and George Lloyd, who came from England to the Canadian prairies and settled the area around what later became Lloydminster on the Alberta–Saskatchewan border. They brought Bob and his eleven-year-old sister Mary, who married Peter Bishop and eventually moved to Malaspina Inlet (see Chapter 13). Trained as a cabinetmaker in England, Bob did work for Chief Billy Mitchell at Church House. The Klahoose people there taught him how to build dugout canoes, and later his children rowed back and forth to Church House for visits. They maintained the friendship long after the family moved to Powell River in 1924, when Bob got a job at the mill there.

In 1914 there were enough children at the cove to qualify for a school. The Blacks themselves had seven: Ollie, Florence, Jennie, Beatrice, Bill, Bob and Morris. Miss G.H. McGregor came for a salary of $60 a month. Donna Jackson Murphy succeeded her in 1921 at the same salary.[57] In her memoirs, Murphy said it was "the most miserable ten months of my whole life." Apparently the food was awful and the living conditions spartan. She and the children found a human skeleton behind the school and used it for health lessons.[58] The school board consisted of Mrs. B.M. Black, who was the secretary, Mrs. A. Hoyel and Mrs. S. Tosr.[59] The school closed in the early 1920s but reopened for nine pupils in 1949. It closed in 1950 and then reopened again a year or two later.[60]

The 1918 Minister of Lands survey reported that the Smith family on Lot 4936 had a good house and garden on six hectares (fifteen acres) and were doing very well. They supplemented their income by trapping and handlogging.[61] James B. Smith obtained the Crown grant for this lot on December 19, 1923. The timber was excluded as it had already been granted in 1908 to John Duncan MacNeill. The same report says that the people at the head of Teakerne Arm, north of Refuge Cove, were also doing well, though it didn't identify them.

It was this level of activity that prompted Robert Donley (1874–1955) to open the first store in the area in 1918. He called it the Donley Trading Company. As well as selling groceries and hardware, he acted as a fish buyer and a gas, kerosene and oil depot. Shortly after the store opened, he added a post office. Settlers from miles around congregated in the dance hall behind the store on Saturday evenings in the 1920s. By 1931, a year after J.R. Tindall (1907–1954) bought the store from Donley, the BC Directory reported the population of Refuge Cove as two hundred.[62]

Many settlers sold their excess vegetables and fruits through the store. "We grew wonderful strawberries," said Maria Christensen Zaikow, who spent her childhood in Salt Lagoon, on the east side of West Redonda Island.[63] "They were more than we could use, so we sold the extras at the Refuge Cove store. We'd make as much as thirty dollars a season, which was a lot of money in those days." They also sold early apples, other berries and tomatoes. "[Jack Tindall] gave us the price he sold them for because he said he made profit on what we bought," Maria said. "That was enough for him. I remember someone complained to Pop that Tindall was selling the strawberries for 50 cents a husk. Pop said, yes that's what I get for them. That's what he did for the strawberries. I don't know about the rest of the stuff, but he said: 'I make profit on what you buy.' Nobody does that nowadays."

The mail would arrive at the Refuge Cove post office on the Union Steamship every Sunday, and many residents would gather to wait for it.

Refuge Cove in 1929, two years before Robert Donley sold the store to Jack Tindall.
COURTESY MARIA ZAIKOW

The McGuffie family in 1903 before leaving England to come to Saskatchewan with the Barr Colonists. Mr. and Mrs. McGuffie sit in the middle with three-year-old Agnes on her father's lap. The eldest boy (top right) did not come. Mary McGuffie (age eleven in white) later married Peter Bishop and settled in Malaspina Inlet. Her brother Robert, a cabinetmaker, stands behind her left shoulder. He homesteaded just north of Refuge Cove 1910–1924. Beside him stands his brother William, a grocer like their father. In front of Mary sits twelve-year-old James and, on the other side beside her father, seventeen-year-old Jessie, a seamstress. After that first terrible winter in tents, the family moved to Kamloops.
COURTESY MARY GUSSMAN

Robert McGuffie's homestead just north of Refuge Cove. COURTESY JOAN FULLER

McGuffie children and friends enjoying a sunny day on West Redonda Island. COURTESY
JOAN FULLER

On one of the frequent foggy Sundays, the crowd could hear the steamship's whistle sounding as it felt its way in. Maria's father, Carl Christensen, a mariner himself, understood the captain's dilemma. He picked up an oil drum and banged it loudly. When the ship docked, the captain thanked him for the help in finding the dock, and the storekeeper put up a three-cornered gong as a more permanent aid to mariners.

Jack Tindall sold the store to Norman and Buster Hope in 1946 and invested the proceeds in Jim Spilsbury's radio business, becoming Spilsbury's partner.[64] The Spilsburys and Tindall were ham radio enthusiasts and had been friends for years, often spending Christmas together. The Hopes were two of five brothers—Reginald, Stan, Buster, Norm and Herbert—who grew up in North Vancouver. Reginald learned Cantonese, Japanese and Russian on the streets of Vancouver and ended up as an official interpreter in Ottawa. Herbert, the youngest, designed Spilsbury's semi-portable Ad-10 radio transmitters, which linked all the ports of call for Spilsbury's Queen Charlotte Airlines.[65] Two Hope sisters, Irene and Winifred, married Spilsburys. Irene married Jim's cousin Rupert, the pilot who encouraged Jim to start his "accidental airline."[66] Winifred, a long-time office manager with the Spilsbury and Tindall radio business, married Jim in 1970.

By 1942, several other floathouses had tied up near the store. COURTESY MARIA ZAIKOW

According to Judith Williams, a member of the Refuge Cove Land and Housing Cooperative, when the Hopes arrived at the cove in 1945, "all the houses were on log floats and strung in rows along boom sticks with cable and chain."[67] Besides groceries, the old store sold logging equipment. Ammunition and contraceptives were kept under the counter. You could also buy a suit of clothes there. Norm would take your measurements and mail them to Vancouver. Some time later, the suit would arrive. In those days, finance and business were male preserves, although Buster's wife, Vivian, and Norm's wife, Doris (1895–1981), worked in the store and post office.

When Joyce Point Logging, just north of Teakerne Arm, defaulted on its credit, Norman (1909–1984) took it over and ran it for ten years while Buster (1910–1980) tended to the store. This diversification was essential as the blasting of Ripple Rock on April 5, 1958, made Discovery Passage much safer for shipping.[68] Many tugs, especially those that had previously transited Lewis Channel, which brought them right by Refuge Cove, now preferred the Campbell River side of Quadra and Cortes islands. Business slumped. When Norman caught Buster

The Refuge Cove store the year before Jack Tindall sold it to Norman Hope. COURTESY MARIA ZAIKOW

embezzling the store's proceeds, he forced him to leave and took over the whole operation himself.[69]

Joyce Mostat, daughter of Dan Parker from Malaspina Inlet (see Chapter 13), remembered her father taking the family to shop for groceries and pick up the mail on a Sunday during the 1940s.[70] They took two apple boxes to put the groceries in. While her parents shopped at the general store or went in to the post office in the back, she made a dive for the comic books.

"The Union Steamship brought in ice cream packed in dry ice," she said. "When he put the ice cream in his propane freezer, Mr. Hope [probably Buster] would empty the ice onto the rocks below the store and a great cloud of smoke came up. We'd buy a brick of the Palm Dairies' ice cream and take it home. Usually we got the Neapolitan flavour, but occasionally we'd have the cherry custard, which was my favourite. We'd rush home with it and cut it into six pieces before it melted.

"I don't know how the Hopes managed, because they gave everyone credit. We all struggled to pay our bills, so they never got rich."

Norm Gibbons first came to Refuge Cove as a child in 1952.[71] He remembered Dorothy and Ed Thomas living on the other side of the cove. They lived on the *Devon*, which Ed had built and which was powered by an Easthope engine. The Thomases used it to run loggers between the Union Steamships and their camps at Homfray Creek and up Toba Inlet. Dorothy (1897–1981) was a tiny woman who had survived three husbands. Once a year she would buy a case of fifty cans of sardines from the store. Her diet was one fish a day plus gallons of tea and tons of goose grass (sea asparagus). She was very limber and hiked everywhere. Even in her mid-seventies, she preferred to sit cross-legged. There is speculation that her third husband, Ed (1889–1969), may have been escaping another wife and family.[72]

Another character was Alice, who came to live in the cove when Joyce Point Logging, where she had been the cook, shut down. She baked fresh bread for the Refuge Cove store.

A big family of Thompsons lived on Lot 5591. Thompson Lake near Teakerne Arm is named after them. They also lived in Tenedos Bay in the late 1940s. Many of the Thompson children moved to Quadra and Cortes.

Agnes Bishop, who grew up in Malaspina Inlet, and her fisherman husband, Nick, lived in Refuge Cove for three or four years in the 1950s. Gibbons remembered her as "a pretty outrageous wild woman and a real party girl. Dressed in a tattered fisherman's sweater and old pants, she had no teeth and was not attractive."

Barb Bloom, who lived in Galley Bay in the 1960s, thought of the Hopes as "a centre of information."[73] They took care of everyone. "You'd ask if they'd seen someone like the Lindbergs and they'd say, 'Oh, yes, they came down and got the mail three days ago. Eric's arthritis is bothering him,' and you'd know that later, when someone asked about you, they'd say something similar." This tradition continues today, though many of the permanent residents have satellite e-mail, and of course there's always the VHF radio.

In 1968 the store burned down. The Hopes' old black cat was a casualty and may have caused the fire by sitting on the ancient electrical wiring, causing it to short. Doris was away when it happened. Norman woke up in time to scramble into his pants and retrieve the cash box before the flames reached it. He reopened on a twenty-six-metre (eighty-seven-foot) barge that he docked at the government wharf and later pulled up on the land.

Big changes were happening on the coast at this time. In the 1950s, the Cove had a population of forty to fifty people living on boats, floats and cottages ashore. By 1971, when Denise and Norm Gibbons arrived there for an eight-month vacation, the population had shrunk to six. Bigger fish boats had refrigeration on board, so the fish-buying station at Refuge Cove closed.

The camp at the Teakerne Arm log sort, just north of Refuge Cove, also closed, but the workers commuted every day from Squirrel Cove and Lund until the early 1990s, when the Stillwater dry sort, south of Powell River, replaced this water-based sort. Bigger tugs replaced the smaller ones. They carried enough fuel and food for three- or four-week trips, so the crew no longer needed to come in to replenish supplies every three days. Big forest companies replaced individual gyppo loggers and handloggers.

"The Hopes were freaking," said Gibbons. "They wanted to retire but couldn't get their money out of the place." Gibbons persuaded them to give him a six-month option to buy the fifty-three-year-old operation. He took a one-year job in Vancouver while he looked for financing, and the final sale went through in 1972. Gibbons and Ken Ferguson bought the store, which included a sinking barge, a laundromat and a diesel generator that didn't work.

In a separate transaction, Hope sold his seventy-five hectares (186 acres) of land, including 2.4 kilometres (1.5 miles) of waterfront, to the Refuge Cove Land and Housing Cooperative. It is now one of the longest-lasting housing co-ops in the province. The buyers were a group of back-to-the-land university types whose learning processes provided much amusement for themselves and for the Hopes. This was largely due to the storytelling abilities of the legendary Doris Hope and to the writing down of Doris's stories by Judith Williams, one of the co-op members. The resulting *Dynamite Stories* is a coastal classic.

Another of the co-op members, John Dixon, said that "'Uncle Norman,' as we all called him, was tireless in his patient tutelage of us greenhorns—even though he was known to use foul language. My favourites: 'That motor is so weak that it couldn't pull a limp dick out of a lard pail' and 'It'll stick like shit to a blanket,' along with Doris's favourite: 'Stiff as a wedding prick.'"

Doris Hope was full of curiosity about the outside world. Periodically she dressed up in black city clothes, including a large hat, and boarded a floatplane for Vancouver. When television first became available, she bought a set. The only place she could get reception was out on the point where the light beacon was. An extremely long cord from the generator next to her house powered it. She rowed out to the beacon, set the TV on the point and patched it into the cord. Then, wrapped in a sleeping bag, she lay back in her boat to watch opera. Soon a man in another boat joined her and rumours rampaged through the settlement.

"We was in separate boats, for heaven's sake," she would say.

Old-timers like the Hopes thought the newcomers would blast spaces for twelve-metre (forty-foot) trailers, which were their idea of heaven. Gibbons and his friends had different ideas. "We built our log house just with a hand winch and a chain saw," said Gibbons. "People like Norm Hope thought we were mad."

The Hopes lived in a house that was one of the well-travelled relics of the coast. Originally built to house workers constructing the Powell River mill in 1910, it and others like it were sold off and mounted on floats. Before Norm Hope acquired his, it was occupied by the Murrays while they looked after the Powell River Company's booming ground at the head of Teakerne Arm. When Norm brought it to Refuge Cove, he pulled it up on land. It is still in use, situated west of the store and set back from the boardwalk. It has a yellow highlight board running around the front just below the level of the porch. The Refuge Cove Co-op members enjoy its original 1940s décor as they play poker on Doris's table.[74]

Norm Gibbons remembered people from the Galley Bay commune coming in and asking for mail "for the Rutabaga Families" in the early 1970s. He said they "didn't wash very much." Many of these people had given themselves new names. One of the women called herself Sunshine. Norm thought she was on drugs and perhaps had a mental illness besides. Once she brought a huge load of laundry and walked right into the water with it, where it floated around her and some kids who were swimming.

Bud Jarvis, Norm Hope's nephew, met the same woman out on the water when a strong southeaster was blowing up a storm. He was in a small runabout, but she was in a canoe that was awash. "She was a tough case," Bud said. "With her, she had Sam, her four-year-old son, and her baby, Moonbeam. 'Would you stay with me till we get through this stuff,' she asked. 'Yes.' 'Thank you.' So I stayed with her till she was nearly back at Galley Bay and in the shelter of Zephine Head. Years later, I heard she had got her life together and returned to her wealthy US family."

The three years prior to the oil crisis of 1973 were busy ones for the store. Suddenly a lot of blue-collar workers were able to afford five- or six-metre (eighteen- to twenty-foot) boats for day trips. They needed ice, water and fuel every day, and they came in to Refuge Cove to get them. The nerve-racking boardwalk was replaced in 1973. Once the oil crisis drove gas prices up, the customers disappeared. The tourists who did come were in nine-metre (thirty-foot) boats that could carry lots of fuel and food. In the late 1970s, a scheduled plane service started from Campbell River. Residents, no longer so dependent on the local store, bought less.

Today, the Refuge Cove store is a conglomeration of retail outlets including a general store, post office, gift shop, showers, laundry and hamburger stand. At a cost of five dollars a bag, you can even drop your garbage off. From mid-June to the third week in August, the store is packed. All the yachts from Desolation Sound come to replenish their booze supplies, buy groceries, gifts and hardware, and give the crew an ice cream. After that, there is so little action that the current owners, Bonnie MacDonald and Colin Robertson, who live on Cortes Island, close down from October to May, though they hire a local to keep the post office open all year round. Most of the co-op members retreat for the winter to less-isolated residences.

The story of Refuge Cove is not complete without "the cougar story." This is a comedy of errors that I have heard told by several people. The gist of it is that a young female cougar in search of a meal followed two delicious smells right into Reinhold Hoge's house (Hoge operates the hamburger stand at Refuge Cove). As his visiting brother-in-law plunked a nice fat salmon down on the counter, the crowd in the living room became aware that he had been followed in not only by the dachshund, Fritzchen, but also by a cougar. An uproar ensued as the cougar grabbed the dog's head. Hoge jumped on the cougar, and Fritzchen bolted out of his dog door. Confusion reigned as some wanted to open the front door to let the cougar out, and others tried to close it to keep the animal from pursuing Fritzchen. Hoge's eighty-two-year-old father whacked the cat with a newspaper as it banged into every window in the place in a fruitless effort to escape. Meanwhile, Hoge searched for bullets for his .22. The cougar was standing dazed and motionless when he shot it.

Everyone with a radio telephone heard Hoge telling the story and inviting people to come and view the results. Newspapers around the world spread the word. The game warden was not amused. Unfortunately, Hoge did not have a cougar licence. The warden informed him that cougars were no longer considered vermin and there was no bounty on them. He ordered Hoge to bring the carcass to Campbell River forthwith, but Hoge committed it to the deep in Lewis Channel. Fritzchen's scratches soon healed.

There hasn't been quite as much excitement in Redonda Bay, previously called Deceit Bay, above Teakerne Arm.[75] In 1835 it was the site of a Salish village. In his history of Redonda Bay, written in March 1975, Tom Manson stated that the remains of a Native fish trap could be seen at the mouth of Lillian Russell Creek, which empties into the bay. Lillian may have been the wife of Alex Russell, a handlogger with Crown grants on several islands, notably Maurelle.[76]

There is a large cluster of dykes along the north shore of West Redonda Island.[77] This geological phenomenon emerged millions of years ago, when a darker rock was intruded into the surrounding granitic rocks, forming stripes called dykes. Hot liquids present when the dykes were formed introduced new minerals and altered existing ones in the surrounding rocks. This altered area near the dykes contains iron and copper minerals that have attracted prospectors for years.

In 1892, the Elsie mineral claim, subsequently known as the Redonda Iron Mine, was staked three kilometres (two miles) east of Connis Point on West Redonda Island. A year later, 568 metric tons (626 tons) of magnetite ore were shipped to Oswego Iron and Steel Company's furnace in Oregon, but this was the first and last shipment. The owners of the claim, De Wolfe and Munro of Vancouver, must have remained optimistic, as George De Wolfe obtained a Crown grant in 1895.

Writing in 1913, J. Austin Bancroft reported seeing an open cut, sixteen metres (fifty-four feet) long, made into a body of magnetite for six metres (twenty feet) at a spot west of Hepburn Point and south of Elizabeth Island in Pryce Channel.[78] This was the De Wolfe and Munro operation. Bancroft described the shore rocks as porphyritic granodiorite, shading off into light grey hornblende granite, and wrote that "a much dilapidated chute extends to the beach." Two bunkers controlled the descent of the ore from the outcrop 135 metres (450 feet) up the steep 914-metre (3,000-foot) cliffs. By 1920, when 7,664 metric tons (8,450 tons) of limestone were shipped to the Whalen pulp and paper mills, there was no trace of the cabin or chute used by the mine.[79]

Bancroft also noted that there was pink granite at Walsh Cove, "similar but more pleasing than that found at Lago de Maggiore in Italy," and two similar deposits at the head of Pendrell Sound on East Redonda and near Dean Point on West Redonda.

Bancroft's conclusion was that although many claims were staked along the shore, they were seldom developed. "In some promising areas practically no development work has been carried on." Most prospectors seemed to be reluctant to get out of their canoes, and Bancroft admitted that he was the same way. In the summer of 1907, his gasoline launch, appropriately named *The Dawson* (after George Dawson; see Chapter 3), logged 2,478 kilometres (1,540 miles) of coast, of which 1,094 kilometres (680 miles) were on the mainland and the rest were islands. He travelled from the mouth of Powell River to the entrance to Kingcome Inlet.

Between 1907 and the 1930s, various logging companies and a cannery set up operations in Redonda Bay, and ships would wait there for suitable tides on which to go through the Sonora Island and Stuart Island rapids. The Redonda Canning Company was established in the 1920s or earlier.[80] Its steam power came from boilers in the rotting hulk of an old paddle wheeler, SS *Transfer*, which in its heyday ran a ferry service between New Westminster and Chilliwack. The ship was drawn up on the beach, where it sometimes acted as a bunkhouse for cannery workers as well.

To serve these transient locals, Syd Vicary (1878–1958) and his daughter kept a store and post office in the bay in the 1920s and 1930s.

During the Depression, all the enterprises except the store closed down.[81]

In 1938, Gerry Olmstead (1885–1956), a logger, brought his wife and four sons to camp on the beach until they had time to build a large house and other buildings. Olmstead "truck logged," using an ingenious combination of plank roads and trestles over the gullies. Olmstead brought Margaret Sinclair to Redonda Bay to teach school in his home till a separate building was erected in 1941. This served as a community recreation centre, and one of the Olmstead sons was married there.

Frances Millerd and Company reopened the cannery in the early 1940s. Workers built a dam above the bay to maintain a steady water supply and dismantled the *Transfer*, which was still rotting on the beach, so they could move the boilers inside the cannery.

The cannery foreman was Albert Wilson, a fisherman who lived with his wife and his brother Charlie in two little houses off to one side of the cannery. The crew were mainly Salish people from Church House, Sliammon and Squirrel Cove. They cleaned and filleted the fish and stuffed the cans before sluicing all the waste back into the ocean.

Redonda Cannery where Elsie Paul experienced the 1946 earthquake. In the 1960s, the Galley Bay co-op salvaged lumber from the cannery to build their cabins. BRITISH COLUMBIA ARCHIVES, D-09320

In 1946, the Timothy family—grandparents Jim and Molly, uncle Willy and granddaughter Elsie—spent the summer working at the Redonda Bay Cannery.[82] They lived in a small cabin on the walkway behind the cannery. At night they could hear the waves washing the pilings underneath. At the end of the walkway was an outhouse with a series of holes over the water. Young Elsie was always nervous that a boat would come in too close while she was using it and she'd be seen.

On June 23, Elsie heard a big bang. Everyone thought a boat had struck the building, and they rushed outside, but there was no sign of an accident. Later they heard that the noise was caused by the most damaging earthquake in BC history. The epicentre was northwest of Courtenay, and the magnitude of the quake was 7.3. Landslides occurred in the mountains, chimneys were knocked askew in towns, and a two-metre (six-foot) tsunami washed up on Sisters Island.

By the late 1940s, the Redonda Bay population edged up to the one hundred mark. It was a regular stop on the Union Steamship route, and the Imperial Oil barge, the RCMP boat, the Columbia Mission boats and others came in frequently. Ashore, passengers played canasta while waiting for the steamships to dock.

In 1949, Olmstead sold his logging company to Giroday Sawmills, a large company with equipment that could reach farther inland, to Baile Lake. A government wharf was built, and scheduled air service brought in mail and movies. Around 1950, loggers building a road on Mount Perritt struck molybdenum. Prospectors rushed in but the claims did not uncover anything viable.[83]

This second boom ended in the mid-1950s. The cannery closed, though the store remained open till 1964. L&K Lumber bought out Giroday but closed down in 1966. A forest fire burned much of the timber. Squatters came and went. Some of the derelict buildings were demolished for safety reasons, while others provided building materials for the Galley Bay commune. In the 1970s, the BC Forest Service set up a minimum-security camp for twenty inmates whose job was to thin out the timber, but in the early twenty-first century, the area is uninhabited.

7

SALT LAGOON
(ROSCOE BAY)
Home of the Christensens

Roscoe Bay is a long, narrow, sheltered inlet on the west side of Waddington Channel, which runs between East and West Redonda islands. At low tide, the entrance to the bay shrinks and dries up.

In the fall of 1927, Roscoe Bay was known as Salt Lagoon. This is what Carl and Bertha Christensen called it when they took up residence on the sixty-six hectares (164 acres) of Lot 4972, which Carl had pre-empted the year before.[84] The lot spills over into Black Lake, a landlocked continuation of Roscoe Bay. (A previous Black Lake settler, a boat builder by the name of Ellingsen, had drowned several years earlier.) The Christensens lived on their land for sixteen years.

Carl (1893–1975) was a Norwegian merchant seaman who served on the last sailing ship on the Vancouver to Sydney (Australia) run. His daughter Maria told me that when he immigrated to Canada, he changed his name from Olson "or something like that" to Christensen because his father's name was Christen. Carl grew up in a place called Husaas, just north of Oslo. Many of his school friends took that as their last name, but Carl used it as a middle name for his son, Karl Husaas Christensen, whom everyone called Joe.

From Montreal, Carl went to Minneapolis, then Biggar, Saskatchewan, where he got a job as a hired man. The food was so poor that he was reduced to sucking eggs for nourishment. In 1924 he went to Harrison Hot Springs in British Columbia, where he met pretty, young Bertha Horner (1898–1983) from Vancouver. They were both there for arthritis treatment in the hot pool. Later that year, they married and went to Guadalajara, Mexico. Bertha hated living there, so she moved to San Francisco while Carl went to sea on freight boats, tugboats and eventually his own boat, a gas boat with a big cabin that served as a floating store. He and his partner, Morris Rude, used to display and sell loggers' boots and gloves up and down the BC coast. As they travelled, Carl looked for a place to settle down. He liked Roscoe Bay, so he took out a pre-emption in 1926 and reunited his family.

The Christensens spent their first Desolation Sound winter in a temporary tent-house located at the end of Roscoe Bay, where a park bench now sits. During the second summer, Carl built a nice house on Black Lake. Their nearest neighbours were the Stanifords, who lived over the hill on Refuge Cove Lagoon.

Disaster struck in August 1928. Carl was away from home, being treated for a logging injury, and Bertha was alone with the two children,

In 1940, young Joe Christensen could row his boat anywhere he liked within Salt Lagoon. The family recently erected a memorial plaque to him in Roscoe Bay. COURTESY MARIA ZAIKOW

three-year-old Maria and baby Joe. As Bertha made jelly, Maria stuffed paper into the stove.

"What's that crackling?" she asked her mother, but Bertha was a bit deaf and didn't hear anything.

"Go outside and see if there's a bird on the roof," she told her daughter.

"There's flames out there," cried Maria, running back inside.

Bertha picked up the bucket of water that was always kept handy, leaned a ladder against the house and climbed up. Maria climbed up behind her mother. She had a little pail of water, but unfortunately spilled it.

"It's too late," said Bertha, climbing down. "Take your brother and go to the water and stay there." Maria grabbed Joe and took him to the well because she'd been told many times not to go near the lake.

Bertha ran back into the house and threw out two chairs and the sewing machine. Flames blocked the door. She was trapped. Throwing a felt mattress out the bedroom window, she jumped down onto it and ran to the lake to find the children. When she discovered they weren't there, she panicked and called out their names, then found them at the well.

All three ran down the trail by the creek to Salt Lagoon, where Jamieson Company operated a logging camp on Crown land. The men were out on the logs using a saw and didn't hear Bertha's cries, so she took her bloomers off and waved them. That got their attention.

Today, the only remains of this house are a moss-covered stove and an old bedstead in the woods behind Black Lake.

After the fire, Bertha took the children to visit her mother, in Vancouver, and her sisters, Bessie in Seattle and Elva in Tacoma. While they were in Vancouver, Carl met with a pole logger (a man who looks for straight immature trees to cut for telephone poles) who had some floating cabins on Black Lake. Carl bought them, towed the cabins to where the house had been and tied them to the shore with stifflegs, logs fastened between the float and the shore to keep the float the same distance away from the land. The family spent the next winter in them.

The children played a game that involved chasing each other along the stiffleg, round the float, along the other stiffleg and back along the shore. Bertha heard the *thunk, thunk* of their feet till all went quiet. She went outside to find that Joe had fallen in. Maria was stretched along one stiffleg trying to pull him in. That was the end of that game.

The two children travelled back and forth to visit their grandmother and their aunts many times. When Maria was five, her Aunt Peggy brought her back from Vancouver on the Union Steamship SS *Chelohsin.* "One of the worst moments in my life," said Maria, "was when we arrived at Salt Lagoon and I looked down at the log boom where Pop was standing far below me. The water was sloshing up and down, and up and down, between the logs. You know how narrow logs are, and there was wash from the boat. And they told me to jump and I wouldn't jump. I was too frightened. The terror haunts me still." The men threw her off and Carl caught her.

The same year, Maria watched goggle-eyed as her father used a donkey winch to pull a bunkhouse up from the beach on the north side of Salt Lagoon. Two years later, between 1932 and 1934, he added a

After fire destroyed the Christensens' original home on Black Lake, Carl hauled this floathouse up onto the beach in Roscoe Bay and added onto it. COURTESY MARIA ZAIKOW

lean-to on the back of the bunkhouse. It held a kitchen and two more bedrooms. Using a froe and a mallet, he split cedar shakes for its roof and walls. The froe was like a big cleaver. Carl would drive the froe into a cedar block with a mallet. Then he slipped a stick through the hole in the froe's handle and wiggled it a little so that it twisted and split the shake off the block. If the shake wouldn't budge, it meant there was a knot in the wood and it wouldn't make a shake.

The Christensens went to Mike Shuttler's now empty Melanie Cove homestead to harvest red cider apples and plums. There was a rat's nest in the rafters of the cabin, and Maria begged to keep one of the four babies as a pet. "Pop said no, but Mother said yes. The rat was a lovely little thing. It liked to eat and be petted. Unfortunately, it squeezed out one night and went through a vent hole under the stove and died, leaving an awful smell. Pop said you're not bringing anything else like that home."

In 1933, Carl applied for his Crown grant but was turned down because Ernie Cowie, the forest ranger, said he hadn't cleared the necessary two hectares (five acres). Decades later, Carl's grandson, realtor John Zaikow, visited the place with his mother and told her that more than two hectares had been cleared. Maria believed her father didn't pursue the matter because he had decided to move on, although he stayed another ten years.

When Maria was eight, she and Joe started correspondence school because Bertha decided it was "easier to teach two kids the same thing at the same time." In Grade 2, Maria spent May and June living with the Palmer family at Salmon Bay (Brem Bay in Toba Inlet) in order to swell the number of students there and keep their school open. "That was the year the Dionne quintuplets were born in Quebec," she remembered, "and everyone was talking about them. I slept in a bunk bed in the girls' room."[85]

Maria also remembered rowing up Salmon River with Billy Palmer and shooting back down on the swift current. "No life jackets of course." Bear droppings were everywhere. Billy fired a .22 at the pigeons, which they then ate. "Those were Depression years. You ate anything, but they were good," she said.

When she came back from Salmon Bay, she ran around looking for Bertha. "You couldn't call because she was deaf," she said. "I looked in the chicken house and everywhere but she wasn't there. I asked Joe where she was and he said, 'Oh, she's gone, and if you hadn't come back there would be just us men here.'" Bertha was down in Vancouver, visiting her family and getting treatment for her chronic rheumatoid arthritis.

In 1934–1935, the Christensens visited back and forth with the

A teenage Joe Christensen gathers oysters in Pendrell Sound with Mr. Stedman who, together with his wife, came up every year in a boat called the Mountaineer. COURTESY MARIA ZAIKOW

Chapmans, who spent two winters on Mink Island. They had two children who were also doing correspondence lessons. Previously there had been a mink farm on the island, and the family recycled the mesh netting from the mink cages to make bunk beds.

In the fall of 1935, Bertha, Maria and Joe moved into a small cabin on the south side of Galley Bay, where the children could attend school. Unfortunately, after six weeks Bertha's arthritis landed her in hospital again, so Maria and Joe returned to Salt Lagoon and switched back to correspondence lessons. These came in units of thirty-six lessons, and the Ministry of Education made Maria start at the beginning again. She was not pleased.

Bertha returned to Salt Lagoon only to have her arthritis flare up yet again. At the same time she developed heart problems, which made it impossible for her to live in the rugged conditions of Desolation Sound. In 1935 she moved to Vancouver to live with her mother so she could be closer to the hospital. The children hated Vancouver and did not want to move there, so the family decided that they were better off with Carl in Salt Lagoon. Both children, especially Maria, regularly visited their mother, aunts and grandmother until Bertha's death in 1983.

On their own in Salt Lagoon, Carl and the children grew their own vegetables and tended their chickens, pigs, sheep and goats. According to Maria, "Joe had thirty hens one year and he had names for all of them." They shared a series of billy goats with Phil Lavigne, pasturing them on Graveyard (Copplestone) Island. These goats were successors to the one eaten by a cougar (see Chapter 5). Maria told me that "Graveyard Island was where the Native people put their dead wrapped in cedar garments and crouched in little huts. Later, they'd remove the bones."

The Christensens had gardens on both sides of the creek, and at the top of the bluff they fenced in a big plot with cedar pickets. This was the upper garden, where they grew strawberries. In those days they had mattocks with blades to chop roots. Nowadays the only mattocks available are those with picks on them, which are used by miners.

Electricity came from a water wheel in a flume fed by the creek that ran down from the top of the bluff. The Christensens cut tin cans at an angle and nailed them to the wheel. Water running through the flume filled the cans, which caused the wheel to turn. It was connected to a car generator, which stored energy in a six-volt battery that ran a light and a radio. The radio could receive news from stations in California and Vancouver. Earlier, they had had a crystal radio with headphones. Maria said her uncle in Vancouver made it. It was mounted on a board, and they used a pointer to jiggle the cat's whisker till they heard a sound. A San Francisco station often came in loud and clear in the evenings.

Their other entertainment was homegrown. Before 1935, while Bertha was still with them, they went to dances. Maria remembered a Halloween dance at Galley Bay. The school was decorated for the occasion, and the kids played a game with dishes. There was also a Squirrel Cove picnic and sports day where there were races and free ice cream. Dinner at the Squirrel Cove hall included a salad made with fresh garden peas and vinaigrette. "Oh, that was good!" Maria remembered. "Joe and I both liked that one. You paid to get in, and then after midnight they passed the hat around for more money so the music could continue. The cloakroom, which was in an alcove off the hall, had a shelf with little troughs for the babies."

Like everyone else, Carl turned his hand to anything that would either feed the family or generate cash. Maria remembered that he even trapped, and she herself set traps along the beach for mink. Mink and raccoon skins were stretched on a board and scraped clean twice before being taken to a fur buyer at Bliss Landing. "Pop shot weasels whenever he saw them as they were bad on chickens. Then we sold the fur. It fetched a good price."

The *Chelohsin* and later the *Lady Cynthia* came into Refuge Cove twice a week, on Sundays and Wednesdays, before calling at logging camps on the way up to Redonda Bay. "At one time those boats stopped at Salt Lagoon," according to Maria. "Any place there was a big camp, they'd stop." The Christensens and all the neighbours were there to meet the ship, eager for their mail and grocery orders from Woodward's.

Once, the Barrows visited the Christensens in Salt Lagoon and they all had their pictures taken together. "Pop didn't like them for some reason," said Maria. "They were collecting Indian arrow heads and Joe gave them two nice ones. They promised to send him two others, but none ever arrived."

When Maria was eleven years old, she went for a holiday to stay with her friend Clara Mae Palmer and her family on their boat, which was tied up to Phil Lavigne's dock. It was summer and she had a red bathing suit that her father had made by cutting an old pair of his own bathing trunks in half. Maria got the top with the straps and a stitch in the hem to make a crotch, and Joe got the legs. They were functional rather than fashionable, but Maria didn't care because she was just with the Palmers.

During this time, they took her up Theodosia Inlet for a weekend to visit some Palmer relatives (see Chapter 12). They went up the inlet and then up Theodosia River. "I remember an old lady and a Mrs. Arnold, who was Clara Mae's great-aunt," Maria told me. "The old lady, Sarah Palmer, was her great-grandmother. She made the most beautiful quilts, which they sold. Her needle was a-going all the time, and I remember her tiny stitches.

In addition to these pigs, which Carl Christensen is admiring, the Christensens also kept goats, chickens and turkeys. COURTESY MARIA ZAIKOW

"I don't remember which pattern the old lady was using for the quilt, just that she was making such lovely tiny stitches and I admired those little stitches. Both of them worked on quilts, but the old lady, of course, was doing it all the time because Mrs. Arnold was either cooking the meals or was out with the animals. She also had a herd of black and white cows. She told us to be wary of the bull. 'Even I am afraid of the bull, but I don't let him know it,' she said.

"Clara Mae and I used to roam around there through the orchard and everything. We were all standing around outside and talking and eating plums when the grandmother came out of the house. I don't know who, whether it was me or Clara Mae or Clara Mae's mother, Gudrun, who picked a plum and gave it to the old lady, and she was just devouring it. It was just dripping juice. Mrs. Arnold came out of the house and said, 'Oh no. You'll attract the wasps. Take that and get in the house.' She grabbed the old lady and made her go into the house. The old lady could hardly walk on her own, and Mrs. Arnold grabbed her and into the house with her. They didn't want wasps around because they kept

Winters in Salt Lagoon sometimes were cold enough to ice up the flume that provided water and power. COURTESY MARIA ZAIKOW

bees. I can remember that so distinctly. Poor old lady, I thought. How can people treat old people like that? She only wanted a plum. That's how I remember Salo's place [the Palmer farm up Theodosia Inlet].

"There was another man eating there when we visited. I don't know who he was or where he lived because he never spoke. He used to go out prospecting for gold till one time he never came back."

Back at Salt Lagoon, there were people coming and going as well. Some lived there for a few years and became friends with the Christensens, often helping by babysitting or keeping an eye on each other's places during temporary absences. Others were just travelling through and sometimes weren't aware that there were people living in the area. These transients were not always very thoughtful.

The Christensens' nearest neighbours for several years were the Tredcroft brothers—Arthur, Ed and Ernest—who lived on the north side of Salt Lagoon. Once, when the Christensens went to Vancouver for a week, they asked the Tredcrofts to milk their goats. While Maria and her family were away, a yacht called *Sylvia* came in and anchored. The crew painted

Carl Christensen with his children, Joe and Maria, and the visiting Amy and Francis Barrow. Ginger, Maria's cat, is in Amy's arms. Francis described this visit in his diaries.
COURTESY MARIA ZAIKOW

the *Sylvia's* name on a rock and stole all the plums. As the Tredcrofts lived out of sight, they did not notice what was going on. The following year the yacht returned, and the crew asked the Christensens if they were new-comers as there had been no one there the previous year.

"When the same kind of theft occurred in 1934 at Deep Bay," Maria told me, "my father gave [the culprits] heck for stealing vegetables and fruit from the one-armed man trying to make a living there. It was dreadful. They had great big yachts and yet they had to take from a poor little guy who was scrounging along the shoreline."[86]

The Tredcrofts left in 1939 when war broke out, but they only moved as far as Quathiaski Cove on Quadra Island. Maria's brother Joe wrote to them for years afterward. He told Maria that although Ed, an artist, remained in Quathiaski Cove, Arthur, an engineer, went on to build dams on Vancouver Island. Ernest had gone home to England earlier, after he got sick.

While Art and Ed lived at Salt Lagoon, they built double-ended rowboats, one of which is in the Campbell River Museum. They were working on yet another rowboat at the time they moved to Quadra Island, but Carl bought the pieces from them. The Christensens finished it with cedar slabs felled in Salt Lagoon and milled in Lund. When they launched it in the summer of 1940, they called it the *Kelp*. It was ten metres (thirty-two feet) long with a cabin for shelter. The original engine was a two-cycle affair that didn't work well, so they replaced it with an Easthope. Later, they also enlarged the cabin. There was a mast, but it was not for a sail but rather to bring the fishing poles up.

"When I was sixteen, Pop and I fished all summer with it," said Maria, "but there was such poor fishing that we couldn't make a living off it even then. We got up every morning at 4 a.m. to troll by hand till the fish stopped biting. Then the seiners came in and picked them up. Pop hated the seiners. He said they were going to kill the ocean and, by golly, I think they just about did, didn't they? And he said that in 1940. Some of the time we fished in Tenedos Bay and walked up to the lake, which, then as now, was full of driftwood." Before the *Kelp*, the family used a gas boat with a Columbia River Fishing Boat hull and a cabin.

Carl logged the area around Church Point on Waddington Channel, so the family got to know the Jensens who lived just north of there. They were boat builders. As well as building trawlers, they also had an oyster farm. There was another Jensen brother who lived at Doctor Bay at the head of the channel. The big Japanese oysters, which thrived in the warm waters of Pendrell Sound, spread down to Salt Lagoon while Maria lived there.

"The Stedmans came up every year from North Vancouver. Arthur was the night watchman for Cates [a tugboat company based on Burrard Inlet in North Vancouver]. They came up in a small open boat called the *Mountaineer*. It had a motor, but they sailed most of the time. May was a little hunchback. They always arrived in the first two weeks of August because she said it very seldom rained then. They came up on the east side of the Strait of Georgia, went further north and then returned down the west side, calling in to see friends all the time. Arthur was a well-travelled man and a keen mountaineer. Joe kept in touch with him till Stedman died."

Other visitors were the Osgoods, who came from Seattle with their two kids a couple of times around 1941 (Mr. Osgood was a woodworking teacher), and Dr. Rikken from Seattle or Tacoma. Both came in big yachts.

There was a shack on the Martin Islands used by transient fishermen. The Christensens caught a big octopus there but must have cooked it too long as it was "like rubber." Sometimes they kept a goat on the islands.

One equinox, Desolation Sound lived up to its name. In 1940 a terrible storm blew in from the southeast, rattling the windows and rampaging around the house till Carl said, "Come on, you kids. Get your blankets and get outside." All night they huddled in the cold under the bluff. No one got a wink of sleep. As the wind slammed into the mountain above them, it was deflected down onto the homestead. "In the morning," Maria said, "everything was down. The boathouse, which had stood on stilts over the beach, had gone, and the wind had picked up the five-metre dory and flung it clean over the *Kelp* to the other side, somehow without damaging either one. The shack housing the water wheel below the flume went too, and all the fences were flattened. The house itself still stood, along with the chicken house and the goat house. These remained because they were protected by the bluff." Phil Lavigne told them he had once had a similar experience when spending the night aboard a boat in Salt Lagoon. A strong wind came up and almost drove him ashore, even though he ran the engine all night. After that he would never stay there overnight.

By 1943, war made it impossible to buy ammunition, and the family couldn't survive without it. Deer came into the garden and they couldn't stop them. "We could have survived if we could have got the deer out of the garden. They even ate the green tomatoes." Carl got a job at Pacific Lime's Blubber Bay quarry on Texada Island. He worked in the quarry's sawmill first, then as a truck driver and finally as a boatman because they found out that he had a skipper's ticket. He persuaded Phil Lavigne to stay with Joe while he and Maria searched for a house. He bought a lot in Van Anda on Texada, but as Mr. Loman, the foreman, wouldn't give

The Christensens bought a partly finished boat from their neighbours, the Tredcroft brothers. When they launched it in 1940, they called it the Kelp *and used it rather unsuccessfully for fishing.* COURTESY MARIA ZAIKOW

him time off to build a house on it, he quit and went to Vancouver for eight months. He worked on the *G.H. French* and on the *holm* boats— the *Southholm, Eastholm, Westholm*—freighters that travelled to Seattle, Tacoma and San Francisco and back up to Port Hardy at the north end of Vancouver Island. When he returned to Texada, he built the house and then became hoist man at the Little Billy Mine.

After the Christensens moved to Texada, hunters burned the house at Salt Lagoon. The family returned to visit, but could find no traces of crockery or glass. Later Joe took a course at the University of BC. In the library, he found a set of encyclopedias identical to the one they'd had at Salt Lagoon; it was even missing the volume on Sweden that they had lent to the Lindbergs. He felt this was proof that someone had raided the house. There is still some ivy and some lemon thyme where the garden used to be, but all other physical traces of their sixteen years in the area are gone.

8

EAST REDONDA ISLAND
Hard Work in Pendrell Sound

On East Redonda Island, Mount Addenbroke rises sheer out of the waters of Homfray Channel for 1,590 metres (5,247 feet), dominating the landscape. Northwest of the mountain, a narrow neck of land connects it to the rest of the island, which is almost bisected by Pendrell Sound. The waters of Pendrell are so sheltered that they register the highest temperatures in Desolation Sound. They are so warm that oyster spat has been produced there and distributed to oyster farmers around the coast since 1948.[87]

Charles and Fred Thulin handlogged Pendrell Sound during the summer of 1889 before they settled in the place they later christened Lund. Others came and went, including Pete and Helen Anderson, newlyweds who built a cabin somewhere on East Redonda. Helen was used to life in the wilderness; she was the eldest daughter of the Hansons of Galley Bay (see Chapter 11). Although the hunting was good and the larder was always full of venison, grouse or ducks, after a year in a drafty cabin (Helen reported that "the cedar shake wall shook so much when the wind blew that the guns would fall off it"[88]), the Andersons moved to Thurston Bay and then Port Neville in Johnstone Strait. Pete earned money from his handlogger's licence, and they also fished commercially whenever they were near a buyer. They had a gas boat called the *Elephant,* so there was no need to row anywhere. In 1924, they settled at Turner Bay on the west side of the Malaspina Peninsula.[89]

In the early decades of the twentieth century, Joseph Edwin McCauley (1873–1960) settled at the head of Pendrell Sound and planted an apple orchard. He got his Crown grant for Lot 3697 in 1918, but he and his family stayed only a few more years. Their next-door neighbour, James Heatley (1870–1944), pre-empted Lot 4180 on July 6, 1915. At the time, his rapidly growing family was living in West Vancouver. By the time they arrived in Pendrell Sound in 1920, the McCauley homestead was deteriorating, though the family was still around. Rita Heatley, born the year her family moved to Pendrell, remembered meeting the McCauleys later.

James Johnstone Heatley was born in Selkirk, Scotland, in 1870. He longed to see the world, and as soon as he was old enough, he got a job on the cattle boats, travelling back and forth to Canada, earning free passage in exchange for feeding the beasts. After some years of this, he decided to settle in Canada and went to work on the railroads, especially in the Okanagan. When he reached Vancouver, he got a job in a bakery. One of his customers became his wife.[90]

Elizabeth Gordon Dawson (1883–1956) came from Inverary, Scotland. She was "brought up to be a lady" by her uncle John, who was a Presbyterian minister. When her fiancé died two weeks before their wedding, Elizabeth left on her own for Canada shortly afterward. She was staying with friends who lived near the Orange Hall in Vancouver when she met James Heatley.

The Heatleys settled in West Vancouver, where their first five children were born (Lily in 1912, Gordon in 1913, John in 1914, Jean in 1917 and Rita in 1920). In 1920 they moved to Galley Bay to help the Hansons qualify for a school. Lily, Gordon, John and Jean were old enough to attend and boost the number of children to the ten required for government funding.

The Union Steamship brought the seven Heatleys to Lund on Halloween. The family spent the night at the hotel, while all their possessions were stored in the hotel's freight shed. When James got up to give two-month-old Rita her bottle, he glanced out the window and saw the freight shed in flames. He rushed to get help, but everyone was at a dance and he couldn't make them understand that there was "a fire down there." Elizabeth panicked. James saved the gramophone player and little else. The family had to borrow clothing and blankets before they set off for Galley Bay.

They didn't stay there long, but moved almost immediately to Pendrell Sound (still there were not enough children—the first Galley Bay school did not open till three years later). The Heatleys decided not to homestead on the land James had pre-empted, perhaps because the McCauleys had already left. Instead, they chose a

Rita Heatley, at the age of 13, lived to go dancing on Saturday nights. She and her sister, Jean, and their friends danced at Manson's Landing and Squirrel Cove. Her two favourite teachers, Ingrid Andersen and Eleanor Lusk, both retired to Powell River where they still live.

place in a sheltered bay farther south on the west shore and lived in a tent. Soon they paid a brief visit to Forbes Bay, where a logging outfit was selling some of its floathouses. James bought a cookhouse and a bunkhouse and towed them to Pendrell Sound for the family to live in.

Rita remembered that they had two levels of gardens just up from the beach. As well as the floathouses, James built a log house on land. He copied the design of a house at a place called Tanbark, halfway between their new home and the McCauleys'. In the fall, when the berries were ripe, the family picked blackberries there—with the bears. "Just clang your pots together and make a lot of noise and they won't come near you," James told the children. It worked.

One day they made sandwiches of butter, peanut butter and Rogers

Golden Syrup. "It must have been a special occasion," Rita said. "We would never have had more than one of those things at a time otherwise." Elizabeth didn't like going anywhere in the boat as she couldn't swim. However, this day they persuaded her to jump in and they went to "Johnny Rock," a rock just in from the little island at the mouth of the lagoon. The picnic was delicious.

For twelve years the Heatleys lived up Pendrell Sound, scratching out a living as best they could. Apples from the McCauley orchard were a welcome bounty. Bob and Daisy were born at Pendrell Sound in 1922 and 1924, and Lily, who had dropsy, got sicker and sicker. One night when the children were playing the card game Fish on her bed, she had an attack, and James threw everyone except Lily out of the room. She died not long afterward of "chronic intestinal nephritis."[91]

Rita first went to school when she was about ten years old. The school was part of Will Palmer's logging camp in Deep Bay (later called Tenedos Bay), and Eleanor Lusk, one of Rita's two favourite teachers, was in charge (see Chapter 12). When the settlement and the school were floated up to Salmon Bay (Brem Bay in Toba Inlet), the Heatleys didn't go with it. Instead they spent a short time in Salt Lagoon (Roscoe Bay) before returning to Pendrell Sound. However, as Will Palmer couldn't keep his school open without more kids, he soon came and got Bob, Rita and Daisy. Bob lived with his family, but Rita and Daisy lived with Mrs. Anderson. "She and I did not get along," said Rita. "She treated me like a servant. Once when I was scrubbing the floors, her daughter Julie hit me over the head with a chair. I managed to keep my temper, but only just. Privately, I called Mrs. Anderson the barracuda."

Elizabeth and the four younger children moved their floathouses to Galley Bay on March 1, 1932, which Rita remembered as the day Charles Lindbergh's baby was kidnapped.[92] The older boys, Gordon and John, were away most of the time, logging with their father in Teakerne Arm, Toba Inlet and the surrounding area, and Elizabeth wanted the other children to have a chance to get an education without living away from home. Every morning they rowed across the bay to the school for classes with Rita's other favourite teacher, Ingrid Andersen. In summer they swam out to the rock at the entrance to Galley Bay, which is submerged at high tide.[93]

Long after the children were past school age, the Heatleys remained in Galley Bay. James told the family he had pre-empted Lot 1474. It had, however, already been granted to someone when the Department of Lands map was drawn up in 1923. That grant may have lapsed, which would have allowed him to pre-empt it. If so, he never purchased the Crown grant. and the property reverted to the province when he died in 1944.

One blustery day when Rita was about fourteen, Elizabeth Heatley was fretting because she wanted her mail. Rita and Jean couldn't stand her complaints, so, taking Bob to bail, they launched the rowboat into the storm. "There was water coming in top and bottom," Rita said. "It took us more than an hour to get to Refuge Cove, and when we arrived, Jack Tindall, who was usually a quiet man, was mad at us. 'What are you doing out on a day like this?' he asked. 'You're not going back in that. You wait till Bill Emery comes back in the *Pug Pug*. He'll take you home.'" So Emery took them back in Tindall's boat, and their mother got her mail.

For a short time the Bishop children, who spent most of their childhood in Malaspina Inlet (see Chapter 13), lived in Galley Bay. While they were there, they invited Rita Heatley for supper. Young William Bishop said, "Help yourself to whatever you see and don't ask for what you don't see because we ain't got it." Later, Rita "beat the hell out of Agnes Bishop and was banished" from the Bishop house. She no longer remembered the cause of the quarrel, just that Agnes annoyed her so she "smacked her a good one." Agnes ran, with Rita yelling after her: "You better git if you don't want more." When she heard about it, "Old Lady Bishop wanted me tarred and feathered. And my dad said: 'The poor kid didn't know any better, leave her alone.'"

From the time Rita turned thirteen, she lived for Saturday nights. "I'd work hard to finish the chores so I could go. I loved dancing. A whole bunch of kids went to the dances at Squirrel Cove, Lund and Manson's Landing. To get to Manson's Landing, we went to Blind Creek [Cortes Bay] and hiked across the land. We'd start really early in the morning,

dance till 6 or 7 a.m., come home and work all day. We danced schottisches, waltz (my favourite), polkas (Jean's favourite) and the Lambeth
Walk."

Elizabeth's mother, whom she always called Tib, visited the family twice—both times in Pendrell Sound. Rita only remembered one
of those visits, and she found her grandmother quite intimidating. Although she was very quiet and never seemed to have much to say, she
looked at Rita with a piercing gaze and didn't act like a grandmother.
She wore a long string of pearls that Rita thought was out of place in
the afternoon.

Ingrid Andersen Cowie remembered Mrs. Heatley coming to tea in
1933 wearing diamonds. Rita said her mother had no jewellery except
a cameo brooch and matching earrings that are still in the family. However, she did have a faint memory of hearing that her father had "sold the
jewellery," so maybe Elizabeth did have diamonds to wear at that time.

There were a lot of mysteries and family secrets. "You were never
told anything," said Rita. Rita and Jean tried to look at the big old family
Bible that had all the family dates in it, but Elizabeth wouldn't let them.
Once they glimpsed Elizabeth's birth certificate, which had "illegitimate"
written on it. Their mother's uncle John had registered her birth, and
he brought her up while Tib worked in the woollen mills. Aunty Chris
came along later from a different father. She was the opposite of Elizabeth—not secretive at all. Chris also immigrated to Canada. She lived on
Lulu Island in Richmond and later moved to Steveston. It was she and
her husband, Jim, who would have brought Tib up to Pendrell Sound to
visit. Tib had two other daughters in Scotland, Fanny and Jeannette.

Pendrell Sound, where the Thulins, the McCauleys and the Heatleys
were active, was not the only area of East Redonda Island that was settled.
The steep slopes of the Homfray Channel side of the island, dropping
from Mount Addenbroke's 1,590-metre (5,247-foot) height to the channel's 726-metre (2,396-foot) depths in a mere six kilometres (4.5 miles),
were ideal for loggers like Archie Stewart and John Bunyan Scott.

No one now living remembers Archie Stewart (1861–1927). The
writings of the late Jim Spilsbury are the best source but only give us

glimpses. He described Stewart as "an old handlogger who had a beat-up cod boat with a four-horsepower Easthope in it."[94] Stewart had two timber claims just south of Booker Point on East Redonda Island, one on the beach and one higher up. Working alone, he'd choose trees that he thought would easily slide down to the water. After felling them, he peeled the bark off one side to make them slippery, rolled them over and used a jackscrew to start their downward trajectory. Stewart pre-empted Lot 3628 in 1907 and registered his Crown grant seven years later. John Waters and James Berg signed that he had "been in occupation, as required by the 'Land Act, 1884.'"

Like most people, Stewart bought his groceries at the Refuge Cove store. In February 1927, when the storekeepers realized he hadn't been in for a while, someone went to his place to investigate. His boat was still tied to the dock, and fresh skid marks led up the hill. There they found his body pinned under a log, where he had died about three weeks before. Respectfully, they piled rocks on his remains and left him in peace. He was sixty-six when he died.

On the coast just south of Archie Stewart's property, John Bunyan Scott (1856–1938) pre-empted Lot 5018 in 1901 but never proved it. He may have been too short of cash. Maria Christensen Zaikow said that after Scott's wife, Ida, died in 1931, he let the Christensens pick his cherry crop. Maria remembered that he had an Airedale dog and used to spread his sheets on the grass to bleach them in the sun. Scott remarried and later had a stroke, which forced him to move to the small community of Squirrel Cove on Cortes Island. "The land was then sold to a man who logged it, ruining the garden," said Maria.

On September 19, 1991, Scott's land was the scene of a spectacular drug bust.[95] For some time it had been common knowledge in Lund that the landowners always had large wads of cash to spend on replacement motors for several high-speed boats that commuted to and from the Lower Mainland. The RCMP went up to check the place and found six camouflaged buildings hidden in a ravine. Inside was one of the largest grow-ops found on the coast to that time. They seized 4,300 marijuana plants, three vehicles, two boats and a helicopter along with a large quantity of hydroponic equipment. Watering systems were intricate, involving several kilometres of black plastic piping. Lighting was run from four large diesel generators. The operation was producing three crops a year, valued at a million dollars each. It was thought to have been active for about three years. Four Powell River residents, one person from Kamloops and another from Washington State were arrested and charged. They were not the first people arrested for running a grow-op in Desolation Sound; a similar, smaller operation was confiscated in 1983 and there have been others. Growing pot seems to be a popular activity on this island.

The land subsequently changed hands and in early 2007 was for sale again with an asking price of nearly a million dollars.[96] This and one other deeded parcel of land are the only places people can live on East Redonda Island, which has been designated an ecological reserve, but no one lives on the island now.

9

HOMFRAY
CHANNEL
Lindbergs and Loggers

On the east side of Homfray Channel, across from East Redonda Island, there are two distinctive bays, Forbes Bay and Atwood Bay, which were the site of logging activity early in the twentieth century, a hippie commune in the 1970s, and a Sliammon camp since the 1990s. About three kilometres (two miles) south of Forbes Bay there's a distinctive black cliff overlooking an old homestead. The homestead was the Lindberg brothers' farm, which they called Lloyd Point. This is somewhat confusing as Lloyd Point on the map is three kilometres (two miles) farther south.

For much of the first half of the twentieth century, Herman (1885–1970) and Eric (1889–1974) Lindberg ran a prosperous farm that supplied many logging camps and other establishments with meat and fresh produce. Long before big trucks hauled food all over the highways of North America, the Union Steamships took turkeys from the Lindberg farm to the Hotel Vancouver. Cash was the bane of all pioneers' lives. They could grow their own veggies and hunt or fish for meat, but they needed cash for staples like sugar and flour, or for clothes, that they couldn't produce themselves. It was this need that caused the Lindbergs to ship their turkeys to the Hotel Vancouver and elsewhere.

The Lindbergs were Swedes who arrived via Minneapolis.[97] They had fled their native country to avoid the Great War but found themselves next door to loggers blasting a road in Forbes Bay. Regardless, they pre-empted Lot 3787 in 1915 and cleared a small flat area below a distinctive wall of black rock.

Unfortunately, their goats liked to climb to the top of the cliff, where they became wolf fodder. Afterward, the wolves would stand on the highest point and howl their appreciation. This did not sit well with Eric. One night when the leader of the pack was in full song, Eric shot him. After that, the wolves were never seen again and the goats roamed unmolested.[98]

Ernie Cowie, the district forest ranger, told his daughter-in-law, Ingrid Andersen, that in hot weather the Lindbergs wore hats and boots but nothing else when logging.[99] He'd arrive at their dock and invite them aboard for a drink. "Yin, yin," Herman would yell to Eric, who would come running. When the Lindbergs applied for their Certificate of Improvement, Cowie told them they had not cleared enough

The black cliff on the left is where the wolves stood on the top to howl their appreciation of the Lindberg farm goats—but not for long. Don and Phyllis Munday tied up their boat to a float in this cove, which they visited in 1932.

land to qualify, but they disputed this and got their Crown grant in 1925.

In addition to turkeys and goats, the brothers raised chickens and geese and grew fruit and vegetables. When the Blanchet family visited the farm, they found orchards of apples, pears, peaches, hazelnuts and walnuts and a vegetable garden full of variety.[100] Eric canned, pickled and stored this bounty, along with venison and salmon, in a double-walled storehouse and a fine root cellar.

Blanchet said Herman was the chattier of the two and the spokes-man. Eric told her that Herman always had a "scheme" on the go. Full of energy, he would pour all his effort into one thing till he had the next idea. He planted acres of walnut trees, intending to sell the young trees, but they grew too big. Next it was Cascara saplings, but falling prices quashed his dream.

Eric welcomed the family and shared a batch of newly baked bread and fresh cherry jam with them. After a tour of the farm, the children were invited to pick and eat as many cherries as they liked. When the brothers discovered that Blanchet was taking the *Caprice* up Toba Inlet, they scared her with talk of aggressive bears at the only anchorage in the inlet. In the end she diverted to the Yucultas instead.

Around 1930, Carl Christensen took a trip over to Lloyd Point to

Eric or Herman Lindberg with the turkeys they raised to supply the Hotel Vancouver.
POWELL RIVER HISTORICAL MUSEUM AND ARCHIVES IMAGE PH005239

see the Lindbergs. As he walked up the trail to the farm, he thought he saw a man he hadn't met before.

"No, there's nobody here besides Eric and me," said Herman when Carl asked about the stranger.

"Well, that's funny. I'm sure I saw a man move up there," said Carl.

"No."

Later, Herman arrived in Salt Lagoon to ask Bertha Christensen how to treat diarrhea. He said he had his father with him illegally, and he was afraid to take him to the Powell River hospital. Bertha told Herman to boil brown rice and make his father drink the water from it, a common remedy. Eventually, when the old man died, the brothers dug a grave for him on a ridge above the property.

The Lindbergs were reputed to be wealthy. Maria Christensen Zaikow had heard that Herman's brother-in-law invented puffed wheat.[101] She thought Herman's refusal to buy cigarettes for Eric (see Chapter 5) was evidence of a rich man's parsimony. Eric, who never left the farm otherwise, regularly rowed over to Laura Cove to ask Phil Lavigne to buy tobacco for him.

On their way to Bute Inlet to make one of many attempts on Mount Waddington, the mountain climbers Don and Phyllis Munday anchored in the Lindbergs' cove one night in 1932. Coming up Homfray Channel, the Mundays passed the cove, then turned back into it. When they asked the Lindberg brothers if they could spend the night there, the reaction was hostile.

"You'll find a fine place to camp right over there on Redonda Island," Herman said pointedly. "The place is vacant, the owner is dead and there ought to be lots of fruit in the orchard." But the Mundays didn't want to go there as it was off their course and would have delayed them in the morning. There was a float in the cove with a red shed on it. Don asked if they could tie their boat to it and sleep in the shed.

"It's full of bugs and cooties," Herman said, but he admitted that it did not actually belong to the Lindbergs. They had towed it from somewhere else, a place where the steamers had stopped calling.

As they cooked supper, Don watched the brothers round up a big flock of goats. The men were dressed only in "black bathing-suits, their bodies smeared with charcoal and sweat from land-clearing fires."[102] With the ease of long practice, one of them drove an axe into a block of wood, raised it over his head, twisted it and drove the other blade into another block. It was the easy way to carry firewood home.

Herman came over to warn them that cougar were plentiful. "I see you use those 'poison pots,'" he said, nodding at their aluminum pans. "You folks must have a lot of sickness."

"No, we're very healthy."

"But using those pots must have stiffened up your joints," Herman insisted. "My brother and me had all kinds of trouble till we got rid of all our 'poison pots.'"

To convince him he was wrong, the Mundays described their mountaineering activities, pointing to the ice-axes, climbing ropes and boots that they had tossed on the float. When they said they were on their way to "Mystery Mountain" (Mount Waddington), Herman realized that he had heard of them.

An hour or so later, washed and fed, the brothers reappeared, looking more presentable. They explained that some of their neighbours had told the police they were brewing bootleg liquor, which had resulted in repeated unwelcome visits. They had thought the Mundays were the police. Now, having discovered that their visitors were well-known, experienced climbers, they wanted their advice on a mystery.

During the First World War, a draft-evader had hidden up in the mountains behind Lloyd Point for a long time. The Lindbergs were careful not to name him or to say who had assisted him, and they gave no indication of support for the war. Instead, they told the Mundays, "The draft-evader came in to see us one evening. He was worried and scared. He had been hunting goats on top of the mountain up there in the big snowfields … The fellow said right out in the middle of a snowfield he had found a big patch of snow soaked with fresh blood." At first he thought someone had killed a goat up there, but the only tracks he could see were his own. The man was in quite a state. He was continually worried about being found by the authorities and thought he was losing his reason.

The brothers did not believe his story, but to reassure him they agreed to go up the mountain with him. Next morning, they climbed to the 1,500-metre (5,000-foot) level, where they found exactly what he had described. Now, years later, they were still mystified.

"Can you tell us how such a thing could be?" they asked.

"Climbers usually call it 'red snow,'" Don said. He explained that it was a well-known phenomenon caused by an algae called *Chlamydomonas nivalis*, which produces the red colour in response to ultraviolet light.[103]

The brothers seemed much relieved by the Mundays' explanation. Next morning they gave them a big bucket of plums and, said Don, "meant as an even kinder gesture, they handed us a number of copies of an obscure little United States publication devoted mainly to attacks on the manufacturers of aluminium, and on the alleged dangers to health of cooking in pots made of the metal."

The Mundays were not the only people to be given this pamphlet by the brothers. Twelve years earlier, when the Heatley family arrived in Forbes Bay to buy their floathouses (see Chapter 8), Herman criticized their choice of pans and gave them a copy of the pamphlet too. It was incidents like these that supported the community's opinion that the Lindbergs were eccentric.

Herman Lindberg died in 1970 and is buried beside his father. The brothers had a sister, Anna, who was blind. She came over from the old country at some point in the 1960s or 1970s.

Bud Jarvis, a Tiber Bay resident with family ties to Refuge Cove, first encountered the Lindbergs just after Herman died in 1970.[104] Homer Bergren, a Seattle resident who made money from the development of cable television, asked Bud to return a motor to the Lindbergs. Homer spent his summers in Desolation Sound aboard a big powerboat called the *Glenhome*. He made a point of getting to know the locals and providing financing for small businesses. When he discovered that the Lindbergs had a fifty-horsepower outboard motor that wouldn't run, even though they had only used it once, he took it away and had it refurbished in Lund at his own expense. This took so long that the Lindbergs became annoyed and told people he had stolen it from them. Homer asked Bud to return the motor as well as a box of miscellaneous items for Anna Lindberg.

Bud didn't quite know how he was going to tackle the problem. "Everyone said the Lindbergs were crazy and didn't like strangers," he told me.

When he arrived at the Lloyd Point farm, a tall, thin, old man with a homemade cane greeted him on the dock. This was Ivor Danielsson (1902–1984), who had a shock of iron grey hair and looked older than he was. He needed the cane because a log had rolled on his hip and broken it years earlier when he had a logging camp. Because he was the camp owner, Ivor hadn't taken time off for medical treatment, and though the injury healed, it was still difficult for him to walk. During his life, he operated a series of such camps, making and losing several fortunes. The last time he went broke, he was able to salvage a floathouse, and when Herman Lindberg died in 1970, Ivor floated it across Homfray Channel and put it by the creek on the Lindbergs' property. He looked after the farm for Eric and Anna, who were older than he was and were now unable to run it themselves. On his monthly trips to the Refuge Cove store, he'd buy a sack of flour, two kilograms (five pounds) of sugar and a case of milk. At the same time he picked up mail for the Lindbergs.

It was all Bud could do to lift the heavy engine out of his boat and onto the dock. He was astonished when Danielsson picked it up with one hand and hefted it ashore.

Ivor Danielsson looked after Eric and Anna Lindberg in their old age at the Lloyd Point farm. PHOTO BY JOHN DIXON

"Where do I find Anna?" Bud asked.

"Go along the boardwalk," came the gruff reply.

It was a hot August day, and Bud was wearing an old pair of shorts held up by a safety pin. As he came to the end of the boardwalk, he saw an old guy standing in the doorway of a cabin.

"Who are you and whadda you want?" yelled Eric Lindberg.

"I'm Bud Jarvis, Norm Hope's nephew." The old man didn't hear, so the whole exchange was repeated a few decibels higher. Bud sweated.

Behind the old man, he could see a tiny, bent-over woman with a widow's hump peering between Eric's legs. "Who is it, Eric?" she asked. The situation seemed bizarre to Bud.

"Did you bring me any money?" asked Eric.

"If I brought you money, what would you do with it?" Bud asked.

"Buy whiskey," said Eric, retreating into a tiny room, only three metres (ten feet) square.

Although a wood-burning stove was going full blast, the two old people were wearing long johns and shawls. Bud figured they must suffer from bad circulation. He put the box on the kitchen table and squeezed onto one of the chairs.

"These aren't mine," said Anna, rummaging around in the box. Then, "Oh, that's mine," she said as she hauled out a salt shaker.

That was the turning point. Anna and Eric were just back from Chicago. Their niece had taken them there because she had decided they were too old to live by themselves. They had escaped somehow, but had left all their papers, in particular their wills, behind.

"Could you help us?" Anna asked Bud.

"With what?"

"Our niece has stolen our money. She's got our bank books."

"But she can't get your money. You have to sign for it. I know. I'm a lawyer."

"You were sent from heaven," shrieked Anna.

"I'll make you a new will. Just give me your instructions."

"What will it cost?"

"I'll just do it for you," said Bud, thinking that they were poor. He asked if they would like to leave anything to Ivor Danielsson for looking after them.

"What about $10,000," Anna said.

"Make it $5,000," said Eric. "He won't know what to do with it."

Later, when Bud probated the estate, he found they were worth half a million dollars. The money had accumulated because they never bought anything.

After that first visit, he returned several times. On one occasion he asked if Eric had known Henry Tiber or the Schofield who had owned the first Crown grant at Tiber Bay.

"I heard of [Henry Tiber] but never met him," said Eric. "I knew Schofield, though. Do you want to know something interesting?"

"Don't tell him," screamed Anna.

"Schofield was a member of the Jesse James Gang."

"Are you sure?" said Bud.

"Yep. Absolutely sure," said Eric. Anna was very upset and scared. Bud later told this story to some Americans, who confirmed that there was indeed a Schofield in the Jesse James Gang.

Bud heard a story about Schofield's death that seems to corroborate this. One evening, Schofield was shot in the jaw by unknown assailants when he was out fishing in his rowboat. Bleeding profusely, he had time to write in blood on the floor of his boat: "Don't know what happened. Pipe exploded." June Cameron, who spent her childhood summers on Cortes Island, disputed this event, saying that "Mr. Scofield, an Englishman who had spent time in the navy ... died in 1930 at the age of 68 after a prostate operation at the Powell River hospital. This calls into question the rumour that he was shot in his rowboat because he belonged to Jesse James' gang."[105] The BC Archives records the death of Edgar Schofield on May 25, 1931, in Powell River. Perhaps this is the man Cameron knew.

Eric would always ask Bud to bring bananas when he visited, but the last time Bud saw him, the old man asked for some "short of breath pills." Bud didn't know what to do: he couldn't write prescriptions, and Eric wouldn't leave the property to see a doctor. Two weeks later, Eric died of pneumonia.

Former fisheries officer Hans Rosenbloom remembered picking up groceries in Lund for Anna and Eric in the early 1970s. Rosenbloom said Eric had "an old way" about him. "He was shy, gentle and funny." Anna told him that the reason Eric never married was because as a young man he had fallen in love with a girl who married someone else. Forty years later her husband died, but she married an Italian. "Now he's waiting for the Italian to die," said Anna.[106]

Ivor Danielsson reminded Rosenbloom of Abe Lincoln. He had a ten-metre (thirty-foot) troller tied up in front of his house. As he didn't use it to fish commercially, the Department of Fisheries and Oceans turned a blind eye to it.

Brenda Finch of Portage Cove was not sure whether she had met the Lindbergs, but she remembered Ivor Danielsson. "He was a wonderful man, tall and lanky, very strong. He smoked a pipe and had a craggy face. He was a very gentle, lovely person." She thinks Anna went back to Chicago after Eric died.[107] Danielsson remained at the Lloyd Point farm for some years afterward and likely buried Eric on the property beside his brother.

John Dixon from Refuge Cove visited Danielsson at the Lindberg farm around 1983. Dixon thought he looked like a gnarled old tree with a matching pipe that seemed to grow out of his mouth.[108] With great pride, Danielsson showed Dixon his firearms. He had a Savage 99 rifle and a .303 Savage, both of which he kept in mint condition. Predators were a big problem. He shot many cougars and a big black bear on the sill of his cabin. It was a bit too close for comfort.

Karl Ivor Danielsson died in Comox on May 24, 1984, at the age of eighty-two. "The $5,000 he inherited from the Lindbergs was untouched in his account," said Bud.

Beth Hill visited the farm in 1993. She said the buildings remained, though the orchard was overgrown and the grape trellises were rotten. The property had changed hands at least twice since the Lindbergs had it. When Maria Christensen Zaikow and I visited the cove in August 2006, the summer residents had lots of deck chairs on the verandah.

Unlike Lloyd Point, Atwood and Forbes bays, farther north in

Homfray Channel, have not had year-round residents in the past century. For hundreds of years, Forbes Bay was the site of a Klahoose village. It was called Ahpookwum, which means "having maggots," because the white splotches on the cliff at the upper end of the bay looked like maggot eggs. The Klahoose people built a rock tidal weir in the bay, which they used to catch salmon. Later, this village was downgraded to a summer camp for the Klahoose, Sliammon and Homalco people who came to smoke-dry the fish. They last did this in the 1960s.[109]

In 1906, Fraser R. Tannery Ltd. took out a thirty-year hemlock lease in Forbes Bay.[110] It was the first of many logging operations, some of which were innovative for their times. By the 1920s, motorized trucks were replacing horses in the woods. They could haul heavier loads more frequently and were much cheaper than building railway lines. Their soft pneumatic tires gave them access to many hitherto inaccessible places. Forbes Bay was one of the first places on the coast to experience such benefits when Robert Campbell brought in five British-made Leyland trucks.[111] He was convinced that trucks were more economical than other methods, even though it was astronomically expensive to build the roads they required. It cost $40,000 to build the first three kilometres (two miles) of road, and the loggers had to put a Berringer snubbing device on the truck brakes to prevent them from overheating. Campbell thought it was worth it because he put sixty thousand board metres (two million board feet) of lumber into the water each month, more than enough to cover his high costs.

When the Heatley family visited Forbes Bay in 1920 to buy two floathouses (see Chapter 8), there were only two other settlers in the bay as well as the Klahoose village. Two years later, Jim Spilsbury, his friend Jim Anderson, and Anderson's little brother Terry spent three months cutting shingle bolts up Homfray Creek, between Atwood and Forbes Bays.

Jim and Terry's father, Louis, and his Palmer in-laws had just finished a logging operation there.[112] It was one of the first high-lead operations. The men removed the branches and the top from a tall tree, the spar tree, overlooking the worksite, then attached a system of wire lines and pulleys that they would use to pull felled trees off the ground and over to where the loggers wanted them.[113] Donkey engines reeled the lines in and out, while a carriage attached to the lines carried the chokers that loggers would attach to the logs so they could be lifted into the air. It was a big advance over trying to shift the logs bit by bit with jacks. Loggers came from all over the coast to see how they did it.

After the workers had transferred their attentions to Theodosia Inlet, Louis arranged for George Palmer to take the three boys and their equipment to Homfray Creek. Unfortunately, Palmer's converted dugout canoe met with an accident near Prideaux Haven, and the boys had to finish the journey in Spilsbury's little kicker. It took two trips back and forth across Homfray Channel to get everything across. After the first one, the two Jims deposited Terry in a cabin up the creek. First, however, they filled his ears with wild stories of grizzlies, cougars and wolves. When they returned after dark, he had barricaded himself in the cabin so securely that they had to break a window to get in.

All summer the boys cut shingle bolts and sent them one by one down the mountain using a three-hundred-metre (one-thousand-foot) spool of wire. At the bottom, they fell off into Homfray Creek. The idea was that when the fall rains came, Roaring Creek, as Homfray Creek was known, would force the bolts down to the sea, where they would be contained by a standing boom at the creek outlet. The three boys went home satisfied that they had earned big money. Unfortunately, the weather did not co-operate. The rains came very suddenly and the boom broke, spewing the bolts all over Homfray Channel. It took a long time to corral them, and they never did get them all. Consequently, the summer's work was not nearly as lucrative as they had hoped.

Twenty years later, Doris Hope at Refuge Cove reminisced about another big logging camp at Homfray Creek. Workers were dropped off by the Union Steamships at Refuge Cove, and then Dorothy and Ed Thomas ran them over to the camp in their eleven-metre (thirty-six-foot) freight boat.[114]

There were occasional logging operations in Atwood Bay as well. It was part of a large timber lease, though most of the logs were taken out

High rigger George Palmer balances on top of an A-frame. Sarah Palmer who, like her husband James, was short-statured, called him her "big strapping grandson." UBC RARE BOOKS AND SPECIAL COLLECTIONS/JIM SPILSBURY FONTS/ALBUM BC1938/3

on the Toba Inlet side of Brettell Point. In 1962 it was the scene of a spectacular fire. For two weeks, loggers worked in the bay, piling the wood they had cut into a very large cold deck. Unfortunately, it contained a lot of highly flammable cedar. It caught fire and burned with a glow visible in Powell River, forty-eight kilometres (thirty miles) away. Young Garry Hubbard had just graduated from high school in Powell River.

"Do you want to work fighting fires?" an official from the Ministry of Forests asked him. (At that time, the Ministry of Forests had the power to go into pubs and commandeer firefighters when they needed them.)

"No, not really."

"Either come with us or go to jail."

Garry grew up in a hurry and later returned to explore many parts of Desolation Sound by canoe.

By the 1970s, Atwood Bay was empty, but fisheries officer Hans Rosenbloom remembered seeing a hippie colony in Forbes Bay when he went there to check the spawning chum in the creek.[115] For four or five years, twenty to thirty Americans from California, including a couple of draft dodgers, lived there during the summers. The winters were too wet and cold. The commune residents kept goats and rabbits and grew radishes and other fast-growing vegetables. Smoking pot was a favourite pastime. The people at the commune were always very pleasant and very friendly, unlike the group at the Galley Bay commune ten years earlier (see Chapter 11).

"I have no bad memories," Rosenbloom said. "One time I remember seeing a naked young woman trying to milk a goat. She was having an awful time because the goat kept kicking over her bucket.

"Another time, I took a very attractive woman up there from Lund. She was a writer from a Hollywood studio who had been sent to live in the commune while writing a film script about it. Before I left, she came running back to my boat and begged me to take her back to Lund, where she checked into the Lund Hotel." He thinks she still tried to write the script, but the political situation with draft dodgers changed so the film was never made.

Although the Klahoose village in Forbes Bay has not been inhabited for several decades, the Sliammon people have been using the site for cultural training sessions since about 1994.[116] I asked Gerald Blaney of the Tla'Amin Health Unit about the sessions, and he said, "Each year in July, we take up to twenty youth, ages thirteen to eighteen. To qualify to go, they have to be attending school. I go, along with an elder and community youth worker Judy Gaudet. For seven days we work fourteen- to sixteen-hour days teaching the kids about fishing, traditional crafts like basketry and how to make cedar head bands, etc. Every morning the kids jump in the river for a spiritual bath. Then we have a talking circle for them to discuss any issues they have. Under Judy's supervision, the kids do all the cooking. Three or four years ago we had problems with mice, so we built a storage shed. Apart from the outhouses, it's the only building as we live in tents.

"We invite the Klahoose to come. We always ask permission from their chief as it's Klahoose land. Recently we've had requests from the Musqueam, the Nanoose and even from northern Ontario to send their kids to the camp. We've talked about doing it for men's support groups and for couples, but so far that's just in the planning stages."

Although no one lives there now, the location of Forbes Bay and Atwood Bay, almost at the mouth of Toba Inlet, makes them popular destinations for yachties and powerboaters exploring the area. Most people never get this far unless they are going up Toba Inlet.

10

PORTAGE COVE
A Hundred Years of Settlement

Joe Copeland has been an elusive figure. When the Ragged Islands, just north of Lund at the entrance to Desolation Sound, were re-named the Copeland Islands in 1945, nobody seemed to know who he was. Then Howard White and Jim Spilsbury wrote *Spilsbury's Coast*. Spilsbury remembered that Joe Copeland "used to meet the steamboat dressed in a full Confederate Army uniform, complete with the little cap that kind of folded in the middle. Old Joe was a bugler on the Confederate side and his Dad was a colonel on the union side."[117] According to Spilsbury, Copeland was later "in one of those renegade gangs that went around robbing stagecoaches." Liv Kennedy, author of *Coastal Villages*, says that when he arrived in Vancouver, Copeland bought a rowboat, outfitted it and rowed north to Desolation Sound, where he spent most of his time logging, trapping and bartering with the Natives.[118] He was usually seen wearing his grey Confederate uniform, armed with a Luger pistol. He lived alone, but when company arrived he loved to tell stories of his exploits, chewing tobacco or spitting snuff in between anecdotes.

Amidst the dry dust of historical records, Copeland springs to life under a variant spelling of his name. James H. Copland first appears in the 1911 Canadian census.[119] Born in October 1844 in the United States, he was of Irish stock. He immigrated to Canada in 1900 and was naturalized in 1906. In 1910 he spent the full year working sixty hours a week at Yuill's Logging Camp in Okeover Arm, earning $900. He had enough education to be able to read and write. The 1911 provincial voters' list records him as Joseph Henry Copland, labourer. The 1916 list describes him as a farmer, and in 1928 he was registered as a rancher on the Lund list and a trapper on the Toba Inlet list.

In 1910, as Joseph H. Copeland, he pre-empted Lot 4933, which was thirty-two hectares (eighty acres) at Portage Cove in Desolation Sound. Ten years later, his neighbours Sheridan and Dewey Vaughn of Okeover Inlet witnessed that he had "made improvements in the aggregate to two dollars and fifty cents an acre," and he received his Crown grant. By 1928, old Joe was finding Portage Cove too populated for his taste. He sold the place and moved up to Toba Inlet, where he trapped until his last illness. He died in Powell River in 1936. The *Powell River News* obituary said the cause of death was pneumonia. He is buried, without a headstone, in the Cranberry Cemetery in Powell River.

Joe Copeland sold his Portage Cove lot to Ross and Harry Brister.[120] Their mother lived with them and planted daffodils everywhere. When she died, they buried her on the property behind a neat white picket

Joe Copeland pre-empted this traditional First Nations Portage in 1910. The Finches later built the house, barely visible in the trees.

fence.[121] Ross fell in love with Mary Gorman, a teacher at Galley Bay, and married her. Somewhere along the line, Harry faded out of the picture. Ross and Mary farmed the land from cove to cove. They raised deer inside fences and butchered them for meat, which they sold to logging companies. They also grew potatoes, apples, pears and peaches. When their daughter reached school age, they moved to Oregon so she could have a good education.

For several years during the 1960s, no one lived at Portage Cove in the winters. Bob De Pape and Ray Schluter had a contract to log a small area northwest of the cove around 1965–1966. "We lived in a trailer and worked ten days on, four days off," De Pape, a short, wiry man, remembered.[122] "From the hill above the cove we sent the logs down into the water on the Desolation Sound side and gathered them inside boom sticks. Although it was January, there was only a little ice on the water and we thought nothing of it till we decided to go out for groceries.

"We kept our boat on the Wootton Bay side, not realizing that the fresh water from the Theodosia River made it more prone to freezing. There was two and a half inches of ice on it." At first they tried using logs to break their way out, but this method didn't work. Then they attached a 3.5 metre (twelve-foot) plank to the boat and pushed it ahead. The plank slid under the ice, then popped up and broke it. They had to do this halfway down Lancelot Inlet before the ice got thin enough for the boat to power its way through.

In the early sixties, the Bristers sold the place to Bill and Brenda Finch, teachers from California. Ross Brister removed his two-storey house on a barge and asked the Finches to respect his mother's grave, but he never told them where it was.

Initially the Finch family came up only for summer months. With no power, just two saws, two hammers and two pairs of hands, they built a house. Water came from a spring that ran out of a rock in the cedar grove all year long.

Between them, the Finches had six children from previous marriages. Some were the same age as Barb Bloom from Galley Bay and Joyce Parker from Parker Harbour, so they were a welcome addition to the community. The kids would get together at Galley Bay or Refuge Cove to play.

Around 1971, when the Finches became year-round residents, Brenda's daughter Rhonda was in Grade 8. Bill home-schooled her using the California curriculum. The BC government never knew she was there. Things were different in those days.

To sustain themselves, the Finches grew a market garden and sold lettuce, beans and zucchini to stores in Refuge Cove and Powell River. As they were digging the garden, they found places where there was up to a metre (three feet) of clamshells, likely the remains of hundreds of years of First Nations' aquaculture. They also found a few artifacts that they gave to a friend who collected such things and who "may have passed them on to a museum somewhere." One of these items was an awl with a hole in the end of it, like a sewing needle. There were also arrowheads and glass bottles of the kind the Chinese kept laudanum in. Perhaps they came from the Chinese loggers employed at the Merrill and Ring logging camp in Theodosia Inlet (see Chapter 12).

One day the Finches' dog dug up some human bones, including a small skull. The RCMP collected them and passed them to the Sliammon people, who reburied them elsewhere. Although these could have been Mrs. Brister's remains, Maria Christensen Zaikow remembered skulls being dug up at Portage Cove when she lived in Salt Lagoon in the 1930s and 1940s. The skulls of Native people born in the nineteenth and early twentieth centuries are often elongated due to the way the babies were swaddled.

The Finches' dog, Virginia Wolf, was white with tan ears, a mixture of Samoyed, husky and lab, and came from the Sliammon Indian Reserve near Powell River. She mated with a wolf and had eight puppies. The Finches raised them and gave all but one away. The one they kept was very destructive and would even pull up the plumbing and eat the putty off the windows. After a year, they give her to the Sliammon kids, who had more time to spend with her than they did.

Whenever a bear came around, Virginia Wolf would bark and tree it. Bill would then take his big gun and shoot the bear, and the dog would jump on the body as if she had done the deed. Once, after Bill had shot a bear, they strung it up in the tree by the house. Brenda, who regularly canned bear meat, dressed part of it but planned on finishing the work the next day. After she and Bill went to bed, they were awakened by the dog's barking and a great thrashing around the house. Bill opened the bedroom door and went outside.

"Dolly, come look," he called. "There's a monkey in the tree." Sure enough, Brenda saw a long tail, twitching back and forth, hanging down from the tree. Above it was a cougar, looking down at the dog barking at the bottom of the tree. Bill shot the animal, and they buried it, because, Brenda said, "eating it didn't seem right." It was a very thin female and was probably starving. It had come for the bear but the dog scared it. Bill and Brenda were sorry to kill it, but the animal was a threat to themselves and their livestock.

To supplement the income from their garden, the Finches also tried raising pigs, starting with two females: Gertrude and Gloria. When they brought the pigs home, they towed them on a barge behind their boat. Instead of landing them right away, they anchored offshore and went away to do some other chores. Gertrude and Gloria swam to land. Later they ran off, but the dog rounded them up and brought them back. Brenda thought they stayed because of the food, which included mash from the Finches' beer-brewing operations.

Although pigs are tame and very affectionate, they are difficult to handle. They have very thick necks, which make it difficult to put a rope round to lead them. Drunken pigs are easier to winch into a boat than active sober ones with other ideas, so the Finches' mash often came in handy.

Eventually Agnes, Alice and a boar joined Gertrude and Gloria. Although the Finches put them all in together, the females never got pregnant, so Bill and Brenda got them drunk and took them to a friend in town to be fattened up and butchered.

By the mid-1970s, the Finches needed more cash, so Brenda went to work for the logging camp at Theodosia run by Don Percy and Nick and Pete Molenko.

Virginia Wolf, the white dog, tells Bill Finch that she killed the cougar he shot. COURTESY
BRENDA KING FINCH

The Finches kept a vehicle at Okeover and collected their mail in Powell River. Like Bob De Pape, they found it more convenient to moor their boats in Wootton Bay—the backside, as they called it. It was closer to the government wharf at Okeover and more sheltered from winter storms. In unusual years they had to break the ice.

"A lot of interesting people came and went in the sixties and seventies, including some draft dodgers," said Brenda Finch. "They'd squat for two or three years and then move on. Many didn't stay. There was a young couple on the left side of Theodosia, on a point. Both were doctors. He had been in the military and she had started out as a nurse and then become a doctor. They didn't stay long. Everyone knew each other and helped out when they could. Rick Tyrrell from Galley Bay would house-sit for us. Dan Parker sold us lumber from his Malaspina Inlet mill. Sometimes we went across to the store at Refuge Cove for supplies so we got to know the Hopes. On the way back, we'd call in on the Fosters on Mink Island."

In the early 1970s, a woman came ashore claiming to be the "first white baby born at Portage Cove or Theodosia." (Since Charlie Fletcher was the first white baby born in Theodosia, she must have meant Portage Cove.) Brenda can't remember her name. The woman, who came in from the "front side" (Desolation Sound) and walked over the portage to Wootton Bay, remembered a shack. Presumably this was the floathouse the Bristers took with them. Was she the Brister daughter, searching for her grandmother's grave?

The portage was a problem at times. Before the Finches became full-time residents, people would come and camp and were shocked to find that someone actually lived there. Bill and Brenda put up No Trespassing signs, which were ignored. Some people felt that even private land should be accessible to everyone. There were occasionally confrontations.

People would also come and pick oysters off the beach. Once the Finches watched a group of ten or fifteen Native people in two or three boats dig for clams in the bay at Portage Cove. As they didn't cover over their holes, all the young clams were exposed to the elements and died.

There were no clams for years after. Elsie Paul, a Sliammon elder, said that these people had apparently never been taught the proper procedure for clam digging. They had probably been forced to attend residential school when they would otherwise have been learning from the older generation.[123]

When the Finches first moved to Portage Cove, there was talk that the provincial government was going to create a park in the area between Prideaux Haven and Malaspina Inlet. The locals feared that the government would be expropriating property for the park. Bill and Brenda wrote letters of protest, but the fear turned out to be unfounded as the government preferred to negotiate with landowners. The Finches eventually offered to sell their land for market value, but the government wasn't prepared to pay this amount, so Portage Cove remained private property, even after Desolation Sound Marine Park was created in 1973.

The Finches finally left Portage Cove in the early 1980s because "it became too crowded" for them. Too many park visitors wanted to portage through their property. In the United States at that time, individuals could own waterfront land right down to the low-tide line, but this was not the case in Canada. However, the Finches may have tried to impose this view. In 1981 they sold the property to Doug Day, a Vancouver and Squamish developer, who still owns it.

11

GALLEY BAY
Entrepreneurs and Dreamers

G alley Bay is a sheltered nook on the east side of Zephine Head in Desolation Sound. The trees there were even bigger than those Axel and Amanda Hanson remembered from Finland. This amazed them when they arrived. In the most protected corner of the cove, they built a snug house and raised ten children.

Axel Andtbaka (1880–1975) grew up on his family's farm in the Kronöby region of Finland. Amanda (1881–1966) grew up within sight of it. Their wedding photograph shows them in their best black clothes. She was sixteen and he was nineteen. In those days, Finland was under Russian domination. Finns fleeing the country often claimed to be from Sweden. Axel and Amanda may have gone to Sweden for a short time after they left Finland. In 1899 they travelled to the United States. Immigration officials couldn't handle Axel's surname, so they asked what his father's name was. When he told them his father was Hans, they christened him Hanson.[124]

According to their son Ed, they first settled in Jennings, Michigan, for seven years.[125] Their son Ragnar and daughter Helen were born here. Axel worked in a sawmill for around $2.50 a day, which didn't go far. Overalls and shoes both cost about fifty cents at the time. Amanda ran a boarding house to help out, and they also kept chickens and pigs. One of the Hanson family characteristics was a consciousness of money—what things cost and how much effort was needed to pay for things like work clothes—probably because they were often in short supply. At least three generations have been entrepreneurs.

A year before they left Michigan, Axel's brother Bill came to British Columbia. He liked it so well he persuaded Axel and Amanda to join him. Bill started the Hanson Logging Company of Vancouver, which did most of the logging on Hernando Island and some at Lloyd Point and in Forbes Bay. He had cigar boxes made with the firm's name embossed on them as advertising.

At that time, around 1907, there was a rumour that paper money was no good. Before leaving Michigan, to the bank's consternation, Axel withdrew his savings of $1,500 and put the money in a trunk. It was in the form of silver dollars, which made the trunk very heavy. When they arrived in Vancouver, he talked to people in the hotel who said, "My God, Axel, you don't have to pack that around. There's nothing wrong with our Canadian dollar. Take it to the bank." He opened an account at the Royal Bank, which he maintained until he died.

After withdrawing some money in paper dollars, he and Amanda caught the Union Steamship to Lund. Their eldest daughter, now Helen Anderson, told me that the family built a house in Lund, and she started going to school there at the age of five to make up the numbers so that the school qualified to have a teacher.[126] "That's why I'm so smart," she said. She liked geography and spelling but hated history and grammar.

When the Hansons first came to Lund, Axel handlogged a ten-mile stretch of Galley Bay, beginning at the beach and working inland. There were good stands of cedar and fir. He worked other places too, but kept thinking of Galley Bay. In 1909 he and Amanda moved there, and in 1912 he pre-empted Lot 2839, seventy-six hectares (188 acres) that included the northwest side of Galley Bay and Zephine Head. As only Canadian citizens could apply for Crown grants, he became a naturalized citizen the following year. On May 17, 1917, after he paid $182 for the land, his grant was registered.

Axel built a snug cottage with a loft for the children to sleep in. Years later, an inspector from the Health Department told him it was

Axel and Amanda Hanson, seen here in their wedding picture, were the doyens of Galley Bay for half a century. COURTESY PAT HANSON

too small for all his children, so he built a substantial two-storey house with a verandah. Maria Zaikow remembered him showing off the new house when she went to live in Galley Bay in 1935. In addition to the house, he planted two hundred fruit trees and some purple lilac bushes that eventually overhung the verandah.

"An agent used to come round to visit all the people who had recently pre-empted land and sell them fruit trees, so everyone had the same varieties," said his daughter, Helen. "I can still identify them by taste."

Axel's son Ed remembered that they got a dollar a box for apples. [127] They tried making the boxes out of cedar shakes but ended up buying them in kit form for forty cents a box. By the time the freight was paid, there wasn't much left out of the dollar. It was Ed's job to load forty to fifty boxes of apples in the old gas boat and go to Powell River to try to sell them. It brought a little bit of income.

Alongside the orchard they planted a large vegetable garden and a hay pasture. They kept chickens, goats and cows, including a Jersey because Amanda couldn't drink coffee without cream in it. Every morning Axel took the milk cows up to the top of Zephine Head to forage.

Somewhere along the trail between the dock and the house, he had his wine cellar. As he grew older he had a number of liquor stashes around the property and would invite visiting men to partake with him. Some, like Dan Parker, were teetotalers, so they would just have a sip or two to be friendly.

Because he had grown up on a farm, Axel had many of the skills necessary to be a successful homesteader. Both he and Amanda were very strong physically. Their son Hugo remembered his father "hoisting a seventy-five-pound jack on his shoulders and away he went to the top of the hill." Amanda gave birth to all ten children at home.

After he built the house, Axel went back to handlogging. In about 1910, Bill and Axel logged the Sliammon Indian Reserve. They had one of the first steam donkeys on the coast. It was a steam winch, off an old sailboat, that had been used for hauling the anchor. There was just a single spool on it with no haulback line. Fortunately, there were some very strong women on the Sliammon Reserve who were able to pull the line out into the woods. Later they used a line horse that was so well trained it would walk on the logs to pull the mainline back. There were some fantastic timbers at Sliammon—sixty-six-foot boom sticks. One was eleven logs wide. There's no timber like that any more.

"He hardly worked a day in his life for wages," said Ed. "He was quite a good faller and bucker and an excellent woodsman. He could have earned $5.50 a day, but by working on his own, he got more. He had one claim in Pryce's Channel that he took two million feet off. You weren't allowed to use any kind of mechanical power whatsoever. You could use a hand winch to pull the swifters, but most handloggers weren't wealthy

The Hansons' orchard after the Blooms took it over. Pa Hanson's stashes of the strong cherry liquor he distilled are all long gone. COURTESY BARB BLOOM

enough to own one. It was really beautiful timber. It had to be, because when you handlogged it, if he didn't get fifty thousand board feet, he figured it was junk. Well nowadays, you'd never see anything that good.

"I used to go up and help him on my Easter holidays when I was eight or nine years old. We lived on the old gas boat. I wasn't much help, I guess. Just got in the way. One time he had this two-section boom of 100,000 board feet. About 3,000 board feet were No. 3 and the rest were No. 2 and No. 1. He got $1,200 for it and he was so proud. He felt so wealthy that he went and bought a Heintzman piano. Amanda was pleased because she had a good voice and liked to sing.

"We had our school at Galley Bay and we usually tried to get teachers who had some knowledge of music. My sister and I took music lessons. It was a beautiful piano but we didn't take much interest in music. There was codfish to catch, deer to hunt and looters to shoot."

The school Ed mentioned took a while to arrive. When the family first pre-empted their land, those of the ten children who were of school age used to attend school in Lund. They'd stay in town during the week, and Axel rowed them home for weekends. The journey took two hours.

A rainbow ends at the roof of the second Galley Bay School, which was barged over from Refuge Cove in 1923. COURTESY BARB BLOOM

Helen continued in the one-room school till the big exam in Grade 8, which was the equivalent of today's Grade 12.

By that time she was rowing to and from Lund on her own. One day as she rounded Zephine Head, she saw a school of blackfish in Malaspina Inlet. "They were squirting and splashing about so I waited, hoping they would go away," she said. "After a while, I crept around the shore to cross at the narrowest point. I thought they had disappeared but I ran into them again at Sarah Point, so they must have swum under me."

In the early 1920s, Helen's parents sent her sister Kay to board with the Smiths in Refuge Cove, where she went to school, but in 1923, the Refuge Cove schoolhouse was towed to Galley Bay and Kay was able to live at home while continuing her education.[128] Helen was appointed trustee for this school. "You don't look like a trustee," the young teacher said when she arrived. Helen was twenty-one years old at the time and working as a waitress at the Lund Hotel.

In 1933, Ingrid Andersen spent a year teaching at Galley Bay.[129] Only three out of two hundred student teachers in her year got jobs, and she was one of them. More than twenty years earlier, her father, Prairie

Ingrid Cowie's 1933 class at the Galley Bay School. Their Christmas concert was followed by a community dance. L to R, Back Row: Ethel Bishop, Agnes Bishop with Willie Bishop in front, Rita Heatley, Jean Heatley. Front Row: Irene Bishop, Daisy Heatley, Bobby Heatley, Mary Bishop. COURTESY INGRID COWIE

farmer Jens Andersen, had fallen in love with Karen Rasmussen, a dress designer who had her own salon in Copenhagen. In 1916, when their daughter Ingrid was three, Andersen moved the family from Lethbridge to Corbie's Point (now Junction Point) on Cortes Island. "Corbie joined up in the First World War and never came back," Ingrid said.

Her father went fishing all over Desolation Sound and became friendly with many of the old-timers. Often Ingrid went with him when he visited them. "My mother, Karen, was so lonely she thought Desolation Sound was aptly named." Fire burned their cabin, so the family moved to Lund, where Jens pre-empted land and built another house. After Ingrid graduated from the Vancouver Normal School, she returned to teach at Galley Bay.

Among Ingrid's nine students, there were some of the Hansons, on whose property the school was located; four of the Heatleys, a well-read family, who lived in a floathouse drawn up on the beach behind the islands on the eastern side of Galley Bay, across from the Hansons (see Chapter 11); and the Bishops from Malaspina Inlet (see Chapter 13).

Ingrid sold a car she had won in 1927 and bought a little open gas boat, *The Flying Bathtub*, which drew thirteen centimetres (five inches) and was powered by an Easthope engine. She got her brothers to transport her to and from Lund in this boat so that she could go home to Wildwood for the weekends.[130] If the weather was bad, she remained in her little rented cabin by the ocean at Galley Bay.

"There was no running water or electricity, just a Coleman lamp," she said. "When a rat caused a commotion in the attic, a friend rigged a trap with a couple of planks and caught it.

"Ma Hanson was used to running things. She said: 'I'll tell you when the Inspector's coming because I always dream about him,' but she didn't this time. I heard a gas boat approaching and thought it was the Reverend Greene but it turned out to be Mr. Daniels, the inspector."[131]

On December 22, Ingrid combined her school Christmas concert with a dance. Grade 1 performed the opening recitation ("When Ma is sick, everything grinds to a halt"), followed by plays (with titles like

Father Hangs a Picture and Sends Everyone to Get Nails), then songs and carols. According to Ingrid, "some kids could sing and some couldn't."

When it was over, the kids trooped up to the Hanson house, where they were put to bed in a circle on the floor in front of the big corner fireplace. Meanwhile, back at the school, their parents stacked the desks to one side in preparation for the dance. People came from miles around. On arriving, the men changed into suits, ties and street shoes; the women into dresses and slippers.

"Pa Hanson made delicious wine which tasted like cherry heering [Danish cherry-flavoured liqueur]," said Ingrid. "He served it a tumbler full at a time and it tasted like pop, but when you tried to get up your legs wouldn't work." Elmer Ellingsen from Gorge Harbour on Cortes played his accordion for the dances—foxtrots, French minuets and schottisches. A Coleman light illuminated the dance floor; when its fuel ran out, Ellingsen played the moonlight waltz while it was being refilled. At the end of the evening, he walked down the dock playing "The more we get together ... " and stepped off the planks into the ocean. The onlookers rushed to rescue the accordion first.

In 1938, a ten-metre (thirty-two-foot) wooden ketch, *Te Rapunga*, sailed into Galley Bay. On board were George Dibbern, the owner and master, along with Eileen Morris and Gladys Nightingale.

Georg Johann Dibbern had followed his father to sea in 1907.[132] After jumping ship in Australia he moved to New Zealand, where he ran a successful taxi business, bee farm and other enterprises before being interned at the end of the First World War. Repatriated to Germany, he married and had four children, but the mixture of unemployment, low-paying jobs, rampant inflation and the beginnings of Nazi politics convinced him that his family would be better off without him. With a crew of three others, he embarked aboard his Baltic double-ender *Te Rapunga* in 1930. (In Maori mythology, "Te Repunga" means the dark sun of the first dawn, which signifies the "Asking" or "Seeking" third stage of creation.) After many adventures, Dibbern arrived in New Zealand in 1934 to find that his employment prospects had evaporated.

He continued to sail with a new crew. Roy Murdock became the mate and Eileen Morris joined as navigator. Murdock described his adventures in letters to his cousin Muriel in Vancouver. She read them aloud to her co-workers at Westinghouse, one of whom was Gladys Nightingale.

When *Te Rapunga* docked in Vancouver in 1937, Gladys met the boat. She and Dibbern fell in love as she typed his book *Quest*. Dibbern's wife, Elisabeth, wrote to warn him against returning to Germany because of the political situation. Consequently, he looked for land in British Columbia, and a year later *Te Rapunga* anchored in Galley Bay with George, Gladys and Eileen on board. (Pictures show *Te Rapunga* and M. Wylie Blanchet's *Caprice* sailing together, though neither Dibbern nor Blanchet mention the meeting in their writing.) Rita Heatley remembered that they enjoyed a convivial visit with Pa Hanson, drinking his wine. At one point, one of the women said, "I'm perfectly sane and sober, I'll have you know." The Hanson wine was known for its intoxicating qualities.

On discovering that the eighty-one hectares (two hundred acres) of Lot 2644 were for sale for back taxes, they scraped together $472 between them and made the purchase.[133] The money came mainly from

The Blanchet's Caprice *rafts up with George Dibbern's* Te Rapunga *and the* Ivanhoe *in 1939. This was just before Dibbern's request for landed immigrant status was denied and he was escorted out of Vancouver harbour by the police.* COURTESY RICHARD BLANCHET

Gladys's cashed-in life insurance policy and a small inheritance belonging to Eileen. Dibbern himself had no funds. (Ragnar Hanson had obtained the Crown grant for Lot 2644 in 1926, but he had not been paying taxes because he had since gone where the logging and fishing jobs were.)

The *Te Rapunga* crew planned to make the place an artists' retreat, where all who came in peace and friendship would be welcome. George visualized winters of log fires and real German Christmas trees lit with candles, his wife and children gathered round; summers, when he wasn't lecturing or writing, would be spent fishing and sailing. It was not to be. George's and Eileen's visitor permits ran out, and immigration officials took a dim view of a German national who stated that he would not be willing to fight for his adopted country. A police boat escorted them out of Vancouver harbour.

Dibbern became known as the "man without a country." Refusing to fly the official German swastika flag, he designed and flew his own. When his passport expired, he refashioned that as well, stating: "I, George John Dibbern, through long years in different countries and sincere friendship with many people in many lands, feel my place to be outside of nationality, a citizen of the world and a friend of all peoples.

"I recognize the divine origin of all nations and therefore their value in being as they are, respect their laws, and feel my existence solely as a bridge of good fellowship between them.

"This is why, on my own ship, I fly my own flag, why I have my own passport and so place myself without other protection under the goodwill of the world."[134]

Unfortunately, his brave words did not stop the New Zealand government interning him for the second time when he took Eileen Morris back to her country. Wartime hysteria and disapproval of her presence aboard a married man's boat were no match for common sense. After the war they had a child together, but Dibbern never returned to Germany, though he had his friend and fellow writer Henry Miller sent much-needed help to Dibbern's wife and three daughters, who were poverty-stricken in the post-war conditions. (His eldest child, a son, died before the girls were born.) Dibbern died of a heart attack in Auckland, New Zealand, on June 12, 1962.

Although Gladys visited George and Eileen in San Francisco, she returned home to Vancouver. She continued to pay the taxes on the Galley Bay land until 1954, when she and Eileen sold it for $6,000 and split the proceeds. By this time Gladys had made a lifelong commitment to Mallory Daniels. Both became Kabalarians and changed their names to Sharie and Allen Farrell. They became well-known personalities on the coast, sailing the Chinese junks built by Allen.

By 1961, the Hansons were too old to manage on their own. Before moving in with their son Ed, in Okeover, they put their beloved home up for sale.

Just north of San Francisco, Gilbert and Kathryn Bloom were becoming increasingly worried about how the escalating conflict in Vietnam would affect their sixteen-year-old son, Carl.[135] They packed him and his two sisters—Barb, aged fourteen, and Elizabeth, ten—into the car, drove north, crossed the Canadian border and continued till the road ran out at Lund. In the hotel pub they heard of the Hanson property and took the water taxi to see it. Impulsive as always, Gilbert fell in love with the place and bought it. Kathryn, who had grown up on a farm in Indiana gardening, cooking and canning, supported him. She had a degree in home economics.

The Blooms returned to California, where Gilbert made a verbal agreement to sell their thirty-two-hectare (eighty-acre) property to a man who was to pay them interest on the principal for the first few years. This was their income. In a nine-metre (thirty-foot) yacht, they sailed to Galley Bay.

Kathryn, who was scared of boats, was glad to get ashore. Only when they landed did the children realize they would be living in a place with no electricity, no phones and no roads. They moved into the two-storey Hanson house with its spectacular view of Mount Denman. Downstairs, the floor of the living and dining area had become wavy as the house settled with age. "You could watch the cat come up and over the mountain," said Barb. The kitchen still had the same big wood stove on which Amanda used to bake her famous "handlogger cookies," made with oatmeal and a good twenty centimetres (eight inches) in diameter.

Once ensconced, the family discovered that they were somewhat lacking in the everyday skills required for this kind of life. They didn't even know how to sharpen the saw to cut wood. Dan Parker from Malaspina Inlet became their mentor, and the two families began a friendship that continues to this day. "In California, you choose your friends," said Barb. "Here, everyone was a friend and helped each other. It was a novel concept to us and one that we liked."

When the man who had bought their California property stopped making payments, Gil had to go back to sort things out. Carl became the man of the house, especially in boat matters. He loved the pioneer life and soon assumed the role of the strong guy, which he retained even after his father's return.

"Gil wasn't useful," said Joyce Parker Mostat. "He loved to read. He made plans, but it was the family who had to execute them."

The old orchard continued to produce. It contained mostly apple trees—Winter Banana, King, Early Transparent (which ripened in the summer), Jonathan, Gravenstein—as well as Queen Anne cherry trees, prune plums and pears. Come fall, bears raided the apples till the "watch geese" chased them away. The family had roast goose for Christmas dinner one year, but it tasted "as fishy as a seagull."

"Christmas wouldn't have been complete without the Boxing Day parties at Refuge Cove," said Barb Bloom. "Everyone except the teetotal Parkers went. The action took place at the back of the post office as a sort of 'Honour your Postman' occasion. Norm and Doris were very friendly, kind and generous people who certainly knew how to drink." As a child, Barb was banned from the adult activities, but the kids were happy to play on their own and enjoy the eatables.

After four years, Kathryn had had enough. Carl and Barb were at UBC, leaving only Elizabeth at home with her parents. The family hired a caretaker and moved to Vancouver in 1966. They were glad to become Canadian citizens, especially Carl, who wanted to avoid the Vietnam-era draft.

In the 1960s, Ingrid Andersen Cowie came back for a visit. "The Hansons had moved to Okeover to live with their son Ed. The people who replaced them said the government was giving them a bad time. They couldn't cut a stick of wood or have an oyster bake. Taxes had risen to $1,800. The Tenedos Bay people were similarly squeezed out. The fox farm my father had taken me to see on Mink Island was gone, though the pens were still there. Someone had put a billy goat on the Martin Islands and it smelled to high heaven. The goat bunted my brother into the sea."

In 1967, in his second year of forestry at university, Carl Bloom quit. Uncertain of his future, he returned to Galley Bay to think things out. There he was joined by a number of other idealistic young people, including some US draft dodgers. All were searching for themselves, and many were more interested in taking than giving. Only three or four did much work. The schoolhouse burned down, and several other structures, including the old Hanson house, were cannibalized for building materials or firewood. The group also scavenged building materials from other places, notably the disused cannery at Redonda Bay, and built seven cabins, including a communal kitchen. One person had money, so he paid the taxes. The rest "grooved on the sunset." At one time there were thirty or forty people, far more than the property could sustain with food or water.

Joan Treen, a newly minted public health nurse, remembered going to Galley Bay in 1968 with her supervisor to discuss hepatitis A.[136] They were met at the dock by a man who said, "I hope you don't mind, they're all in the nude up there."

"My supervisor barrelled on up and I followed," said Joan. "I was a little worried as I wasn't sure if she had heard what the man said. But when we arrived, they had thrown some clothes on and we gave them their shots."

Paul Williams wrote a book, *Apple Bay*, about the relationships between the participants.[137] With no strong belief system, there was nothing to hold people together. One by one they left. As happened with many utopian communities, wild rumours circulated about the residents' activities, which the media repeated long after everyone had gone home.

When they died, the Bloom parents left the property to their three children. Carl set up a tenants-in-common legal framework for sixteen participants. He, Barb and Elizabeth hold the majority of the shares. In the last twenty years, only one couple have become permanent year-round residents. The rest are summer people, several of whom have built homes. All want their privacy respected. Nothing remains to be seen of either the Hansons' buildings or the commune.

12

THEODOSIA INLET AND TENEDOS BAY

Ultimate Wilderness for the Palmers

One of the toughest pioneers in Desolation Sound was James C. Palmer (1846–1921), a recluse par excellence who spent his life searching for the ultimate wilderness.[138] Although born in Rome, New York, he grew up in Embarrass, Wisconsin, where his father's family were early pioneers. There he met Sarah Jane Wiswall (1851–1940), whom he married. While still living in Wisconsin, they had seven children, one of whom died in infancy. Three more died in the diphtheria epidemic of September 1881. There was a tall gene in the family, and many of the boys grew to over two metres (six feet) in height. Albert, the second oldest, was nicknamed High Pockets.

Seeking a fresh start in a less-populated area, they took the train to Oregon, settling in Clatsop County near Astoria. There they had five more children. The first of these was William Cyrus. In 1898, when William was fifteen, he accompanied his father to Vancouver, Canada. From there they rowed north to spend a memorable winter trapping beaver and marten along the lakes behind Stillwater south of Powell River. It was a particularly hard winter, with a metre (three feet) of snow, so they roofed their tent with cedar shakes and lived on starvation

James and Sarah Palmer married in 1867 in Wisconsin before moving west first to Oregon and then to Theodosia Inlet where Sarah stayed put while James, always the wanderer, spent winters trapping up Bute Inlet. COURTESY MOYRA PALM

rations augmented by meat from the animals they caught. Once they were down to one cup of flour a day, no bread and no salt. They shot a deer, but eagles ate most of it before they could bring it in.

In the spring they shipped their furs out of the Frolander post office (south of present-day Powell River) and rowed over to Van Anda, where they cut wood for steamships. Gas boats were still a thing of the future in this area. They met Fred Thulin, who, on hearing they had a large family, urged James to bring them to Lund so that there would be enough children for a school. Fred did not realize that only four were of school age. Both Palmers went south to pack up the farm. The family travelled up the coast on the SS *Comox*, arriving at Lund on October 7, 1899, the day before daughter Vira May's eighteenth birthday.

While the family settled in Lund, the men earned a living at "young Mr. Merrill's" logging camp in Okeover (see Chapter 4).[139] Conditions were poor, as the cook went on benders after distilling moonshine from potato peelings. In spite of this, the Palmers liked the area for its plentiful fish and game, and James pre-empted sixty-five hectares (160 acres) at the head of Theodosia Inlet in 1900. Theodosia is a well-hidden

The reclusive James Palmer built this barn soon after he pre-empted his land up Theodosia Inlet in 1900. COURTESY MOYRA PALM

extension of Lancelot Inlet, which runs into Okeover and Malaspina Inlets. James felt comfortable with its remoteness.

He may have believed he was the first to homestead in there, but he was not. On June 9, 1893, Charles Harding pre-empted fifty-three hectares (132 acres) on Lot 1830, receiving his Crown grant for it in December 1898, but he was long gone by the time the Palmers arrived.

To reach the Palmer land, the family had to wait for a high tide in order to go up the Theodosia River, past the 178-hectare (440-acre) Sliammon Indian reserve. Clearing sixteen hectares (forty acres) for a farm was a priority, so the family lived on a houseboat. Once a month they sailed a dinghy to Lund for groceries. Soon they had a herd of sixty to a hundred purebred Aberdeen Angus cattle, fed from their own hay. They sold the meat they didn't need to neighbouring logging camps and stores. Their extensive vegetable gardens made them largely self-sufficient.

Sarah planted a flower garden full of "sweet peas and annuals" and told her husband that she was not moving any more.[140] She was just as capable of rowing a boat or shooting a cougar as he was and often did so. Many years later, Eleanor Lusk, who married one of Sarah's grandsons, said Sarah always "ran rather than walked." Toward the end of her life, her hair thinned so she wore a cap above her circle of braids.

James continued to be driven by wanderlust. Each winter he rowed alone to the head of Bute Inlet, where he ran a trapline. The local Native people, fearing a

Sarah Palmer just before her death in 1940 at the age of 89. She only saw a doctor once in her life and died of pneumonia soon after surgery for a hernia. COURTESY MOYRA PALM

Vira May Palmer (photographed with her first husband Fred Thulin and sons Oscar and Clarence) survived three husbands before taking over her parents' farm. She was handy with a gun and not afraid of anything. COURTESY MOYRA PALM

repeat of Waddington's ill-fated attempt to build a road through their land to the interior (see Chapter 3), turned him back, but the furs were good so he returned every winter until he became too ill to continue. Although he died in Powell River in 1921, he is buried on the farm, across the river from the homestead.

Sarah outlived him by nineteen years. She was healthy all her life and only consulted a doctor once, in 1940. At her daughter's insistence, she underwent an operation for a hernia and died of pneumonia soon after. She is buried under a horizontal headstone in the Cranberry Cemetery in Powell River.

As Will, their oldest Oregon-born child, was more a logger than a farmer, it was their daughter Vira May (1881–1968) who took over the farm when James and Sarah grew old. She was their seventh child, the last to be born in Wisconsin, and the oldest surviving daughter. As strong as her pioneering mother, she always knew what she wanted and made sure she got it. In 1900, she married Fred Thulin (1873–1935), with whom she had three children (Oscar Frederick, Clarence August and Harold Wilfred). When the marriage broke up, she married Samuel Blake Arnold, a hotelier from Oregon, with whom she had two more children (Katie and John). After living in Seattle for a while, she returned home and married Charles Salo in 1920. They ran the farm together until he backed off the Lund wharf in his car and drowned in 1941.

By this time the old Palmer homestead had been sold to a Mr. Molenko. Vira May bought a floathouse from Ed Hanson, who was moving into Lund after living on it in Okeover, and pulled it up on her brother Will's property in Theodosia, where she lived in it alone.

In 1955, as she was carrying a beam to rebuild a fence, she knocked herself unconscious when she slipped on wet grass. "When I came to, I finished the job," she said. "Got some wood and lit a fire, then, because I was wet and cold, got into bed to rest. Shouldn't have done that, because my leg stiffened up. I'm sure if I'd kept walking, it would have been alright."[141] When staff at the Powell River hospital X-rayed her leg, they discovered she had broken her hip. They also saw two old breaks that had healed on their own. A lump on her hand, which took a year to grow, marked another broken bone, but Vira May claimed the hand was "as good as new." After she came out of hospital, she lived for some time in a trailer at the back of her son John Arnold's place at Pebble Beach, south of Powell River. She died of heart failure on September 11, 1968.

She told stories of numerous encounters with cougars and wolves, some of which she shot. Once, when she had a new Savage rifle, a cougar appeared two metres (six feet) away. She pressed the trigger but the gun didn't fire. Coolly, she loaded another cartridge and shot it. She carried the head home, but when she went back for the body next day, another cougar had moved the carcass and partly eaten it. She set a bear trap to

Will Palmer's float home in Squirrel Cove. When he had it in Tenedos Bay, young teacher Eleanor Lusk remembered eating superb meals in there. She taught school while Palmer towed the whole community up Toba Inlet. COURTESY MOYRA PALM

Will Palmer pre-empted land on Savary Island in 1902 and eventually had fifteen logging outfits along the coast, including one in Tenedos Bay. His wife, Mildred, was known for her excellent baking and nursing skills. COURTESY MOYRA PALM

catch the second cougar, but it just sat on the trap to finish its meal. On another occasion she shot two wolves and then heard "about a hundred others in the bush." As she had only one shell left, she quickly went home by way of the creek, where she would have been able to climb a tree if necessary. Next day "an acre of bush had been flattened" after a pack of wolves fought and trampled it.

Not all the Palmer children stayed in the area—the two oldest boys went back to Oregon—but Will Palmer (1884–1966) stayed. He pre-empted sixty-five hectares (160 acres) for himself on Savary Island (his brother-in-law, Louis Anderson, pre-empted an adjoining lot), earning the Crown grant in 1909, and over the years he registered other properties, including at least one in Theodosia, and many handlogging licences.

Will had logging shows as far north as Kingcome and Knight inlets, and at one point he had fifteen outfits with donkey engines. During the 1920s he and his wife, Mildred, lived in a large floathouse hauled up on the beach in Tenedos Bay, which was then called Deep Bay. The commissary and the schoolhouse were also hauled up on the beach. The rest of the camp floated nearby.

Fresh out of Vancouver's Normal School, eighteen-year-old Eleanor Lusk came to Deep Bay for her first teaching job in 1929.[142] She lived with the Palmers and had fond memories of their pretty dining room with its view of the water and the seagulls. When the Columbia Mission boat came, the Reverend Heber Greene held Sunday services in that dining room. Later, Eleanor and Jimmy Anderson, a grandson of James Palmer, were married on the Columbia Mission ship.

Unfortunately, when she developed quinsy, a painful throat infection, the boat with its medical service wasn't around. Mildred Palmer dosed her with hot rum, and Eleanor lost a lot of weight. She soon regained it, though, as Mildred was a good cook. "The cakes, pies and puddings were out of this world." Even skating around the islands in Unwin Lake in the winter didn't stop her from gaining weight.

Fred Fletcher and Nellie Palmer posed for this formal portrait to celebrate their marriage. Their son, Charlie, was the first baby of European descent to be born in Desolation Sound. COURTESY MOYRA PALM

The school consisted of ten to twelve kids in various grades between one and twelve. There were eight or nine families in camp, and more came for the school. Apart from the three Palmer children, there were the Jones and Lindsay families as well. The government only provided school texts, but she bought additional books herself. The children provided their own scribblers.

"I had Mr. McLean as an instructor at Normal School," Eleanor said, referring to the man whose "McLean Method" of teaching cursive writing was popular across Canada for many years. "He volunteered to mark my pupils' writing, and issue certificates."

In 1931 the whole camp was towed up Toba Inlet, and Eleanor taught all the way. During a spelling test, the kids kept seeing interesting things and rushing to the windows. "I just let them," she said, "because it was such a wonderful experience. I thought they should take advantage of it."

Lusk taught in the area for three years. At the end of each term she boarded the *Chelohsin* from a raft outside the bay and went down to Vancouver on it.

Will Palmer's nephew, Charlie Fletcher, remembered the camp at Deep Bay, where he worked one summer before he went to Vancouver Technical College.[143] Fletcher was the first European baby to be born in Desolation Sound. The happy event occurred on August 24, 1909. His mother was James and Sarah's daughter Nellie, and his father was Fred Fletcher. He was such a novelty that the whole population of the Sliammon reserve turned out to see him. When he cooed at them, they called him "Ahamoo," which means "Little Pigeon."

Having learned to run the Stillwater logging railway engines while he was growing up, Charlie was well qualified to run the steam donkey that dragged logs down a chute from Unwin Lake to Deep Bay. He had to start early in the morning to take advantage of the offshore wind that pushed the logs out to where they could be gathered in a boom. It was also his job

Merrill and Ring built and operated a logging railway 1923–1937 in the Theodosia valley. When they had finished logging along a spur line, they took up the track and re-laid it elsewhere. BRITISH COLUMBIA ARCHIVES D-04906

to run the gas boat over to Refuge Cove or Squirrel Cove for supplies and mail. The Union Steamship *Cheakamus* brought supplies in from Vancouver and tied up to a nine- by fifteen-metre (thirty- by fifty-foot) float. In fog, the captain would blow the ship's whistle and listen for the echo to judge where he was, as he had neither radar nor depth sounder.

There was logging up Theodosia Inlet as well. In 1923, two years after James Palmer's death, the quiet valley where his grave lies rang with the sound of hammers as work crews constructed a logging railway. Did he turn in his grave? The railway's builder, Thomas Merrill, was a Duluth millionaire with extensive timber holdings along the BC coast. He aimed to log "half a dozen Crown-granted properties, carrying some of the finest fir in British Columbia."[144] Merrill had originally planned to do this in 1907, but the construction permit was not issued until 1922.

At its peak, the Theodosia, Powell Lake and Eastern, or TPL&E— one of the few lines that was not named for its owner—was fifty kilometres (thirty-one miles) long. Merrill's company, Merrill and Ring, removed the track when it finished working an area and recycled the materials for the next rail line, a common practice for logging railways. Starting in 1934, the length of track diminished, and after 1937 there is no mention of it in Railway Department reports.

In the railway's early days, before he became a commercial fisherman, Ed Hanson of Galley Bay would cut wood to fuel the steam donkeys. There was always a tussle between the firemen and management. The firemen wanted to burn fir to keep steam up, because hemlock simply wouldn't maintain enough heat. Management hated burning fir. "If you didn't burn it, we could make some money," they'd say. Usually the fireman had two assistants to buck and split the wood, which was then piled alongside the tracks.

Even after the demise of the railway, logging continued in the valley. At one of the last old-style logging shows in the 1950s, Frank White spent two years working for his friend Blondie Swanson, first as shovel operator and later as camp gofer.[145] Every week he'd drive in to Powell River from Okeover to buy fresh groceries at Toigo's store and pick up parts from the hardware store in Cranberry.

Theodosia was so pleasant that he rented a cabin and brought his wife, Kathleen, and three- or four-year-old son, Howard, for a month's vacation.

White remembered dropping in to the old Palmer homestead, now engulfed in honeysuckle vines. The Palmers' daughter, Vira May Salo, served him tea with scones and cookies. "She was quite a character," he said. "She commanded respect and never swore." Her son John Arnold took meat from the cattle they raised to Powell River to be sold at Mitchell's store, where customers asked for it specially. White also heard that her brother Will Palmer, then aged seventy, was seen carrying an oxygen cylinder on his shoulder as he walked across loose logs.

Over the years, White had heard wild tales of former camps in Theodosia. Camp Baloney was so named because the cook fed pigs that he kept under the bunkhouse. In the early 1930s, when the "hurry-up system of logging" was in operation, there was a horrendous accident. Five chokermen died in one day. Instead of shutting down the operation for twenty-four hours, as usually happened when a death occurred, the company simply yarded the bodies off to the side and continued working. At quitting time, a railcar came down the track to take the workers back to camp. The dead were stacked one on top of the other on one side of it; the living rode on the other side.

Jim Chambers, whose family homesteaded in Okeover Inlet in 1916, knew the man who ran a small gas boat between the camp, Lund and Powell River twice a week. "Nearly every time he had a couple of corpses on board," he said. "One time he had five lying on the deck."[146] This is probably the same incident that Frank White remembered.

In 1989 and 1990, the Powell River historian Bill Thompson interviewed Chambers and John D'Angio, whose family arrived in Okeover Inlet in 1910. D'Angio said that the Merrill and Ring camp (then Merril, Ring and Moore) was a large operation employing four hundred men. Moore's son was the super. There was little respect for the workers. If he knew the Union Steamship was about to bring thirty new men to the float in Lancelot Inlet, Moore would fire thirty old ones as they were getting onto the crummy or the speeder to go to work.[147]

Most of the hands were newly arrived immigrants, unfamiliar with the rough life. Although the Workman's Compensation Act of 1916 resulted in a compulsory no-fault accident compensation program, no one enforced safety rules and "the companies got away with murder," according to Chambers.

Conditions were better for the twenty-five to thirty men employed by the Swanson camp in the 1950s, mainly old-timers who had known each other for years. White's friend Bill Diot was there, along with several others. The men lived in the old camp buildings that were now well-maintained, with rules and standards. They slept on single beds, not bunks. There were showers and a dining room but no recreation room. Liquor was frowned on. Rising as soon as it was light, they worked eight-hour days till fire season, when they had to quit by noon. Sometimes during fire season they were shut down altogether. There were no accidents. The logs were trucked down to Theodosia Inlet, where they were assembled in booms and towed to Vancouver.

This was not the last logging show in the area. Merrill and Ring still retains the rights to timber in Theodosia. In the 1990s the company began cutting the second growth. This time the workforce commuted daily from Powell River, and the operation was highly mechanized. No further cutting was done in Tenedos Bay, and no one has lived there since the park opened in 1973.

13

MALASPINA INLET
Bishop Harbour Becomes
Parker Harbour

*A*t the entrance to Desolation Sound, Malaspina Inlet opens to the south. It is the only exit for the tributary inlets of Lancelot and Okeover, which have many secret coves, including Grace Harbour and Theodosia Inlet. The First Nations people of the area had a big winter village, Kahkaykay in Grace Harbour, and there were satellite summer villages in Theodosia and Freke Anchorage (see Chapter 2).

The sheltered waterways of the Malaspina Inlet complex attracted more settlers than any other part of Desolation Sound. Although some established themselves permanently in one place, others moved around, often living in floathouses that could be drawn up on the beach or re-floated as necessary. This meant communities that formed in one area could suddenly disperse and regroup in another.

High, perpendicular cliffs drop straight into the water on the eastern shore of Malaspina Inlet, so settlers like the Bishops and Parkers perched their homesteads on stilts on the western shore. South of them, Coode Island at the mouth of Trevenen Bay marks the end of Malaspina Inlet and the beginning of Okeover Inlet, and the continuation of the inlet, Trevenen Bay, ends in a narrow isthmus that separates it from Penrose Bay on the Okeover side. The Crowther family homesteaded the isthmus (see Chapter 15).

Although he was never able
to prove it, Peter William Bishop
(1871–1946) was convinced his
Bishop's Landing store, just north
of Lund, was destroyed by arson.[148]
To cut his losses, he moved his
wife, Mary, and their three children, Agnes, William and Mary, to
the mouth of Malaspina Inlet.

Born in Peterborough, On-
tario, Peter was the first of three
brothers to come to the Lund area.
He pre-empted the land that is
now called Bliss Landing. In 1911,
when he set up a general store and
post office, it was called Bishop's

*After fire burned his Bishop's Landing
store, Peter Bishop moved his family
to Malaspina Inlet and started over.*
COURTESY MARY GUSSMAN

Landing. He added a telegraph office in 1917 and began dealing in furs,
logs, fish and oil. A year later he married Mary McGuffie (1892–1953),
the sister of Bob McGuffie of Refuge Cove (see Chapter 6). Peter received his Crown grant in 1921. Their daughter, Mary Bishop Gussman, whom I interviewed, was proud that her birth certificate clearly
stated she was born at Bishop's Landing in 1924. Not long after, fire
levelled the buildings, and the family moved farther north and to the
other side of the peninsula.

In Malaspina Inlet, Peter Bishop chose a sheltered cove protected
by some islands and pulled a floathouse as far as he could up the beach
before putting stilts under it. "The tide used to come up under the house
all the time," Mary recalled, while sitting surrounded by family memora-
bilia in her Van Anda home.

Peter's brother Charles and his wife, Margaret, were living in Theodosia Inlet, and his third brother, Abe, worked at the Merrill and Ring
logging camp at the head of the inlet. His father, also called Peter William, came out to visit occasionally. He came the year Peter took his
family up Toba Inlet in his nine-metre (thirty-foot) gas boat, which was

called the *PWB*. This was short for either Peter William Bishop or Public Work Boat, depending on the whim of the day.

Since Peter Sr. was forgetful, the children were told to follow him whenever he went for a walk. He'd tell them to leave him and go home, but "We wouldn't," said Mary. Another year he stayed with Charles. One afternoon when Charles was away, Peter Sr. decided to go for a walk. Margaret sent the dog with him to make sure he came back, but he must have told it to go home. He was never seen again. The family searched for a long time but there was no trace of him.

Peter Jr. went handlogging. It was hard work for a man his family always considered sickly, but it provided a tiny income. It was an ongoing battle to earn enough money. The children's clothes were hand-me-downs, supplied by one of the churches in Victoria, which also sent them Christmas gifts—dolls, books and games. Mary still has a rose-coloured plastic

Peter and Mary Bishop had four daughters. In this 1943 photo, Ethel stands on the left, then Agnes, Mary McGuffie Bishop, Mary, and Irene with her father, Peter Bishop, behind her. COURTESY JOYCE MOSTAT

bracelet with a diamond pattern on it that she received the Christmas she was eight years old. Christmas dinner was roast chicken rather than turkey, and there were no cranberries.

The Reverend Alan Greene of the Columbia Coast Mission knew things were tight for them. Every year at Christmas he would play Santa Claus, as he did for many families on his routes. At other times he brought movies of Donald Duck and Mickey Mouse. In summer, he took the whole family for picnics that included helpings of ice cream that he made on the boat.

For food, the Bishops kept a flock of thirty goats, as well as

By the time Mary McGuffie married Peter Bishop she had survived a Saskatchewan winter in the Barr Colony. COURTESY MARY GUSSMAN

chickens and rabbits. The goats were all named, and it was the children's job to milk them. The family also canned vegetables and fruit from the garden and the orchard. Potatoes, carrots and cabbage kept well in the root cellar. Wild blackberries, huckleberries and crab apples added to their food supply.

"We also fished from our rowboats," Mary said. "We rowed everywhere. On Saturdays we'd row to Squirrel Cove for the dances. On Sundays, when the Union Steamships brought the mail to Refuge Cove, we rowed over there. We'd row down to the Chapmans and hike across the old Indian trail to Bliss Landing.

"Once Agnes and I rowed up to Portage Cove. When we got there, we put blankets on the floor of the old house, which was empty at the time, and slept the night. I remember the mice kept me awake running around for hours.

"I was never scared in the bush," Mary said. "The only cougar encounter that I remember was when one got away with a baby goat. We
rushed after it and I remember throwing stones at this brown thing dis-
appearing in the distance. It had the goat in its mouth and that was
the end of it. Another time, a big grizzly bear attacked the goats in the
swamp near the 'dryback,' the hilly pile of rounded beach rock connecting
the island to the mainland. Only abnormally high winter tides flooded
it. Nick, Agnes's husband, wandered around with his gun trying to get
it, but it had gone off somewhere else."

After Mary's mother gave birth to two more children, Ethel and
Irene, the Bishops decided to move to Galley Bay so the children could
go to school. It was just a short way along the trail to the school or to
their neighbours, the Heatleys. Mary remembered running along behind Agnes and Willie. The next thing she knew she fell down a cliff
onto her head. Mercifully, she was all right. She was not so lucky one
night when she was chasing Agnes in the bush. She tripped over a log
and dislocated her right shoulder.

*Vivian Mackie (with corsage) kept a firm hand on her pupils at the Galley Bay School in
1929 and 1930. Back row: Ed Hanson, Vivian Mackie, Corinne Hanson. Middle row: Dot
Hanson, Patricia Palmer, Violet Anderson, Mildred Palmer. Front row: Billy Palmer, Agnes
Bishop, Lloyd Anderson. Seated on the ground: Willie Bishop.* COURTESY JOYCE MOSTAT

"Ragnar Hanson was a First Aid man, but he couldn't put it back," said Mary. "I had it in a sling for a long time and learned to write with my left hand. Eventually, the pain calmed down and I went back to writing with my right hand, but I still can't lift my hand above my shoulder. Ragnar had nicknames for everyone. Even though I was very little, he called me Aunt Mary."

After a while her father moved them back to Malaspina Inlet. They still went to the Galley Bay school, but to get there they had to row a quarter of a mile across the inlet and then hike a mile along a trail Peter cut for them through the bush. This became a burden, so they reverted to home-schooling for another two years.

"I was in Grade 6 at the time," said Mary, "but I never finished it. We were just starting to take fractions, and Mom couldn't help us. All the exercises came back marked wrong, so I quit." At seventeen she got a job as a nanny in Cranberry and later looked after the grandchildren of Dr. Marlatt, one of Powell River's early doctors, while their parents were away. In 1942 she married Bill Gussman. For several years they lived on a boat, moving between Powell River and Van Anda on Texada. Bill had many skills. He logged, fished, ran the water taxi, worked at the quarry, acted as wharfinger and lived to the ripe old age of ninety-three. After he died, Mary took on the Van Anda wharfinger job.

When Agnes and Ethel (1926–2003) married, they brought their husbands home to build houses on the family property. Ethel's husband, Dan Parker (1898–1986), was the most ambitious. Born in Michigan and brought up in Alberta, he'd worked in the Anyox copper mine and then at Frank Osborne's sawmill in Lund. Now in his late forties, he built a large mill at the mouth of the creek. Since there was no flat land, he built it on pilings over the beach. At low tide he would dig a hole. At high tide he'd pound a piling in, and on the next low tide he would plumb the piling and brace it with rocks. He put in fifty to sixty pilings this way and then, at high tide, took his rowboat out and stood in the boat to saw the tops off level. Afterward, still from the rowboat, he added crossbars and decked the whole thing using beachcombed lumber. Then he put in a walkway

Built with painstaking effort, Dan Parker's mill cut lumber for the Finches of Portage Cove and many others for miles around. It didn't make him rich but it fed his family. COURTESY JOYCE MOSTAT

Dan Parker, who married Ethel Bishop, ran his mill with a variety of engines starting with a Model A Ford. COURTESY JOYCE MOSTAT

and built the mill on the platform he had created. He used a Model A Ford engine on the winch and three or four gas engines of various types for the mill. People came from miles around to have their lumber custom milled.

For several years in the late 1940s, Peter Bishop was unable to pay his taxes, and the family was in danger of losing the land. Somehow, Dan Parker and Willie Bishop scraped together $250 apiece and bought it for the back taxes. From then on, and even sometimes to this day, the place became known as Parker Harbour.

"Uncle Willie never lived on the property," said Joyce Mostat, Dan and Ethel's daughter, "but now the caretaker lives in our house, and when I went back to see it, it had shrunk. The present owner built a new house on the point."[149]

Joyce and her siblings did not go to the Galley Bay school as her mother had done. Joyce spent Grades 1 and 2 living with her aunt Mary on Texada, then moved back home to Parker Harbour for Grades 3 to 5.

Snowfall at Dan and Ethel Parker's house. Dan and Ethel's brother, Willie, bought the Bishop property for back taxes when Peter Bishop couldn't pay. COURTESY JOYCE MOSTAT

Her father converted one of the outbuildings into a schoolhouse. Every day she and her sister, Diana, did their correspondence lessons there from 9 to 3 p.m. under the supervision of Phyllis Hunter, who lived on the property with her husband, Harry.

"Phyllis was one tough cookie," said Joyce. "My mother never would have done it."

Another person who lived in one of their outbuildings was Frank Osborne (1879–1963), who built the Lund Machine Shop in 1907 but had recently retired from it. "He had a black lab dog called Belle," said Joyce. "Frank cooked his own meals in a cast-iron fry pan, which he also ate out of. Then he'd let Belle lick the pan before he put it away in the cupboard, ready for the next time.

"We spent more time together as a family in those days," she remembered. "In the evenings, we'd gather round the coal oil lamp to play cards and board games like Chinese checkers. We learned to count playing rummy, hearts, crib and whist. Sometimes we played

The Reverend Trevor Williams of the Columbia Coast Mission's ship Rendezvous *officiated at David Parker's christening. In the back row, Dan and Ethel Parker, Joyce, and the Reverend. Front row, Bessie, Diana, Barbara, and David.* COURTESY JOYCE MOSTAT

blackjack for matchsticks. We got ten matches to start with. There was lots of hide-and-seek and kick the can. Outside, there was beachcombing for treasures of all sorts. In the spring, we loved to walk along the dryback, where pink and white lady's slipper orchids grew along with chocolate lilies, shooting stars, wild onion and blue-eyed Mary."

Joyce remembered the day her grandmother, Mary Bishop, had a stroke. It was a Sunday, and her father had just left for Refuge Cove to get the groceries. Ethel sent Joyce over to see if her grandmother would like anything.

"No, she doesn't," she reported back.

"Has she had breakfast?"

"I don't know. She's just lying on the floor."

Ethel flew over to find her mother lying very still. Agnes's husband, Nick, jumped in his boat and went down to the home of Brook Hodson, where there was an intercom to the taxi in Lund.

"We need an ambulance," he yelled.

He brought the two ambulance attendants back with him, and they loaded Mary Bishop onto a stretcher. The stroke paralyzed her along one side, so she went to a nursing home on Saltspring. Eventually she was able to live with her son, Willie, in Powell River, and later she came back to Dan and Ethel at Parker Harbour, where she died.

Although the Reverend Alan Greene had retired, the Reverend Titus still brought the *Rendezvous* to see them. Ethel was mortified one time when he came for supper and they remembered afterward that they hadn't asked him to say grace.

"Well, now he knows how we are," Dan said.

Lots of yachts came in, some returning year after year. Hungry for company, the Parkers would go down and greet them.

"Come on up for coffee," Dan would say.

"Oh, Ethel, that's a million-dollar view," they'd say.

"You can't eat it," Ethel responded. The family was still very cash poor. Dan was used to starvation rations. Often, in Alberta, he had gone for three or four days with nothing to eat. Once all he had to eat was a can of peaches. "He never complained," said Joyce. "He accepted his lot in life and did the best he could."

The Parkers still raised goats and chickens, although Joyce reported that "Mom hated goats with a passion, probably because she had to care for them as a child. We kept them for meat and milk and because they could range for themselves. Cows would have been a lot more trouble. Once in a while Dad shot a deer and we canned it—everything. Nothing was wasted. Canned wild meat is still my favourite. We also dug for clams and fished. When we had to have fish for supper, all we had to do was jig for a few minutes and we had one."

Every year they picked blackberries till they never wanted to see another one. Ethel canned them, along with pears and plums, which they sometimes got from the Hansons' orchard at Galley Bay. One year a batch of prune plums didn't seal properly and fermented in the jars. Months went by before they discovered the problem.

"Dad made us wrap the jars in towels and throw them down the beach," said Joyce. "When they hit there was a big *kaphoomph* and purple juice went everywhere.

"Another time, Frank Smith, who was living in one of our shacks, made wine and stored it in bottles under the bed. When it exploded, there was an awful stink.

"We made root beer and dandelion wine but neither was a big hit."

One source of funds for Dan Parker was Blondie Swanson's logging camp up Theodosia Inlet (see Chapter 12). The cook would radio a grocery order to Woodward's in Vancouver, and a freight boat would drop it and other supplies off at Parker Harbour on the weekly run. The sandbar at the mouth of Theodosia was too shallow for the freight boat, so Dan took the order in to the camp.

When the Bloom family settled in Galley Bay in the 1960s, they became really good friends with the Parkers, alternating Christmas and birthdays at each other's houses. "This was quite lovely for Mom, who otherwise had little social life," said Joyce. "Once or twice a year she'd go to Deep Bay [Tenedos Bay] to see George and Jeannine Fidler, who had a logging show there. She also knew an older couple on Mink Island,

and she'd see the Hansons at Galley Bay. Apart from the Sunday trip to Refuge Cove, that was all except for the summer tourists. Most of the loggers and fishermen were men. She read a lot—Harlequin romances, murders, whatever magazines the loggers left, and then we always took subscriptions to the *Winnipeg Free Press*, the *Star Weekly* and the *Powell River News*."

Although the Bishops and Parkers lived in one area, Joyce Parker Mostat remembered "little vacant homesteads and orchards all over the place." She was taken up Theodosia to visit her uncles, Charlie and Abe. She had tea and cookies at the Salo house—and watched. In those days, children were seen and not heard.

In 1966, Dan Parker sold the property to Oscar Greene, who kept it for three or four years, subdivided it and sold off portions. Eventually the portion with the original Parker house was purchased by Betty and Bob Fletcher of Seattle. They hired Walter Franke as a caretaker for about ten years.[150] Franke, who lived in various places in Desolation Sound for thirty years, had a herring skiff with a canvas cabin. He and his old dog, De Gaul, lived in it when they were between jobs. The dog was not so old that he couldn't father pups, which he did when they visited Ivor Danielsson at the Lindberg farm in Homfray Channel.

"Walter was a little crazy," said Bud Jarvis. "Everybody knew him. When I first met him, he was digging clams. He lived in a floathouse on the north side of Teakerne Arm. He was an expert at pruning and grafting fruit trees. He'd learned to play the zither by listening to the radio, and he sure made the instrument sing. All was well till 'they' found him and started poisoning the water.

"It was then that he got the job at Parker Harbour. He moved his floathouse to the east side of Malaspina Inlet and remained for ten years. He was a really nice guy. He didn't smoke or drink. When I was at Tiber Bay, he came to visit me once a month. I thought he had a chemical imbalance problem. Once I suggested he get some medical help, but he wouldn't hear of it, and shortly after that he sold his boat and bought an old school bus that he said he was going to drive to the Prairies because the end of the world was coming."

Karen Gordon of Larson's Landing also remembered Walter and wondered if he drank unfiltered water and contracted beaver fever from it.[151] Beaver fever or giardiasis is a stomach infection caused by drinking contaminated water or eating contaminated food.

In the early 1970s, Jill and Wolfgang Goudriaan, who ran a restaurant in North Vancouver, decided to join forces with another family and homestead in Malaspina Inlet. "The inlet was so empty then," said Wolfgang. "The only other light we saw was from Rick Tyrrell's yacht *Greta*, which he moored in Theodosia Inlet."[152] Like many yachties, Tyrrell was from California. Goudriaan added that a lot of people from Seattle were buying property in the area at that time.

The Goudriaans and their friends had a seventy-square-metre (753-square-foot) cabin with no telephone, electricity or water. "We had to learn to live as a family. We all had equal opportunities to fight for our rights, and we did. It made us very close and very strong as a family. The kids bonded with friends from Galley Bay, Sharp's Bay and Lund. If a storm blew up while they were visiting, they'd stay for three or four days. Now they have coffee with each other in Vancouver and come back for vacations."

After two years of home-schooling, the Goudriaans' two daughters felt they needed to go to school and wanted to live in Powell River to be near their peers. Goudriaan and his wife had never considered such a possibility. Reluctantly, they bought a farm on Wilde Road, where they continue to live with their sheep, dogs and chickens—but they still spend time at the cabin on Malaspina Inlet.

Today, there are few year-round residents in the inlet. The several houses at Parker Harbour are summer places, as are the Malaspina Estates at Selina Point on the other side of the inlet. A handful of oyster growers live year-round above their leases (see Chapter 16).

14

LANCELOT INLET
Desolation Tragedy

Where Malaspina Inlet turns into Okeover Inlet, another short inlet, Lancelot, intersects on the east side. There are two interesting features at the head of Lancelot Inlet: a short traditional portage over to Portage Cove in Desolation Sound and, behind some islands, a narrow secret passage that widens out into Theodosia Inlet.

One of the earliest settlers in Lancelot Inlet was Ed Berglund, who pre-empted Lot 2313 at Thors Cove in 1912 and received his Crown grant for the forty-three hectares (104 acres) in 1923. Around 1916, he built the second Okeover school for $100, and Francis Barrow, a visiting cruiser, reported that he played cribbage with Ed in 1938.

Among other things, Ed was a boat builder. When someone asked him to build a boat, he would get them to order the engine first.[153] Then he'd use it to power the tools to build the vessel. The current owners of Thors Cove, Roger Thorne and Susan Canning, have their workshop in the same southeast corner of the cove as Ed did.

While most people who settled in Desolation Sound had some rural survival skills, Arthur Jones (1889–1939), who pre-empted Lot 4603 in Lancelot Inlet in 1927, did not. He and his wife, Helen (1891–1952), had recently arrived from Britain on a wave of advertising euphoria. They were full of hope that they could make a better life for their large family. Apparently no one told them they lacked the necessary skills to survive

Ed Berglund was one of the earliest settlers in Lancelot Inlet. CAMPBELL RIVER MUSEUM 85-1

in the isolated Canadian wilderness, and Arthur would likely have disregarded such advice anyway.

Ingrid Andersen Cowie remembered Arthur as a very autocratic Englishman, and she thought his wife was correspondingly cowed.[154] She may not have actually met them, but she had heard of them, and that was her conclusion. Ingrid commented that there were two kinds of women on the coast: those in control and those who were submissive. Amanda Hanson was an example of the first kind, and Ingrid believed that Helen Jones epitomized the second. The distinction could be crucial. "The men ran the boats," Ingrid said. "If there was a disagreement, the man would take off, and it was common for the woman not to know when or if he would return. Some desperate lives were lived on the coast." She said Jones made his teenage daughters row all the way to Refuge Cove by themselves for supplies.

Arthur Jones may have been autocratic, and his daughters might have rowed to Refuge Cove, but Ingrid's analysis of the situation lacked some of the facts. And as I looked into the family's history, it turned out that "cowed" Helen was mightier with the pen than with the axe. Her letters to the government are my source of information.

Like many others, the Jones family began their new life in a tent. Before long, Arthur got a job at the Merrill and Ring Lumber Company, whose logging operation up Theodosia Inlet was in full production. Given Ingrid Cowie's characterization of Arthur, it is perhaps not surprising that on May 24, 1928, he was fired from his job because he "struck the foreman for lying about him, and was taken to Powell River by the police boat *Watla* in charge of Constable Byatt, on a charge of assault."[155] According to a letter Helen wrote to the minister of justice in Ottawa:

He arrived in Powell River dock at half past eight, and was tried and convicted and given two months in Oakalla Prison or a $20 and cost fine. Mr. Jones asked Constable Sutton to have a friend brought from one block away, who would pay the fine, as he had only fifteen dollars in his pocket. Constable Sutton said he hadn't time. He was then hustled down to the dock and was taken aboard a boat in company with a Constable Sims of Vancouver police. Before leaving he gave Constable Byatt the $15 out of his pocket and asked him to get in touch with his friend first thing in the morning

Lancelot Inlet, idyllic on a sunny day, was the scene of terrible hardship in 1928 when Arthur Jones went missing for several weeks and his wife and ten children had no idea what had happened to him. They were city folk lacking the skills settlers needed to survive.

and wire the amount to Oakalla so that he could secure his release, but when he came out of jail two months later the $15 was handed to him. Constable Byatt never went near the friend, but just handed the money back to Constable Sims before he left Powell River with Mr. Jones. Constable Byatt also promised to notify me next day but I didn't find out what had happened for three weeks and a half when I rowed my eldest girl four miles and had her take the road to Powell River to find out what was the matter. The next day Constable Byatt called in here with all kinds of lies and said he would get what supplies I needed. I asked him how much I would order, and he said, enough for a week, as he would be in in a week again. I ordered about $12 worth of groceries, and that is the last I saw of him until Mr. Jones was home four weeks later, although I wrote and told him we had practically no food left.

When Arthur returned from Oakalla, he found "the garden eaten by deer, and the potato crop ruined for lack of attention. The result was that instead of having potatoes for the coming winter, [the family] had finished them all by the end of August." Arthur laid a justifiable complaint against the Powell River police, but this only escalated the situation. Mr. North, the Powell River man investigating the complaint, showed Arthur's letter to the police, who threw Arthur back in jail. Two police constables and a man who said he "looked after the welfare of the children" visited Helen, and then the constables returned and took two of the children to Powell River hospital "for treatment as they were thin and rundown." The next day, the police were back to take Helen and her eldest daughter, aged fourteen, to Powell River to attend her husband's trial for child neglect. After what Helen described, in a letter to the provincial attorney general, as an "infamous" trial run by the Powell River police, which never would have gone forward if they had had money for a lawyer, Arthur Jones was sentenced to a year in jail or an impossible $500 fine. The whole family was starving because they were inexperienced city folk who, in Arthur's absence, were unable to build fences, grow vegetables or cut wood.

With her husband in jail, Helen wrote a heart-rending letter to the BC Attorney General begging for justice and help.

If Mr. Jones is kept there [in Oakalla Prison] for a year, what am I going to do? Is it making the situation any better, ruining the outlook of the children by making a criminal of their father. If Mr. Jones has erred at all, it was in being too anxious to get a home made here for the children so that some day they might be independent. Do you think it has been any pleasure to Mr. Jones or myself to sacrifice every kind of social intercourse, who have been always used to it, to come to a place like this and try to start a ranch out of stumps and rocks? Mr. Jones worked from daylight till dark every day he was home, and what has he got for it. Another year coming when there will be no garden, no chickens, no anything on the place. Even if I decided to plant a garden, it would be wasted effort as the fencing isn't finished, and the deer would simply eat it all up. After the trial at Powell River I asked Mr. North why they couldn't give him a job and let Mr. Jones work for his family, and he said it couldn't be done. I then asked what was going to happen to us, and he assured me the government would look after us. If they don't do it any better than they did it last time, we will sure get fat on it.

I am using the last stamp I have to send this letter, and have no money to buy more. The children's lessons can't be returned to the Dept. of Education because of that. We have always tried to be independent of outside help, but now they tell us that we should have applied to the government for help if we didn't have enough. It's the first time I have heard of the generosity of the government.

There is no record of what happened in the next few years except that one more child was born, bringing the total to eleven. The tragedy climaxed in 1939 when everything became too much for Arthur.

John D'Angio, who was working at Higgins Camp across from Isabel Bay, noticed smoke rising from the Jones homestead. Later, when Roy Allen, who ran the police boat, called in at the camp, D'Angio learned what had happened. Arthur Jones had shot himself and set his house on fire.[156] Allen, who had Arthur's remains in a coffin, related the sad news.

The Jones family appears to have stayed in the neighbourhood. Eleanor Lusk Anderson mentioned that Jones children attended her Tenedos Bay school in 1930, two years after the events related above, but didn't remember any details of them. As there was no trail between Isabel Bay and Tenedos Bay, the Jones children may have boarded with the Palmers, as others did. Perhaps Eleanor did not remember them because they didn't stay long. There is also a reference to Jones children attending the Okeover School (see Chapter 15).

Four of the daughters married in Powell River: Violet in 1935, Norma in 1941, and Madge and Adina in 1942. Perhaps Madge Island in Isabel Bay is named after Madge, who was the eldest. Helen died in Vancouver in 1952.

Isabel Bay, where the Joneses lived, has in recent years attracted boaters who are fascinated by the biffy built conveniently over a creek—a kind of ultimate water-carriage system. Derek Poole, a retired BC Parks

Dusty tells Vicki Swan (in the kayak) that he is going to have to move. Floathouses, once common in Desolation Sound, are no longer permitted in Lancelot Inlet.

officer, told me that Parks workers have removed it at least twice—and it keeps coming back![157]

Lancelot Inlet is also now the home of several oyster farms. Dusty, a colourful character who was the caretaker for the farm on the south side of the inlet, lived in a tiny floathouse powered by solar panels and adorned with window boxes of red geraniums. In 2006 he was given his eviction notice. Either he went, the government told him, or they would close down the oyster farm.[158] Sewage is the big issue. The slightest hint of contamination is enough for buyers to refuse a whole shipment of product from an oyster farm. Cruising boats must have holding tanks and are not allowed to discharge them within a certain distance of the park.

It used to be that everyone in Desolation Sound lived in floathouses, either on the water or hauled up onto the beach. Dusty's eviction signals the end of an era, as these residences slowly disappear.

15

OKEOVER INLET
Murder and Fire

O keover was one of the first areas in Desolation Sound to be logged in the late 1890s and the first decade of the twentieth century. The Vaughn brothers on the eastern shore were probably involved in the tail end of this logging. "Young Mr. Merrill's" crew of thirty men clear-cut the whole western shore, so settlers didn't have to cut down big trees in order to cultivate the land. This certainly attracted the D'Angio brothers to the area, and probably the Roos family too. They still had to contend with two-metre (six-foot) stumps, but they accepted that. The Chambers family came soon after, as did others like John Korpi and Alec Johnson, who feature in some of the stories but who left little or no information behind. Another wave of settlers arrived in the 1920s, including the Crowthers of Penrose Bay.

John Oscar Roos (1884–1962) came to Okeover in 1902 and settled on forty-five hectares (110 acres) above where the government wharf is now located.[159] He formally pre-empted it in 1912 and received his Crown grant in 1927.

Oscar was born in a small town near Stockholm, Sweden, in the late nineteenth century. "If I'd known what Canada was like, I'd have stayed in Sweden, bad though it was," Oscar later told his grandson, Sheldon Ahola. "When we got off the ship, they stuffed us in box cars and we couldn't get out till Winnipeg." He worked hewing railway ties. For the

first couple of years he hated Canada and would have gone home but
had no money. "The camps were
horrendous," he told his grandson.
"The beds were just two logs and a
bug-infested blanket."

When he reached "Egg Mountain," as his friend Charles called
Edmonton, things improved a bit.
He was making five dollars a day,
which was enough to buy a suit of
work clothes complete with boots,
pants, Stanfields and suspenders
(nowadays, it would take a week
to earn enough to buy a set of
work clothes). Beer was five cents
a glass.

Oscar liked Vancouver even
more. It was there he met the
Thulin brothers, who urged him

*Swedish Oscar Roos married Finnish
Manni Kangas (Nunny) in Vancouver in
1911. They met at Lund where she was
a chambermaid. For half a century they
homesteaded where the Laughing Oyster
Restaurant is now.* COURTESY SHELDON
AHOLA

to come to Lund. Oscar and Charles went prospecting up Phillips Arm
and were amazed to find an uninhabited log cabin about a week's journey into the bush. They wondered who had built it so far away from the
coast. (It may have been one of the winter trapping cabins built by the
reclusive James Parker of Theodosia Inlet.) Returning to Lund, Oscar
hiked the trail to Okeover, where Merrill and Ring had logged the whole
west side of the inlet. "You could stand on the ridge and see everywhere,"
he said.

For a while he worked as a bartender at the Lund Hotel, and it was
there he met Manni Kangas (1888–1982), "Nunny," who was a chambermaid. They went to Vancouver to get married on June 28, 1911.
They and all five of their children—Engla, Helga, Oscar Jr., Arnie and
Lillian—are now dead.

In 1912, Oscar pre-empted forty-five hectares (110 acres) where the

Laughing Oyster Restaurant is now. He chose that location because it had a natural spring so he didn't have to dig a well. (Some writers have claimed Oscar had property in Lancelot Inlet, but there is no record that he did.[160]) Although he was a fisherman and required access to the water, his waterfront consisted of one small corner of his square of land. He made good use of the limited access. Taxes were one dollar a year.

Oscar's tiny beach, where the government dock is now, was a shallow cove. Today's breakwater was not there, and the wharf wasn't built till the early 1960s. To provide shelter for his ten-metre (thirty-four-foot) gillnetter, *Me*, he set two logs on the bank, leading up into his net shed. There was enough room between them for the keel of the *Me* to slide in. He drew the boat up between the logs as close to land as possible, then built a dock beside the logs so he could work on it. Behind the *Me* he towed a 2.5-metre (eight-foot) skiff called the *Me Me Two*.

In the days before he got a gas boat, he had a big rowboat. When he needed a forty-five-kilogram (hundred-pound) sack of flour, he rowed round Sarah Point to Lund to buy it and rowed all the way back. Only once did he upset in big waves off the point. He also used the rowboat to

The completed Roos homestead in Okeover. Oscar built the pantry first, then added the kitchen, a big living room, a study and four bedrooms upstairs. After Oscar's death, it was rented out and burned to the ground. Twenty feet away, the cherry tree, now behind the Laughing Oyster Restaurant, was scorched in the fire but still produces fruit. COURTESY SHELDON AHOLA

get his cow to pasture on the rich grass at the head of Theodosia Inlet. He built a raft for the cow to stand on and towed it across Okeover Inlet, up Lancelot Inlet and then up Theodosia. It took him two days each way. He'd start out with the tide and row till it changed. Then he'd anchor till it flooded again. He'd leave the cow up there while he went fishing for two months and collect it when he returned. (In those days, the Theodosia River was a good salmon stream with lots of coho over 4.5 kilograms/ten pounds. Until the 1980s, cod fishing was good in the inlet too.)

Up the hill, Oscar started the house by building the pantry. He then added the kitchen, followed by a big living room. Behind the living room was a study where he wrote letters and kept a few books. Doors on either side of the living room and study were kept open in summer to let a breeze through. They also let the swallows fly in and out. Although Oscar said they never stopped inside, Nunny told of an occasion when she was resting and a bird alighted right beside her. Next day they all flew south. She said it had come to bid her goodbye.

Upstairs there were four bedrooms. The one in front had a balcony. One bedroom was never used. The ground-floor area of the house was around a hundred square metres (a thousand square feet.)

A short distance down the hill from the house, Oscar built a root cellar that sloped down into the ground. The logs were carefully interlocked with vee-notches. Above the dirt floor, he built shelves for canned goods. The chickens were able to get in at the top to lay eggs.

"We made money any way we could," Oscar told Sheldon. In the 1930s and 1940s after the road went in, Oscar bought an old Chrysler Royal car that he used to run a taxi service for the Merrill and Ring logging camp.

"They killed about one man a week," he said. "Most of the workers were untrained greenhorns, mainly Chinese. They'd be given an axe and told to work. No training, no safety. When the men died, they'd put the body beside the track till the end of the day. Then they brought it out. Many more were injured." Oscar took the men either to the funeral home or the hospital. He also took them to the house of ill repute or the bootlegger in Wildwood.

That was when he started making his own wine out of raisins. The process took a while, and he needed to stay awake to tend the fire. To make sure he did, he sat on a round log. If he fell asleep, it rolled and woke him. Soon word got round that it was pretty potent stuff. One day the sheriff showed up. Nunny pretended Oscar was away, so he left. Then she crawled up the hill to the spring, where Oscar was making a batch, to warn him.

The taxi business came to an end one fall when Oscar came home from two months' fishing to find that Brook Hodson, who lived up on the highway, had scooped the business. A telephone line ran from the dock up to Brook's house, so customers just had to crank it and he'd come and get them. Oscar was mad for a while, but he eventually recognized that people needed service all year round.

Lots of people lived on the shores of the inlet. They'd tow in a floathouse, pull it up on the bank and stay awhile. Gordon Bloom and his wife and son lived in one beside a sawmill that Billy Palmer built in the vicinity of what is now Tux'wnech Okeover Arm Provincial Park. Alders mark the site.

When the Roos children grew up, they all left home. Both older girls went to Vancouver and got married. Arnie went into insurance in Vancouver, and Oscar Jr. became a logger in Powell River. Lillian married Ed Ahola, a Finn who was born in Sointula and spent part of his childhood in Ocean Falls. Later his father moved down to Powell River, where he bought Cranberry Hardware. Oscar was about forty-five when Ed first met him, and he was very strong. "He used to do handspring somersaults from the net shed all the way up the hill to the house." Lillian and Ed eventually divorced, and Lillian went to California, leaving her son, Sheldon, behind. When Oscar was away fishing for the summer, Sheldon lived with Nunny.

The family claimed they never knew Nunny's maiden name or much about her except that she came from Finland. Her marriage registration papers give her name as Manni Kangas, and her wedding picture shows an exceptionally beautiful bride standing proudly beside her slim, handsome husband. Even when she was an old woman, her face retained the beautiful lines of her youth. On her death certificate she is identified as Nanni Gustava Roos, aged ninety-four years.

Her English was always heavily accented and never fluent.[161] Oscar used to say she spoke "Finglish." One day, when he was working in the net shed below the house, he heard loud voices and rushed up the hill to defend his wife from her attacker. It turned out she was just having a friendly conversation in Finnish with their neighbour, Mrs. Korpi.

Another time, when Nunny had packed a lunch for Oscar before he left for his two months of fishing up Rivers Inlet, she told him she had put in a "pinanna." As usual, Oscar teased her about her pronunciation. "That's a pinanna, you urkly-looking Swede," she said, holding up the curved yellow fruit. She never could say "banana."

The family thought Nunny must have come from a "dirt poor" family as she never threw anything out. She insisted on using a pot with an

Oscar and Nunny Roos on the right with their daughter, Lillian, her two boys: Sheldon and Tommy with their friend Tommy Knorr. When Lillian and her husband, Ed, split up, Ed and Sheldon helped Oscar and Nunny modernize the house with a propane fridge, an oil stove complete with hot water heater and even an indoor bathroom. COURTESY SHELDON AHOLA

uneven bottom until one day Oscar grabbed it off the stove, emptied it out and flattened it. After that she called him a "goddamned pot masher." She would scoop up anything left on the table, including money, and hide it away. By the time they were each getting the princely sum of sixty dollars a month in old-age pension, Oscar discovered a thick roll of one- and two-dollar bills in a tobacco tin by their bedside. It totalled two hundred dollars.

"Where did you get that money?" he asked her.

"I saved it," she said.

"Well, put it in your purse," he said. She kept her purse in one of the kitchen drawers.

After that the teasing took a new twist. "Come on, Ed," Oscar would say to his son-in-law. "Let's go to Lund for some drinks. I got money," and he'd move toward the kitchen drawer.

"Don't take it," Nunny would scream. If she realized he was just teasing, she never let on.

Nunny couldn't read English, though she could sign her name. One day a peddler came round and helped Nunny make out a cheque to subscribe to a whole lot of magazines. Oscar was livid. The next time Ed and Sheldon arrived for the weekend, they were greeted by a big sign with every word spelled wrong: "No soliciters or paddlers aloved insid gait!"

Oscar had a small generator off which he ran twelve-volt lights that dimmed as the evening wore on. The radio, which they listened to for about thirty minutes a week, was battery operated. At Christmas, the tree was lit with candles that they burned for only half an hour at a time because of the fire hazard. This was what they had done in Europe, so it was natural to them.

Although down quilts kept the beds warm at night, the house, which was not well insulated, cooled down fast and was cold in the morning. Deer meat, chicken, fish and other foods were kept cool in either the root cellar or a pantry that vented to the outdoors.

When Oscar and Nunny got old, Ed Ahola came up from Cranberry every weekend and undertook several major renovations of the house. He installed a propane fridge and an oil stove complete with a hot-water heater, and he encouraged Oscar, who was a good carpenter, to build another room on the back of the house so that they could replace the outhouse with an indoor flush toilet and a bath. It was ready in two days. Oscar loved the oil stove and Nunny exclaimed over the bathroom.

One Wednesday after the oil delivery, as Oscar rolled the oil barrel up the ramp, he slipped, fell and broke his collarbone. Despite the pain, he soldiered on, cooking the breakfast porridge and making sure that Nunny had her morning coffee in bed. On Saturday, when Ed and Sheldon arrived for the weekend, they found him grey-faced and huddled under a quilt, looking very sick. The collarbone was sticking up out of his back. Ed rushed him to hospital, where a doctor taped the bones.

Oscar's twin brother, Eric, settled in Longview on the Oregon–California border. They hadn't seen each other for forty years, but one time Ed drove Oscar down for a visit. In less than an hour, Oscar had picked a quarrel with his twin and refused to sleep in the house. "He hasn't changed," Eric said.

After Oscar died in 1962, Lillian took Nunny to live with her in California and the house was rented out to tenants. During this time, a fire levelled the place. Later the root cellar burned too. All that is left is the cherry tree behind the Laughing Oyster Restaurant. It was within six metres (twenty feet) of the house, so it got scorched in the fire, but recovered. Cherries still ripen on it.

About eight years after Oscar Roos arrived in Okeover, John (Giovanni) D'Angio (1887–1962) moved into the area. One day in 1910, after a breakfast of seagull eggs from Mitlenatch Island, Chief Tom Timothy of the Sliammon guided John and his brother, Raffaele (1894–1921), over the trail to the Native village at Freke Anchorage at the head of Okeover Inlet. The D'Angios had considered buying land for thirty cents an acre around the Sliammon Lakes, but they were put off because there were huge trees they would have to fell before planting any crops. About three years earlier, fire had cleared the land on the west side of Okeover Inlet, which made it more favourable to farming.

John pre-empted Lot 3919, which consisted of twenty-six hectares (sixty-five acres) and two hundred metres (seven hundred feet) of waterfront. His brother pre-empted Lot 3913, sixteen hectares (forty acres) on the slope above him. The pair cleared about eight hectares (twenty acres), then ditched and planted it. To get a stump out, they'd dig a hole in front of a fifty-centimetre (twenty-inch) tree, put a big block beside it and wait for a strong southeast wind to blow the tree over, popping the stump out.[162]

A lot of the trees were cedar, which they cut into about three hundred cords of shingle bolts and sold to their neighbour, A.A. Plummer. Plummer had a long pier sticking out into the water over the mud at the head of the inlet. He also had a flume going back five kilometres (three miles) to Southview Road, where he operated a logging camp employing Japanese workers.[163] The creek running into the head of the inlet still bears his name.

After John D'Angio married in 1918, he went to work for the Powell River mill and lived in town. Raffaele, or Ralph as he became known, continued to live on the Okeover property until December 15, 1921.[164]

On December 14, Ralph and his friend Alec Johnson paddled a canoe across the inlet and went hunting up the Bunster Hills. In the evening, when Alec didn't show up at their meeting place, Ralph climbed the mountain again to look for him. Darkness fell so he spent the night up there. In the morning he returned to the canoe, paddled back across the inlet and hiked up to where Alec Johnson and Frank Gustafson shared a cabin. When he opened the door, he found Alec safe at home in bed.

"God!" Ralph said. "I've been looking for you all night. I thought you were dead." Alec told Frank to make some coffee for Ralph.

"Are you hurt?" Ralph asked Alec and then repeated, "I was looking for you all last night. You shouldn't work so hard."

"I don't think I work hard enough," replied Alec. "I ought to work some more."

Frank got up to put some wood on the fire. When he turned around he saw Alec reach for something. Then a shot rang out. Ralph put his hands to his head. Nothing was said. It was rather dark and Frank couldn't see clearly, but he did see Alec point at him and fire a second shot. (Years later, the bullet holes were still in the door.)

"I thought he hit me," Frank said a few days later at the inquest in Powell River. "I fell down like I was stunned. I tried to get out of the door but it was hard to open. It took me about three-quarters of a minute to get out of the house. Finally I got out and thought I heard another shot fired, but I'm not sure as I was so much excited I ran for about ten minutes in my bare feet and then stopped to rest. Then I heard a rifle shot and started to run again."

Frank didn't stop until he reached two neighbours, Joe Devito and John Herman Korpi.

"When I finally reached Joe Devito's house," he testified, "I told him that Alec was crazy and he had better look out as he could come over there."

"Well, I'm not moving," said Korpi. "I'm staying right here." He put his gun at the ready, just in case. Around midnight, Alec came over and shot five times at Joe Devito's house.

Joe, also testifying at the inquest, said: "After I heard one rifle shot I went into the house. I grab my wife and two children, still more shots were coming striking the shakes of the roof. I put my wife and children in the cellar. I called my cousin Devito, who lived next door, to help me and he came. I told my wife and we beat it for Lund, leaving Frank in my house."

Korpi heard the shots and walked the half mile down to Joe's house. As he reached it, he heard a last shot but no more.

The Devito cousins went to Brook Hodson's house, which had a telegraph, and summoned the local representative of the Provincial Police, Constable W.H. Hadley, who deputized a couple of helpers to accompany him by boat to Lund. The three of them hiked about six kilometres (four miles) over the trail to Alec Johnson's house. There was no smoke coming out of the chimney, so Hadley said, "You just stay ready with your guns. I'm gonna make a run for the house." With his pistol drawn, he did just that, only to find Alec lying dead on the steps. He'd put his gun under his chin and blown his head off.

At the inquest, Frank testified: "I never thought there was anything wrong with Alec, but sometimes he talk queer like there was someone after him, he said 'They wont get me, but I will get them before.' Alec and Ralph were good friends and I am sure he did not mean him when he talked like that. He was always good and kind to me, but two weeks ago I was afraid of what sort of man he was because of something he said about one of his neighbours and I was scared for awhile. Alec had two rifles and a revolver. He was about forty years old and spoke of a younger brother in the United States. He was not a drinking man. He has been living 7 or 8 years in Lund. He made no attempt to stop me from leaving the house."

Dr. Charles Marlatt's autopsy report, which was presented at the inquest, included a description of Ralph's clothing, typical of what was worn by all the men of that time: "Heavy logger boots with hob nails, gray woollen socks, 2 piece suit of woollen underwear, khaki overalls, brown drill shirt, and a red checked woollen overshirt."

After his brother's death, John D'Angio returned to Okeover and commuted to his job at the mill. He got up at 4 a.m. and ran the twenty-four kilometres (fifteen miles) over the trail to the mill, worked all day and ran back in the evening. He'd get a day off after they'd worked a double shift. Once his wife started having children, he quit the mill and got a job breaking rock for the road the government was pushing through. He also cut shingle bolts. The family kept goats and chickens, and grew oats for the animals.

Around August, the family would try to shoot one of the bears, which were getting fat on berries. With no refrigeration, they had to work fast. The meat went into quart jars that they canned outside in an old copper boiler. They cooked fourteen quarts at a time for four hours, batch after batch. Venison was prepared the same way.

To hunt deer, they paddled along the shoreline with an Airedale dog. When the dog smelled a deer, he'd whimper and they'd put him ashore. He herded the animal into the water, where the D'Angios clubbed it and towed the carcass home.

John D'Angio ran a trapline from Sarah Point all the way along the shore to the head of Okeover and Lancelot inlets. His son inherited it and passed it on to his son-in-law.

One January when John D'Angio Jr. was thirteen, they got a young cougar, which they skinned and ate. "It tastes like veal, a very, very nice mild meat," John Jr. said.[165]

The D'Angios had to relinquish Ralph's Lot 3913 because they couldn't pay the taxes on it. John Sr. got a Crown grant for Lot 3919, which he sold in 1970. His son Raffaelle, born in 1922, pre-empted and obtained the Crown grant for Lot 3914, which he sold to a California buyer in 1968. In the early twenty-first century, Frank D'Angio was working for the City of Powell River, and other members of his family still held some land in the area.

Among the D'Angios' neighbours were John and Devina Chambers. They were one of many couples from the Shetland Islands who immigrated to Canada, settling first in Vancouver in 1910. John (1883–1929) was quartermaster on the tug *St. Clair*, one of the first steam tugs to be converted to oil.[166] They must have had a hankering to own their own land, because John pre-empted land near the head of Okeover and got his Crown grant in 1913. While improving the land and building a cabin, he continued to work on *St. Clair*. Devina (1871–1931) remained in their house on Davie Street in Vancouver.

When the family finally moved to Okeover in 1916, they had three children—John, Mary and James—and Devina was pregnant with their fourth child, Stan. They walked over the trail from Lund, pushing a wheelbarrow containing all their worldly possessions.

John, Devina, Mary, John Jr. and Jimmy Chambers sat for this family portrait in 1914, two years before moving to Okeover. COURTESY DORIS CUMMINGS

On arrival they found a squatter living in the shack that was to become their home. He didn't want to move but left after a fight with John. He had removed the cabin windows, perhaps with a view to selling them later. Happily, the family found them in the bush close by and reinstalled them.[167]

After settling the family, John returned to the *St. Clair*. On its last run before Christmas 1919, a vicious southeaster blew up off the Sandheads light at the mouth of the Fraser River. A scow broke loose, and the captain's brother was mortally injured trying to get aboard it. Chambers helped him write a last letter to his wife before he died off Point Grey.

A year or two later, again just before Christmas, John loaded supplies into a new boat he had bought and set off from Vancouver for Okeover. Captain Johnson of the *St. Clair* lent him a 4.5-metre (fourteen-foot) clinker-built lifeboat to tow behind him for safety. Again a southeaster blew up, this time off the Trail Islands near Sechelt, an area with a fetch the length of the Strait of Georgia. The lifeboat got loose. John was able to retrieve it, but it got loose a second time and he lost it. Down below, an oil lantern tipped over, starting a fire in his bedding. As he threw the mess overboard, the crew on the Union Steamship *Cheakamus*, which had come up behind him, was able to see his plight and escorted him to Merry Island. He tied up at Secret Cove to recuperate. Meanwhile, the family was snowed in at Okeover with no means of knowing what was happening. Three days later, John reached home just before the inlet froze.

The family settled in, and the kids enrolled at the second Okeover school. The first school had opened in 1903 but didn't last long. The Thulin brothers of Lund financed the second one. Permission was granted to place the schoolhouse on "any part except the good part" of Lot 3912.[168] Ed Berglund of Thors Cove built it for $100.

This school ran from 1916 to 1923 and then reopened in the 1930s. (In the intervening years the children were home-schooled.) There were usually around fourteen school-aged children. The D'Angios had seven, the Larsons four or five, the Chamberses three and the Joneses of

Lancelot Inlet eleven.[169] The schoolteacher boarded with the Chambers family.

John D'Angio remembered one winter that was so cold the ink in the inkwells froze. They had to close the school for a time. The ice was so thick that people could drive a horse and sleigh across from the Vaughns' home on the other side of the inlet. Water at the head of the inlet freezes easily because the fresh water from Plummer Creek, which freezes faster than salt water, spreads out on the surface of the ocean water. (In 1968, the inlet froze four inches thick out past the wharf. When it does that now, it can tear the oyster rafts and the dock.)

Devina Chambers poses with a friend.
COURTESY DORIS CUMMINGS

Devina Chambers spun and carded the wool from the sheep they raised and knitted it into socks and sweaters. One needle was held fast by a leather holder attached to her waist, leaving her hand free to weave in the coloured threads that created the traditional Shetland patterns ornamenting the waists and wrists of the dull grey garments. However, one fateful night a cougar killed and ate the sheep. Although wolves howled at night, the family never lost any animals to them. Devina was handy with a gun, so she scared them off.

On the Vaughns' side of the inlet, summer lightning started a big fire in 1923. The whole peninsula between Okeover, Lancelot and Theodosia inlets glowed red. Ash and big cinders fell round the Chambers home. Terrified, Devina made a superhuman effort. She dug trenches a metre deep and buried furniture, clothes, bedding and loaves of newly baked bread to keep everything safe. Fortunately, the fire didn't reach the house.

Five years later they were not so lucky. John lit the wood stove and then went to fix his nets in the shed sixty metres (two hundred feet) away. Two of his sons were gillnetting at the head of the inlet, fifteen minutes from the house. Suddenly a big cloud of smoke attracted their attention. By the time they got home, they could see flames. Nothing was left, and the family went to live in the Lund Hotel.

The fire was the first of four tragedies. Fishing alone off Sliammon in 1929, John got his boot button caught in his gillnet, which pulled him off his boat and drowned him. Devina moved the family, which was still living in the hotel, to a house in Wildwood. Two years later she died of pneumonia. On her deathbed, her last words to fifteen-year-old Stan were "Stanley, you won't be a drinking man." He promised he wouldn't, but he lived with guilt his entire life because he was unable to keep the promise. In 1933, Stan's sister Mary contracted puerperal fever and died, leaving a three-week-old baby. After the war, the brothers lost the Okeover land as they didn't have $149 to pay the taxes.

In 1927, a year before the Chamberses' house burned down, the Crowther family pre-empted Lot 4208, fifty-five hectares (135 acres) at the head of Penrose Bay on the isthmus connecting Coode Peninsula to the mainland. After blazing a trail through the woods, the family split dead snags for logs to build the house. They chose these because they were already dry and wouldn't warp.

Ingrid Cowie believed that Bill Crowther (1884–1961) was a remittance man, someone whose family paid him to stay away.[170] She described him as well educated and well read. He had been a scoutmaster in England and continued to be one in Powell River.[171]

When Crowther and his wife, Doris (1887–1967), arrived in Okeover, their daughter Nancy was four years old. "Mom and Dad had saved a little bit of money, and we earned our living digging clams," Nancy told Murray Kennedy in 1987.[172] "We couldn't afford shoes, so we wrapped cloth around our feet. We could use it to walk on barnacles. We used a spade. We didn't know about rakes."

Okeover in the 1930s was bleak. Three children ended up in the Powell River hospital suffering from starvation. "I couldn't stand up for starving," said Nancy. "It just so happened that a goat freshened that morning, and that extra milk put me back on my feet. Nobody got much work. We were mighty glad when a logging camp moved into the area, because they would buy bread and eggs." It was 1942 before they scraped together enough cash to buy their Crown grant.

Nancy took the BC elementary correspondence course and often did her lessons on the beach, where watching ants and crows took precedence over schoolwork. One September she joined the Okeover school for two weeks when the inspector came so that it looked as if there were enough students to justify keeping it open. She didn't stay because it was "too far, too wet and too cold to go every day."

Irene Apps met Nancy in the mid-1930s when the Anglican minister introduced them at a meeting of the Young People's Association at the church. "I remember her as a quiet girl," Irene said. "I think she had come to town to look for a job, and the bakery at the company store hired her. Later she went to work at the mill. She invited me home once, and I remember walking about three miles down a trail to her house, which was on the water."[173] Nancy commuted by bicycle five days a week to work in the company store in Powell River. She must have left for work at 5 or 6 a.m., and she had thick, strong legs from pedalling over the dirt roads.

After a disastrous marriage, Nancy resumed her maiden name and returned to her parents' home. Soon she became famous throughout the region as "the Cougar Queen of Okeover Arm," though she disapproved of this title.[174] "Living in the bush like I do, a gun is as much a part of my household tools as a vacuum cleaner is in the city," she said. She killed her first cougar at the age of thirteen with a .22-calibre rifle, which she soon replaced with a .303-calibre carbine. "About the only place to shoot a cougar for a sure kill is right in the centre of the neck. It snaps the spine and kills instantly."

When her father died in 1961, she and her mother continued to live at the homestead. They preserved fruit from the orchard, butchered their own chickens, made cheese from goats' milk, kept bees and gathered clams and oysters from the beach. They were especially protective of the goats. "At Galley Bay, Axel Hanson lost thirty goats to cougars in one night," she said, "and Mrs. Salo up at Theodosia lost six calves." From her study of the animals, Crowther found that "every twenty-eight days a cougar will retrace a pattern."

Nancy was good friends with Sheldon Ahola's mother, Lillian, and Sheldon remembered the Crowther family.[175] He told of one occasion when Bill Crowther rowed to the dock to pick up their groceries from the Lund delivery. He was in a five- or six-metre (eighteen- to nineteen-foot) dugout canoe. "He wore an old coat and stank like a goat." Another time Sheldon watched Nancy dive off the old chain floats and swim underwater for a hundred metres (three hundred feet).

In the last months of her life, Nancy became hostile to friends, telling them to stay away, and then wondered why they didn't ask if she needed anything. She'd often sleep in her yellow truck with her dogs. Sheldon thought she was confused, but Nancy died of a brain tumour in 1990. All three Crowthers are buried in the Cranberry cemetery in Powell River.

All of these stories come from the western shore of Okeover Inlet. There is also a shorter eastern shore with its own stories.

In 1920, Dewey and Sheridan Vaughn, brothers and loggers, received a Crown grant for Lot 3767 on the east shore of Okeover Inlet, across from the D'Angios' property. They built a three-hundred-metre (nine-hundred-foot) chute to bring logs down from the Bunster Hills to the water. Above the chute, a donkey engine with about a mile of line in it pulled logs down a skid road.[176] The Vaughns had logging interests elsewhere and eventually moved on. After they left, Edmund Larson drew his floathouse up onto the beach and lived there so long that people stopped calling the place "Vaughns'" and began referring to it as "Larson's Landing" instead.

Up above Larson's Landing, in the Bunster Hills where Alec Johnson and Ralph D'Angio went hunting, there was action of a different kind. Mining—or a form of it—was a common occupation everywhere on the coast. In the early decades of the twentieth century, there were no welfare payments for indigent people. To make some kind of living, many men took out "free miner's" certificates. When they staked a claim, the government would advance them a small sum of money that they had to justify by working on their claim. This work could be anything from digging a hole to digging a ditch. Many settlers in the Okeover area did this, with few expectations of finding anything. James Norris Thompson, who was listed on the 1928 Voters' List as a "mining prospector," may have been one of them.

John D'Angio Jr. was badly bitten by the prospecting bug.[177] He said, "Mining is a lot like logging. The first day you go out to try your luck and each day after that you try to get your money back." Though he once thought he had found strontium and dreamed of marketing it to NASA, there wasn't enough of it. "It's an area of metamorphic contacts and no real mineral in place. The pockets of minerals all pinch out," he said.

Mary and Paddy Boylan also prospected in the Okeover area. They took it up as a hobby after the Second World War, when they were living in Chilliwack (Paddy was an officer at Camp Chilliwack). They wanted to explore the mountains, and a friend who was a prospector got them reading books on minerals and mining. Soon they had their free miner's certificates, and by the time they moved to Powell River in 1947, prospecting had become their favourite weekend activity.

They staked a lot of claims, including some on the Bunster Hills above Okeover Inlet. Sometimes they hiked in, but they also chartered floatplanes from Powell Lake. Loaded with provisions and camping gear, they would fly up to a lake in the mountains to check out the rocks for a few days. After Paddy died in 1971, Mary continued to prospect and staked several claims in partnership with Bob Mickle. "He's younger but he's been prospecting since he was five years old."

Mary Boylan was about to celebrate her ninetieth birthday when I interviewed her in June 1997.[178] She said she still enjoyed driving her Ford Bronco up into the Bunster Hills above Okeover to inspect her mining claims. "I've got a crew coming in this week to do some drilling," she said, "and I like to keep an eye on them."

Like most prospectors, Mary was cagey about her finds, though she admitted to finding traces of copper and lots of small amethyst crystals. Most of the rocks here are granite with flecks of pyrite, copper, silver and tiny bits of gold. Although she never found a gold mine, prospecting was a lifelong fascination and a reason to explore the outdoors. "As the years go by, you can't continue as you were, but it was great fun when you did it. That's the main thing," she said.

Back at Larson's Landing in the 1950s and early 1960s, Ed Hanson and his Romanian wife, O'Tillia (Tilly) Maria Reder, pulled some floathouses up on the beach and started living there. Ed, who had grown up in Galley Bay (see Chapter 11) and was a successful commercial fisherman, decided to initiate oyster farming in Okeover. His son Daniel, who was eight years old in 1952, remembered unpacking a box of oysters that his father had ordered from Japan and spreading them out on the beach.[179] He thought another box from the same order was spread in Baynes Sound. Twice a week, Tilly drove the harvested oysters to market in Seattle. They also shipped product by train to Saskatchewan and Manitoba. It was a gruelling business that likely contributed to the breakup of the marriage.

Living conditions were not great. Their home was two long, narrow granaries stacked one on top of the other. Ed and Tilly's daughter Pat remembered that the walls were painted with pictures of farm fields and fences.[180] Their neighbour, an old-time handlogger/fisherman named Jack Anderson, tended his orchard and grape arbour.

After Ed's grandparents sold their Galley Bay property, they lived in a floathouse drawn up on the beach beside Ed's place. Their granddaughter Pat, who was twelve when they died, remembered them. "As Amanda grew older, she became very stout and didn't move around much," Pat told me. "Axel's voice got more and more guttural when they were older, and Amanda's bulk was such that she occupied two chairs." In 1965, the old folks moved to a house at the end of the Lund boardwalk. Ed moved his family to a two-room house on Pryor Road so that it was easier for the kids to get to school. Vira May Salo bought Amanda and Axel's floathouse and moved it to Theodosia, where she drew it up on the beach and lived in it.

Karen Gordon lived in the old homestead at Larson's Landing in the late 1990s. She was told the house was haunted. A previous occupant had seen a child there.[181] Karen never saw any spirits, but her daughter, Emma, saw a man with a knife several times. Eventually he stopped coming.

There was a 2.5-metre (eight-foot) mural of Vancouver's Point Grey in the kitchen, painted in oils and signed by Edmund Larson. Other paintings on the walls were of sailing ships and busts of women. "He signed them all," said Karen. "The earliest picture I found was dated 1912. The original house was the size of a single trailer. Every family that lived there seemed to have added a piece on, and none of it was insulated. Living was a challenge, especially getting to the government dock before the icebreaker came in. Often there'd be a couple of centimetres of ice on the inlet almost all the way across."

Karen also remembered Helmut Franke, brother of Walter, the latter-day caretaker at Parker Harbour (see Chapter 13). "He lived in another house on the property. A chronic hypochondriac, the terrible scenes he had witnessed in the war-torn Germany of his youth were never far from his mind. He hated noise, especially the constant running of the oyster plant's generator. Happy to live as a recluse, he rarely went to town. In addition to his house, he had a little cabin, which he said was his fire insurance, but he died before his place also burned." Karen herself moved away some time before the house she lived in burned down in 2004.

As the old-time residents die or move away, new residents from the cities replace some of them. Okeover is the only place in Desolation Sound where the population is not only maintaining itself but even growing (see Chapter 16).

PART 3

Latecomers

16

RESIDENTS AND
OYSTER GROWERS

*I*t's not easy to calculate the present-day population of Desolation Sound. The area is divided between two subdivisions of the Canadian census, which include populations outside the Sound as well, so census results are not too helpful. There are at most 100 year-round residents, and many more people either live here only part-time or commute to oyster leases from residences in the nearby communities of Lund, Powell River and Cortes Island.

Most year-round residents want to be within easy reach of civilization, so they live around Okeover Inlet, with road access to Lund and Powell River, or on West Redonda Island. Denise Reinhardt, president of the Okeover Ratepayers' Association, a non-profit society formed in 1996 for people living within the watershed that drains into Okeover Inlet, estimates she has about sixty members, some of whom live here only part of the year. Bob Paquin, for thirty-eight years an oyster grower in the area, disagrees, estimating the year-round population of Okeover at thirty.

About twenty members of the ratepayers' association are retirees, while the rest work as oyster farmers, cater to tourists or telecommute. Some members are from the United States, but the number of Americans is not increasing, due to the strong Canadian dollar and difficulties with travel. Properties are not currently selling well; one waterfront lot has remained on the market for over a year.

In other areas, the homesteaders' big lots have been subdivided in various ways. Members of the Refuge Cove Land and Housing Cooperative—the longest-operating co-operative in the province—share Lot 4936 on West Redonda Island between them (see Chapter 6). Most of them are part-time residents. According to Norm Gibbons, the year-round population at Refuge Cove, the only settlement on West Redonda Island, is around twenty people.

In Galley Bay, shareholders own sixteen parcels of land that were the original Hanson homestead of Lot 2839. The Bloom family siblings, whose parents bought the property from the Hansons, own the majority of the shares.

Malaspina Estates Strata Corporation, on Lot 4600 at the mouth of Grace Harbour, comprises approximately forty designated building sites on the waterfront and is organized as a "strata recreational development."[182] Each fifteen-by-twenty-five-metre (fifty-by-seventy-five-foot) site has access to a further 1.5 hectares (3.5 acres) of surrounding land, where

A great blue heron looks out on the oyster farms that now plug Trevenen Bay.

lot owners can put gardens and fences but no permanent structures. They are not allowed to log, either. These are not designed to be year-round residences. They have water access only, and no services like roads or septic fields are provided.

The former Heatley property in Galley Bay (Lot 1474), the former Crowther property in Penrose Bay (Lot 4208) and a lot adjacent to Larson's Landing have also been subdivided in various ways. A recent example is the Toquenatch Creek Cooperative, a group of five like-minded families whose goal is to live together in an environmentally friendly manner. Elsewhere, most dwellings are individual houses or "weather shelters" above oyster leases.

As the baby boomers have aged, demand for recreational property has grown. Others have been drawn to the area for its quiet waterfront lots and views of diving ducks, eagles and other wildlife.

Al and Arlene Carsten fell in love with Okeover in 1988 and bought land on the former Roos property overlooking the inlet. "There was nary an oyster farm in sight," said Arlene, who can be quite feisty on that topic.[183] In San Diego, California, they had spent twenty years manufacturing casting machines and kilns for the technical ceramics industry. They wanted out of the city, and they realized their product was small enough to air-freight to customers around the world. In 1992 they moved themselves and their family to Okeover, where they rebuilt the business as a Canadian corporation. Three years later they became Canadian citizens.

Knowing that they would soon be retiring, they designed a timber-frame home with windows all down one side. For the living room, they used twelve-metre (forty-foot) lengths of thirty-by-thirty-centimetre (twelve-by-twelve-inch) heartwood that came from the former MacMillan Bloedel drying shed in Port Alberni. Maurice Shapiro put together the mortise and tenon structure, and "many wonderful local craftsmen" then finished the house.

In 1996, Al and Arlene sold the business to a US company. One of their customers didn't realize this and sent an order, which the Carsten son couldn't bear to refuse. From there, using the same site, he built a new company that competes with its US cousin.

Three years after Adam Vallance and Laurie Heide bought Powell River Sea Kayaks in 1997, they decided to move it from its previous location in Powell River.[184] They bought Nancy Crowther's funky old log house at the head of Penrose Bay and moved themselves and the business there. Although a six-kilometre (3.6-mile) drive separates them from the end of the pavement by the Okeover dock, their quiet bay, sheltered from the summer northwest winds, is an ideal location for the lessons they give beginners and for the start of their multi-day eco-tours. Theirs is the closest kayak rental to Desolation Sound, and they are also close to Lund, where they maintain a rental outlet in conjunction with the Lund Hotel.

Another year-round resident of thirteen seasons is Jürgen Köppen, who lives at the head of the inlet and builds beautiful cedar-strip sea kayaks.[185] These are works of art inlaid with marquetry designs in fine woods, mother-of-pearl and abalone. In the shop beside his house, Jürgen does specialty timber framing for decks, doors, kitchens and other "one-off" custom jobs. Together with their neighbours, he and Cindy have incorporated the Toquenatch Creek Cooperative.

The Köppens also breed Leonberger dogs, large, majestic animals with a lion's mane, webbed feet, a love of swimming and a friendly temperament. They are descended from Newfoundland, St. Bernard and Great Pyrenees dogs, among others.

When Barbara Plourde visited Okeover a few years ago, she bought one of Jürgen's kayaks and had it shipped to her Florida home.[186] She was so enamoured of his house that she bought the adjoining lot and hired him to build her dream home—and a second kayak.

Unfortunately, there has been friction between the people who come for the quiet, nature and recreation, and some of those who are trying to make a living in the Sound. Denise Reinhardt moved to the area from New York. She bought her house in July 2000 and three months later discovered via an advertising notice that a large deep-water oyster farm was about to be installed right in front of her property. "It was supposed to be eighty metres away, but it's only fifty metres," she said.[187] "The government have admitted that allowing it to locate there was an error, but the owner doesn't want to move it." The same farm impinges on the pristine view formerly enjoyed by Bob and Rita De Pape and their Y-Knot Charters and Campground.

This problem has galvanized the ratepayers' group and brought its members together. Without it, residents would probably live quietly in the backwoods and never meet. Most are not active on the social scene in nearby Lund, and there is no community hall or other site to create a focus for locals.

"We don't really want more services," said Reinhardt. "It's not a case of city people moving here and wanting urban comforts, but we do have concerns in three areas. We're concerned about the impact the detritus from the oyster operations has on the ecological balance. While one species really flourishes, what is happening to the others? There's a lack of science here. Our second concern is that big farms shouldn't be located in front of houses, especially those built before the farms came into existence. A third concern is health. This is less of a problem here, but in other places oysters ingest cadmium and concentrate it. We want testing to be done in a responsible manner.

When Bob and Rita De Pape retired to Okeover to run Y-Knot Charters and Campground they didn't anticipate the problems they would encounter from the oyster growers.

"We can live with most of the problems if we can have a bit of co-operation from the oyster growers. Some of this is happening. In at least one case, the striking blue and white floats are going to be replaced by less obvious black ones. One thing we don't want is a lot of cranes and generators running twenty-four hours a day by absentee corporations. This is happening in Gorge Harbour on Cortes Island. Some of these corporations are already in Trevenen Bay, and Taylor from Washington State has just bought up a lot of leases on the east side of Okeover. Most of these are mom-and-pop operations and we'd like to see it stay that way."

For the past ten years and more, participants in the Okeover Round Table representing oyster growers, residents, kayakers, yachts-men and hikers have debated the issue extensively—occasionally with some heat.[188] Desolation Sound Resort, an architecturally beautiful complex of luxurious tree houses located just south of the government dock in Okeover Inlet, has protested the unsightly mess left by oys-ter farmers within sight of their guests. The De Papes, whose Y-Knot Campsite is a retirement project, have received anonymous threaten-ing phone calls, and guests using their boats have been harassed by high-speed powerboats, though no charges have been laid. Certainly no one would want to own recreational or even residential property in Trevenen Bay, which is wall-to-wall plastic floats dancing to the music of generators.

From the oyster growers' perspective, their farms are the answer to the question of how one generates an income on the British Columbia coast in the twenty-first century. Beginning in the 1950s, it became in-creasingly difficult for settlers to live off the land (not that it had ever been easy). Big forest companies squeezed out individual gyppo loggers, removing the main source of cash. Fish stocks had declined to such an extent that any locals trying to make a living by fishing had to travel far from home. Mineral prospecting had never been profitable, and the tourists arrived in their own boats and rarely came ashore. Many chil-dren of the pioneers left for the cities. For those who remained, oyster farming seemed a good option, though few realized how gruelling the work could be, especially when harvesting was done by hand during the rainy, windy winters.

The oysters being farmed are imports, the same large, juicy Pacific oysters, *Crassostrea gigas*, so common on today's beaches. The native species, *Ostrea conchaphila*, was harvested by Europeans from wild populations as far back as 1884,[189] though individuals grow slowly—after four or five years they are generally less than five centimetres (two inches) across. No wonder First Nations preferred the more plentiful clams and geoducks.

Starting in 1912, enterprising oyster lovers imported Pacific oyster seed from Japan. This species grows to thirty centimetres (twelve inches) long and matures in two to four years. The seed was transported on the decks of freighters, packed in wooden cases and covered with rice matting for insulation. The crew frequently hosed the cases down with seawater to prevent the seed drying out on the crossing, which could take up to forty days. The box of oysters that Daniel Hanson spread on the beach at Larson's Landing in 1952 (see Chapter 15) was probably one of these imports.

Importation continued until about 1961, though in 1942 and 1958 there were two coast-wide spawnings when Pacific oysters "escaped" from the farms. This likely explains why Maria Christensen Zaikow encountered Pacific oysters in Roscoe Bay in the early 1940s. The newcomers, which reproduce faster than the smaller native oyster, have since overwhelmed the native species. (The clams the Natives loved to gather are still here but are hard pressed by these invaders as well as by the purple savoury clam (Dark mahogany-clam *Nuttallia obscurata*), which first arrived in the early 1980s and is now taking over sandy beaches. Another invader, the mud snail (Mudflat snail *Batillaria cumingi*), arrived with oysters from Japan. In ideal habitats, like the head of Freke Anchorage, snail densities can reach seven thousand per square metre.[190])

Starting in 1948, oyster spawn was produced in the warm waters of Pendrell Sound and sold to oyster farmers all over the coast. Oyster harvesting, which had been a wild fishery, became instead a highly scientific farming operation that was carried out on beaches or on specially constructed two-metre (six-foot) rods in deep water. Although Bob Paquin still gathers spawn in Pendrell Sound, many growers hatch the 350-micron larvae in tanks. After seventeen to twenty days, the spat either falls to the bottom or attaches itself to the rods placed in the tank for that purpose. The loaded rods are removed and attached to long lines beneath floats. They are ready for harvesting in about three years.

Naturally seeded imported oysters contributed to the success of a number of oyster businesses in Okeover. In addition to the Hanson family at Larson's Landing, Fred and Ginny Vey and Tiny Hansen had thriving businesses in the 1950s.

In 1975, the Sliammon Band Council "brought home" a business they already knew. They hired Glen Calvert as an economic development adviser to help them run a mariculture operation, of which one component was oysters.[191] Glen arranged for the band to purchase the Vey and Hansen operations, which, when combined with band members' many years of experience in oyster picking and clam digging, and Sliammon women's expertise as the area's best oyster shuckers, were a strong base for a new licensed processing plant built at the foot of Cannery Road. Soon the band was selling oysters and clams (butter, horse, geoduck and littleneck) to local buyers and shipping 1,360-kilogram (3,000-pound) air-freight containers of shellfish from Sea-Tac Airport in Seattle to Honolulu each week.

Glen left in 1980 to become administrator with the regional district. A year later, a band election removed many of the people he had trained and worked with. The new band chief was soon implicated in selling off the assets of the business, and he and another band employee were charged with theft and sent to jail. The operation, which had been viable, never recovered. The band now leases the operation to non-Native growers.

At Refuge Cove, store owner Norm Gibbons started an oyster business called Redonda Sea Farms, which operated from 1979 to 1985.[192] Norm later moved to Cortes and expanded the operation.

Individual residents of the complex of inlets around Malaspina Inlet also started oyster farming in the late 1970s. "In those days you could select a spot and start almost immediately," said Roger Thorne of Thors Cove. "If you wanted to start an oyster farm now, you'd have so much red tape to go through that it would be easier to buy an existing operation. It's become a bureaucratic nightmare."

Thorne started growing oysters on the west side of the cove while still holding a day job in Powell River. Later he expanded to the east side of the cove, quit the job and built a house above his leases. He used seed from Pendrell Sound and hatcheries on Lasqueti Island and in northern California. Out of this came Thynne Island Seafoods, owned by Roger Thorne, Susan Canning and Jean Coustalin.[193] For eighteen years they operated two oyster farms in Okeover and Lancelot inlets. In April 2006, they sold them to Taylor Shellfish of Washington, which has bought other operations in the vicinity.

Roger and his partners now have a mussel farm in Thors Cove. "We tried scallops," he said, "but the supply of seed was uncertain, and in the early stages of their growth, scallops are very finicky and apt to die on you.[194] Mussels are better. They respond to the same techniques used for oysters. You don't have to do everything by hand. There are mechanical aids that make harvesting relatively easy. One advantage is that mussels can be harvested in fourteen or fifteen months whereas oysters take three years or so."

The Okeover oyster growers show off their product each year at Oysterfest, an annual event held in conjunction with student chefs at Malaspina University College in Powell River. The Future Chef's Café at the college sells plates of a dozen oysters served in different ways, along with plates of clams, mussels and other delicacies washed down with appropriate beers and wines. Tickets for the April event sell out in January.

Local growers also sell to wholesalers, who ship the oysters to tables across Canada and the United States, as well as to Hong Kong, Hawaii, Singapore and Taiwan. In August 2005, the BC Shellfish Aquaculture Industry issued 467 licences, of which 47 were in Desolation Sound. Of these, 32 were located within the Malaspina/Okeover complex of inlets.

Growing oysters is hard work, but the local growers have fun too. About eight years ago around the summer solstice, everyone gathered in their herring skiffs off Lion Rock near Selina Point for a big party. Several of the women had been taking belly-dancing lessons. As the tide uncovered the rock, they put on a performance that has become a legend. This party has become an annual event, though not necessarily in the same location.

In addition to partying, the growers exchange information at meetings of the Active Malaspina Mariculture Association (AMMA). There are a couple of AMMA representatives on the Okeover Round Table.

One of the issues crucial to oyster farming is the need for pristine water quality. Oyster buyers test the quality of the product. If it shows any hint of contamination with sewage, they refuse everything from that supplier, which can be catastrophic. The growers do everything possible to keep the water clean, and this is where they run into conflicts with owners of shore property as well as yachties and paddlers. The big worry is improper disposal of sewage. Some homes are on property that is too rocky for a septic field, which means that contaminants from their outhouses could potentially leach into the ocean. There is still no sewage pump-out station for boaters at Lund and questions have been raised about leakage from the park facilities that paddlers use.

Another concern for oyster growers in the complex of Okeover, Lancelot, Theodosia and Malaspina inlets is the move to return the Theodosia River to its original course. In 1956, a dam diverted 80 percent of the flow to Powell Lake to generate power for the pulp mill. More than four decades later, in 1999, the BC Outdoor Recreation Council and the Sliammon Nation persuaded the province to fund changes that would gradually return the river to its normal flow.[195] This would significantly increase the freshwater content of the connected inlets, perhaps with deleterious effects on oyster-growing operations. So far this hasn't happened. Incremental changes have been made to provide more flow for salmon runs, but no big changes have affected the inlets.[196]

The shellfish growers are here to stay, though corporations are beginning to replace individual growers. Only a persistent mutation of red tide is likely to threaten the industry, which, along with tourism, is now one of the main ways to earn a living locally.

However, the people who want to retire to Desolation Sound, work from homes overlooking the water, visit for recreation or work in the tourism industry are not going to go away either. Those people who live or work or play here will have to continue to search for common ground and a way to coexist. Just as the Sliammon tradition teaches, they need to get along and share what they have, knowing that they all need the Sound to be healthy and available.

17

ON THE WATER

Vancouver Island is a sheltering bulwark that has created one of the most fabulous cruising areas in the world. Within this paradise, Prideaux Haven in Desolation Sound is a mecca for both sailboats and powerboats. It's also a dinghy explorer's dream, with many fascinating nooks and crannies among its islands and inner coves. Every year in July and August, luxury yachts populated by the world's celebrities and beautiful people stuff this quiet anchorage. Helicopters on back decks stand ready at a moment's notice to replenish supplies of liquor and gourmet food. This parade of wealth began in the 1920s and has continued ever since.

Squirrel Cove is the next most popular destination. For several years a series of enterprising floating bakers from Cortes Island have capitalized on this situation by providing mouth-watering cinnamon buns, fresh bread and pies. Customers have flocked to them. Sometimes they are so busy that orders must be placed twenty-four hours in advance. At high tide, dinghies can explore the tidal lagoon in the northeast corner.

Yachts also congregate in Tenedos Bay, Roscoe Bay and Grace Harbour. At the east end of Tenedos, warm pools in the creek flowing out of the Unwin Lakes are often used as freshwater baths.

For those who want to be on their own, there are several tiny one- and two-boat anchorages within eight kilometres (five miles) of Prideaux Haven. These are sometimes missed by travellers intent on reaching the main anchorage.

People have been visiting and writing about Desolation Sound since the early years of the twentieth century. The travels of the early yachties Stewart Edward White, M. Wylie Blanchet, and Francis and Amy Barrow have been described in earlier chapters. White's novel *Skookum Chuk*, Blanchet's vignettes in *The Curve of Time* and the jottings from Francis Barrow's 1926–1941 journals describe the characters who lived in Desolation Sound and, in the case of the Barrows, the area's petroglyphs and pictographs. (The Barrows' correspondence with the provincial and federal governments pertaining to these images is in the BC Archives.)

During the 1960s, in the course of editing Francis Barrow's journals (*Upcoast Summers*), the author Beth Hill and her husband Ray cruised the same waters in their twelve-metre (thirty-eight-foot) fish boat *Liza Jane*. Hill found she had so much material that she wrote her own book, *Seven-Knot Summers*, about their voyages. She was also interested in petroglyphs and pictographs and wrote a book about them.[197]

When *Pacific Yachting* magazine published a four-volume cruising guide to the BC coast in the 1970s, it had Bill Wolferstan, a geographer and resource management researcher, devote a whole volume to Desolation Sound.[198] Articles on the same subject by other authors continue to

Yachts visiting Squirrel Cove often come for the delicious fruit pies, fresh bread and cinnamon buns made by this floating bakery.

appear regularly in the magazine. In the late 1990s, Anne and Laurence Yeadon-Jones, began series of guides named after their eleven-metre (thirty-six-foot) sloop *Dreamspeaker*.[199] Experienced blue-water sailors, the Yeadon-Joneses set sail from England in 1986 on a round-the-world voyage but settled in Vancouver. Laurence's charming hand-drawn coloured maps and plans of the anchorages add a host of useful details for cruisers that are not found on the hydrographic charts.

Desolation Sound was popular enough that celebrities regularly turned up there aboard yachts. As a teenager in 1978, Karen Rossman Davidson of Courtenay met Bob Hope.[200] "He was on a big powerboat," she said. "I was in a sailboat dinghy rowing around and happened to notice him." She also knew that "the very petite woman" who seemed to have two boats was Barbra Streisand. "The stars don't look like themselves because they don't have the makeup on that we see them wearing in the movies or on TV." She said Paul Allan, the co-owner of Microsoft, was also around.

Members of various yacht clubs like to cruise here so much that the Royal Vancouver Yacht Club and the Seattle Yacht Club have purchased outstations in Cortes Bay on Cortes Island.[201] Although the slips remain empty much of the year, they are prized possessions for a fortunate few.

In July and August, Prideaux Haven becomes a showcase of expensive yachts, often with celebrities on board.

Ghosting into Grace Harbour, a yacht passes the Indian village of Kahkaykay to find the protected anchorage behind.

In 2006, the Royal Van club planned a "Dog Days North" cruise from July 29 to August 7 with a maximum of twenty-five boats.

As it takes several days to bring a sailboat up from the centres of population, some enterprising owners find places to moor their boats in Desolation Sound for the off-season. In the early 1980s, Dick Sandwell moored his *Gabrielle III* in Stag Bay on Hernando Island and then flew in to cruise.[202] One of his favourite activities was to call at Refuge Cove for some chilled white wine and then heave to in the middle of Desolation Sound for a leisurely lunch, often with fresh-caught prawns. In August 1987 he motored to Refuge Cove for ice and supplies, then "spent an hour drifting off Redonda Island, eating European sausages and drinking chilled white wine for lunch" before returning to Stag Bay.

New boats arrive all the time. In September 2006, the owners of ten California micro cruisers trailered their sailboats to launch at Powell River.[203] The group, which called itself All the Usual Suspects, put a 5.7-metre (nineteen-foot) length limit on participants' boats and planned to sail through Desolation Sound and round Cortes and Quadra islands. They would cook and sleep on the boats, which included six West Wight Potter 15 sloops (a compact cruiser designed for safety and ease of sailing even in strong winds), two 4.5-metre (fifteen-foot) Montgomeries, a five-metre (seventeen-foot) Venture and a five-metre SunCat.

It's not just the rich and famous who sail in the area. In the 1930s and 1940s, Madge and Bill MacGillivray of Powell River spent weekends and weeks in Desolation Sound in their powerboat *Pat.* "If we found someone else anchored in a cove, we'd go on to find one of our own," their daughter Marge McLeod reminisced.[204]

Between 1968 and 1978, sea cadets from across Canada participated in week-long Easter cruises in ten-metre (thirty-two-foot) sailing cutters of the same clinker-built, lug-rigged design used by Captain George Vancouver.[205] The cadets sailed or rowed from Powell River to camp at Squirrel Cove and Prideaux Haven, following the route set out in Vancouver's and Archibald Menzies' journals. Each cadet had copies of sections of these journals and attempted to identify the various landmarks mentioned as they sailed around Desolation Sound. Some

Sea cadets follow the wake of the explorers in a replica of one of Captain Vancouver's longboats. PHOTO BY JOHN TREEN nights they slept in the boats, using the sails as awnings; other nights they camped on the beach. Each of the eight boats contained thirteen cadets and two officers. If the wind did not co-operate for sailing, five pairs of oarsmen sat side by side and rowed. Each boat had a centreboard that was retracted for beach landings. When they tacked, everyone had a job: the mainsail was sheeted in closer and closer to the centreline; then the foresail was backed, the lug dipped and the running backstays reset. Blocks and tackles controlled all the rigging. These "re-enactments" of Vancouver's explorations in and around Desolation Sound were educational and enjoyed by all.[206]

In 2004, Paula Brook, who camped ashore at night from her small speedboat, had a somewhat different take on Desolation Sound.[207] She described the cruising yachts she encountered as "Winnebagos of the waves, towing Zodiacs and Sea-Doos the way RVs haul cars and ATVs." Surfing their giant wakes through the "gridlocked channels of 'downtown Desolation Sound" (meaning Prideaux Haven) was hazardous. She felt that small boats were "even less likely to be noticed by the inebriated yacht's captain than the motorcyclist is by the oblivious RV driver" and noted that "small-craft campers are basically popping their tents in off-leash dog parks. And if they're not careful about choosing a cove with serious tidal wash, they're swimming in the big boats' toilets." Unfortunately, she is right. I've experienced the dogs first-hand in Roscoe Bay, and I only swim in Laura Cove in June. The same thing happens everywhere yachts anchor. It's a good reason to go in the off-season, preferably early in the year.

Paddling instead of sailing or using an engine is a very old method of transportation in Desolation Sound. First Nations people did it in long, graceful dugout canoes with swept-up ends. The longboats attached to Captain Vancouver's 1792 expedition were often rowed as well as sailed. Early settlers like Mike Shuttler and the Thulin brothers thought nothing of rowing back and forth to Vancouver for supplies and mail.

In 1937, young Betty Lowman Carey, who had started out in the San Juan Islands, paddled from Sarah Point, up Teakerne Arm and on to the Yuculta Rapids in a refurbished dugout canoe.[208] She was on her

Betty Lowman Carey paddled her dugout canoe through Lewis Channel on her way from the San Juan Islands to Alaska in 1937. She spent a night in Teakerne Arm where handsome young loggers took her fishing in Cassel Lake. COURTESY BETTY LOWMAN CAREY

way to see her father, a fisherman in Alaska. When she picked up her mail at the Squirrel Cove post office, however, she discovered that her father disapproved of her solo trip and had reported her to the Coast Guard. Hiding behind the islands, she snuck out of Squirrel Cove and paddled across Lewis Channel to visit "tall, swaggering, brown-eyed, young" Barney Smith at what turned out to be a womanless logging camp in Teakerne Arm. In the evening, the men took her fishing in Cassel Lake. After she had a good night's rest in a comfortable bed in the guesthouse, they lent her a pair of caulk boots and she helped blow apart a Kelly Raft (a type of boom in which the logs were tied together with thick wire cables so that they were easier to keep bundled while being towed). After Betty kissed Barney goodbye, Ernie, the boss, gave her and her canoe a ride back to Lewis Channel and she continued on her way to Alaska. Her father forgave her as soon as she arrived.

Audrey Sutherland from Hawaii, paddling an inflatable kayak, soloed the same route in reverse in the early 1980s, and there have been many other paddling trips in both directions.

In the 1950s, members of the Washington Kayak Club led trips

to Desolation Sound, the Gulf Islands and the West Coast long before Canadians were paddling anything except rivers. Dogwood Canoe
Club members from the BC Lower Mainland followed in the 1960s and
1970s. Dinty Moore, a founding member, remembers an early group of
Montreal medical students who paddled Desolation Sound but ran into
grief on the last day of their trip.[209] They were paddling back to Okeover
from the Curme Islands, where they had camped. As often happens in
the morning, they encountered a strong headwind. To escape this, they
landed at Portage Cove, but the owners, who were in residence, would
not let them cross over into the calmer waters of Wootton Bay. The
canoeists retreated into Tenedos Bay. They ended up staying there until the wind calmed in the evening. Then they paddled round Zephine
Head and up Malaspina Inlet. It was dark by the time they took their
canoes out in the little cove beside the Okeover government dock, and
they were a day late returning their rented craft.

Powell River paddler Garry Hubbard, who regularly paddled Desolation Sound in the 1960s and 1970s, had a solution to the Portage Cove
problem.[210] "I've often slept in the old cabin at Tenedos Bay," he said. "Then
we'd portage the canoe up to Unwin Lake to fish. Crossing at Portage
Cove was no problem for me. I just bribed the caretaker with a few nice fat
trout and he hauled my stuff through in his wheelbarrow. It cuts off seven
miles of stormy water that way." Others were not so lucky. Some tell of
menacing guard dogs or even guns. A local outfitter has been threatened
with a potato gun and has offered to see the perpetrator in court.

"It's a shame," said Garry. "For centuries the Indians portaged their
canoes across there. It should have been included in the park long ago."
Indeed, the name Portage Cove appears on the 1862 British Admiralty
chart.

Jack Wainwright's book *Canoe Trips of British Columbia* promises
warm water and succulent oysters in the Sound but warns of powerboat
wakes in narrow channels.[211] He notes that there is less of a wilderness
feel in Desolation Sound than on other canoe routes—unless paddlers
visit before or after July and August.

In the mid-1980s, the big sea-kayaking boom began, and Lund to

Okeover via Theodosia became a popular long-weekend trip. Warmer and less hazardous than Johnstone Strait with its uncertain winds, Desolation Sound soon became the second most popular kayaking destination after the Gulf Islands.

At first it was relatively easy to find campsites, but soon almost all of them were taken over by oyster leases, which were also expanding at the time. Some owners were hostile to kayakers, claiming that they polluted the beaches. However, debris from oyster operations, both in and out of the water, is just as polluting and can be hazardous to recreationists.

Seventeen sea kayakers who spent the weekend in Desolation Sound in September 1996 looked no different from any others till they came in to land. Four transferred into wheelchairs and were hauled up to the campsite with ropes, four were amputees, and the rest were able-bodied helpers who were happy to let those less mobile cook and do dishes for them. The group was organized by Disabled Sports Northwest, a Seattle-based division of Disabled Sports USA. In their well-worn, slightly damp T-shirts and soft hats, they didn't look like the high-powered group they turned out to be. Two of the wheelchair contingent were medical doctors specializing in spinal cord injuries, and there were other health workers in the group. This was the fourth year Disabled Sports Northwest had run the trip. Participants met one evening a week for seven weeks before the trip to learn about paddle strokes, wet exits, gear, wilderness camping, how to cope without conventional washrooms, etc. "With catheters and a folding porta-potty, we've got that one down pat," said Dr. Steven A. Stiens, an attending physician for spinal cord injury at the Seattle Veterans Affairs Medical Center.

"Getting into a kayak is very liberating," enthused Dr. Lance Goetz, a first-timer. "I just loved paddling close along the rock faces and looking down and seeing jellyfish. We had wet weather and good sun but we had lots of tarps so we were fine." He particularly enjoyed visiting the Curme Islands and Prideaux Haven, where he was able to land on a rock and get ashore.

Steven Stiens had a good time too. "We caught rock cod and two red snapper, which we haven't eaten yet. One of the highlights of my trip this year was when I got towed by a dogfish till he got off the hook," he chuckled. He noted that most of the disabled people on the trip had been disabled for some time. The people with recent injuries dropped out during the training period. "Next year we will try a buddy system so that an experienced person will team up with a rookie and talk to them more about how to cope," he said. He was surprised to learn about the wheelchair trail and campsite at Inland Lake, near Powell River, and thought that another time they might like to use them for the first day or so of the trip.

A couple of years after this, the Powell River Paddlers and I enjoyed a wonderful weekend on the Curme Islands in late June. Keeping well to the west side of Malaspina Inlet, we successfully avoided the strong tidal current and made it round to Galley Bay in Desolation Sound by mid-afternoon. The water was calm, so we paddled a direct line to the Curme Islands and set up camp on a beautiful rock bluff. Next morning, after a leisurely breakfast in the sunshine, we slipped through the narrow passage by Otter Island to explore Prideaux Haven. On the way back we were greeted by about forty seals basking on Pringle Rock.

Turkey vultures are summer visitors.

Paddling into Tenedos Bay, we met a double kayak that had seen a black bear on the island in the centre of the bay, but we had no such luck. Everyone enjoyed the bright green shades of the water in the narrow passage behind the island, but Unwin Lake was a big disappointment, because a log jam prevents access to the warm flat rocks.

Early the next morning, we headed straight over to Portage Cove, where we found several thick, white, fluffy sea anemones and some moonsnail collars. As we edged along the low-tide line to Galley Bay, we stopped to look at sea cucumbers, brown anemones, a scarlet blood star and a small abalone that was well anchored to its rock.

As we ate lunch, we watched a turkey vulture tilting its wings. Later, when we rounded Zephine Head, we caught the infamous tidal current, which this time was going our way. A side trip to Grace Harbour provided us with a welcome rest and the promise of a nice future day trip to the lake above it. As we crossed the inlet back to the government wharf, we ran into a school of tiny jellyfish, which we stopped to marvel

Marg McNeil looks at a batch of newly laid squid eggs below her kayak near the head of Okeover Inlet.

at. Total distance travelled during the three days was thirty-seven nautical miles. This is how it should be.

Today, members of all the major sea-kayaking and canoe clubs in the Pacific Northwest enjoy trips into Desolation Sound, usually in the summer months. Local paddlers can be seen on the water at any time of year, especially in the winter when a high-pressure system brings sunny skies.

18

MARINE PARKS IN DESOLATION SOUND

*T*he popularity of the anchorages in Prideaux Haven, Tenedos Bay, Galley Bay, Roscoe Bay, Teakerne Arm, Grace Harbour and the Copeland Islands led to a general feeling that the area should be pre-served in some way. This happened in the 1970s, with the creation of a variety of marine provincial parks, but perhaps if that status had been formalized earlier, the result might not have been so piecemeal. As it is, areas like Portage Cove and Galley Bay are still privately owned, result-ing in a park with chunks of land off limits to visitors.

Long before any parks were established in Desolation Sound, the University of British Columbia received a gift of land at Melanie Cove in Prideaux Haven, site of Mike Shuttler's homestead, the first in the Sound. After Shuttler died, his land eventually fell into the hands of Reed Hunt of San Francisco, who in 1966 deeded it to UBC "to pre-serve it as a public anchorage and as part of BC's natural heritage."[212] For a while, it seems, the university forgot it held the land.[213]

In 1971, Roscoe Bay and the Copeland Islands became the first two provincial marine parks established by the BC government. Roscoe Bay is a popular destination for boaters because they can use the fresh water of nearby Black Lake to wash their hair or do laundry.

The Copeland Islands, known locally as the Raggeds, are not actually

in Desolation Sound, but boats coming from the large population centres of Vancouver and Victoria generally pass through them before
rounding Sarah Point. The warm pink rocks of the islands are fringed
with arbutus trees. In spring, blue-eyed Mary and pink sea blush add
to the ambience. Mink used to gambol from rock to rock, but most of
them disappeared about fifteen years ago, possibly because bald eagles,
unable to find enough fish to eat, picked them off. However, the islands
are still a staging point for marbled murrelets, which gather in pairs or
small family groups.

It was another two years before Desolation Sound Marine Park
came into being in 1973. It encompasses Prideaux Haven and its sheltering islands, Tenedos Bay and both sides of the Gifford Peninsula, as
well as a jog across Malaspina Inlet to Cochrane Bay, where a branch
of the Sunshine Coast Trail comes down to a waterfront campsite. An
undated thirty-two-page proposal called for nine campgrounds in the
park, and an extensive network of trails connecting them. [214] The writers
assumed that the private property within the park boundaries would be
expropriated, but protests launched by the owners, together with BC

*A glaucous-winged gull contemplates the pleasure boats anchored in Roscoe Bay. They will
not be able to leave till the tide has risen to flood the entrance.*

Parks' lack of money to buy the land at market value, left a hodgepodge of private parcels in Portage Cove, Galley Bay and at the entrance to Grace Harbour. Consequently, there are only four campsites—at Tenedos Bay, Grace Harbour, Cochrane Bay and Galley Bay—and three trails: one between Melanie Cove and Laura Cove; another from Tenedos Bay up to Unwin Lake (a ten-minute walk following the creek; many people enjoy freshwater baths in the deep pools); and the third from Roscoe Bay to Black Lake for the same purpose. The planned road in from Bliss Landing has not appeared either, though there has been an old trail across the peninsula since the 1920s. Although park managers have discussed linking the trails, Hugh Ackroyd of BC Parks says that developing trails is a low priority for the department because "most cruisers just like to socialize on each other's boats and the kayakers spend most of their time on the water."[215]

In 1996, at the urging of local kayakers, the marine park's boundary was extended west to include the Curme Islands, a favourite camping spot for all paddlers. These islands are very similar in appearance, flora and fauna to the Copelands.

Yellow monkey flower, Mimulus guttatus, *grows in places where water seeps out of or over rock faces. It blooms May to August from sea level to the mountaintops.*

A female bald eagle hungrily surveys the water for her next meal. Females are larger than males and this one has nothing in her crop. If she doesn't catch a fish soon, she will take a gull or a duck instead.

Since the area became a park, all cabin structures and fences have gradually been removed. BC Parks usually does a cultural assessment of an area before a park opens. The decision to keep a cabin or remove it depends on the condition it is in and on the cost of upkeep, which is sometimes more than the park budget can bear. Both Mike Shuttler's cabin in Melanie Cove and Phil Lavigne's cabin in Laura Cove had been unoccupied for several decades and were likely in very poor repair by 1973. So although Mike's terraces and fruit trees remain in Melanie Cove, there is no trace of his cabin, and the deer wander freely over his former vegetable patches.

The old loggers' flume at Tenedos Bay was another piece of history. It was built for Will Palmer's logging camp in the 1920s and ran from near the park information board, up along the creek to Unwin Lake. A careful examination of the beach reveals traces of the flume, and upstream it is possible to see where the loggers smoothed out its passage beside the creek.

Marine parks include the upland and the sea bottom.[215] For the most part, the water column is under federal jurisdiction. Plants and animals in the water are the responsibility of either the federal or the provincial government, depending on the species. On land, the Park Act protects them all.

In July and August the anchorages are packed with boats—sometimes as many as 120 in Prideaux Haven alone. Although they are prohibited from discharging their sewage, the presence of large numbers of boats make these areas unattractive for swimming. Pit toilets have been installed at Grace Harbour, Tenedos Bay and the head of Melanie Cove. There used to be a garbage scow in Prideaux Haven, but BC Parks took it out when old refrigerators and what was unmistakably household garbage started turning up on it. At the time, locals and visitors worried that the same stuff would appear in the water or the upland areas, but that didn't happen. Most boaters are pretty good about packing their garbage out.

In 1989, Walsh Cove and Teakerne Arm became provincial parks. Surrounding islands make Walsh Cove a very protected anchorage, long favoured by cruising boats. Because it is the nearest protected anchorage to Toba Inlet, it is a key location for boaters planning to brave the uncertainties of that beautiful place. Teakerne Arm is a favourite cruising destination because it offers freshwater swimming in Cassel Lake or a shower in the waterfall that spills down so invitingly from the lake.

Nearby, round the north end of Cortes Island, Ha'thayim (Von Donop) Marine Provincial Park, established in 1993, provides another sheltered anchorage. Visitors here can walk the short trail through to the popular Squirrel Cove anchorage, where cinnamon buns and other delicacies may sometimes be purchased.

Mt. Denman overlooking Station Island and Lewis Channel between West Redonda Island and Cortes Island, from where the picture was taken.

In 1996, Malaspina Provincial Park was created. It protects the beginning of the Sunshine Coast Trail, which runs 180 kilometres (112 miles) through the forest and over the mountains to Saltery Bay. This is a major hiking trail, comparable to the West Coast Trail and a lot less crowded. A spur from it descends to Cochrane Bay, where there is a small camp spot. It's a safe haven for storm-stayed paddlers, giving them a welcome hiking alternative till the weather calms.

The last park to be established was the small Tux'wnech Okeover Arm Provincial Park. This opened in 1999 and is a joint venture with the Sliammon Nation, whose midden at this location is now protected by a solid layer of fill. Interpretive signs describe First Nations' traditional uses of the area. There are over a hundred First Nations sites in the Desolation Sound area, and the bands are concerned about their fragility. People can damage sites without realizing that they are doing so, which is why the midden at Tux'wnech has been capped.

When Desolation Sound Marine Park was given Class A status in 1973, there were four mariculture operations within its boundaries.[217] These were located at Galley Bay, in Isabel Bay and Edith Island in Malaspina Inlet, and behind the Susan Islets at the mouth of Theodosia Inlet. These farms were allowed to continue, but no new ones were permitted. Today, only the one at Edith Island remains.

And why is East Redonda an ecological reserve and not a park? Because it is a pristine representative of a steep coastal island, and its status as an ecological reserve gives it more protection than park status would do. Recreation is not permitted in ecological reserves; they are open only for scientific or educational projects (which does not include growing marijuana—see Chapter 8).

19

THE FUTURE

*I*n a whimsical world of 2075, Dan Wing and Lakshmi Smith sip their cappuccinos as they look out their picture window at the big round boulder on top of which Phil Lavigne's goat stood sentinel. They are year-round caretakers for the Desolation Sound Natural Heritage Area. Their two-year contract is dependent on their finishing their PhD theses for the biology department at UBC.

Dan's thesis is "The replacement of *Thuja plicata*, western red cedar, by *Sequoia sempervirens*, coast redwood, and its status in the sustainable forest of BC." By 2006, stands of red cedar were beginning to suffer from the reduced moisture of global warming.[218] Redwoods, moving north from California and Oregon, have now largely replaced them.

In her thesis, "The return of *Melanitta perspicillata*, surf scoters," Lakshmi is examining the early twenty-first-century attempt by commercial mussel growers to exterminate scoter populations. Widespread killing of the birds caused a serious natural imbalance, and a ban on shooting, established in 2010, has still not compensated for this catastrophe.

Both students are scheduled to finish their work this year, after which one of the other universities in the province will send its graduate students to complete different studies. A pool of potential candidates and First Nations people help the full-time caretakers during the busy months of July and August, putting on a series of natural and cultural history programs in amphitheatres at the main anchorages in the heritage area.

Yes, the yachts still come. They book moorage a year in advance, and no one can come more than two years in a row. Small groups of four to six kayakers and canoeists are subject to the same rules. Some groups are led by commercial operators, while others come on their own.

Desolation Sound Natural Heritage Area is a combined administration for the parks and ecological reserves. Its territory is much enlarged since the reserves' piecemeal beginnings in the late twentieth century. Now all the Redonda Islands, the south side of Homfray Channel and Desolation Sound between Brettell and Sarah points, and all the inlets feeding into Malaspina Inlet are under the management of the heritage area. Half the members of the governing body's board of directors are elected Sliammon elders, most of whom have university degrees or years of practical business experience.

Some people still live in the park. They are either designated shellfish growers, people who owned property before 2020 (most of whom are dying out or leaving the area), or residents on five-year leases. Many of the latter are artists, writers or retirees. Most live in Malaspina or Okeover inlets in homes built by the baby boomers. These properties were so hard to sell after the boomers died that their heirs gladly turned them over to the heritage area in exchange for a tax break.

The disputes between oyster growers and waterfront owners were solved when the deep-water operations were confined to Trevenen Bay. Soon after, the mariculturists became heroes for growing food locally so that it did not need to be trucked in. When the flow of the Theodosia River was restored in 2030, it did not cause the havoc some thought it would, and all have enjoyed the increased salmon run.

A Sliammon chemist's discovery of a process to convert sewage into power for vehicles, boats and other uses was an added bonus. It means no more septic fields to be pumped out and no more worries about *E. coli* contamination of food. When power produced by the conversion process is augmented by solar panels, it frees most people from the need to buy any outside power at all.

With cheap satellite access to the Internet, many residents don't need to leave their homes to work. Hidden in the forest near the road are a few small manufacturers of specialty products, like the kilns the Carsten family pioneered in the early twenty-first century.

Fred Wing, Dan Wing's handlogging ancestor, was able to survive quite comfortably in Desolation Sound because there were fish in the sea and individuals had access to the forests. Living off the land is once more becoming practical.

Could this happen? Possibly. I grew up in the Midlands of England, where no one in their right mind would have considered swimming in the toxic rivers from which fish had long disappeared. Yet when I returned home in the mid-1980s, much of the pollution had been cleaned up and wildlife was returning. The same thing could happen here. Already there is talk of banning fish trawlers, a long-overdue measure. If we cleaned up all the streams clogged by unsustainable logging practices, fish would return. Twentieth-century forestry practices disturbed the balance of the ecosystem. Careful replanting of mixed species known to

Harbour seals bask on a rock by Feather Cove.

flourish in this area would go a long way to restoring the health of the land.

The Sliammon people, in whose ancestral territory Desolation Sound nestles, are a consistent thread. They were here in the beginning, and they will be here in the future. Treaty negotiations are ongoing, and more and more of the Sliammon are involved in post-secondary education. They are the biggest stakeholders.

In time, the Sliammon Development Corporation may take over the companies now buying out individual shellfish growers. It's hard to predict what will happen when the baby boomers are gone, leaving a glut of recreational property on the market. The rainforest reclaims untended land in a matter of a few years. On the other hand, if immigration boosts Canada's population, these properties may still be enjoyed by generations to come.

ACKNOWLEDGEMENTS

I've sailed and sea-kayaked Desolation Sound countless times since 1979, but I didn't think about writing a book on the area until after I had worked on two articles that appeared in the magazine *Pacific Yachting* in April 2001 and August 2003. The first was on First Nations legends of Desolation Sound and the second on the European pioneers.

I profiled the Sliammon chief Joe Mitchell in September 1999 for the last issue of the *Powell River News*. When I interviewed him, I knew that he didn't have long to live, so I asked him to tell me about Desolation Sound as well. He told me about the Grace Harbour winter village and the legend of the mountain goat and the deer. I sent a query to the editors at *Pacific Yachting* to see if they would like an article on the First Nations legends of Desolation Sound. I had already profiled two other Sliammon elders: Elsie Paul in September 1997 and Sue Pielle in June 1999. Two weeks after the chief passed away, *Pacific Yachting* gave me the go-ahead for the article. The chief's nephew, Murray Mitchell, took me to Feather Cove in his big replica Nootka canoe, telling stories all the way. His aunt, the chief's sister, Sue Pielle, kindly added more stories and went over the final manuscript. *Pacific Yachting* happily took the resulting article.

When I was writing the second article, the children of the pioneers kept asking, "Are you going to write a book?" "No" was my firm answer, but then it seemed a pity to waste so much good material, especially as it wouldn't all fit into the article.

On a cold, bright January day in 2003, John Dafoe took a friend and me to Desolation Sound. He was doing an eelgrass survey for the

Department of Fisheries and Oceans and wanted company. As we approached Prideaux Haven, a small flock of surf scoters burst into the air, scattering diamonds of light. Ours was the only boat. Surely this must have been how Mike Shuttler saw it when he first arrived in the 1880s.

Of course there had to be a book. Maria Christensen Zaikow, Ingrid Andersen Cowie and many others thought so too. Willingly they shared their stories. Soon I realized that Powell River, where I live, was full of people who had spent their childhoods on one of the many homesteads dotted around the Sound. It was just a matter of asking. One phone call led to another and "Oh, you must talk to so-and-so, she'll be in town on Monday." It was never-ending. My apologies to those I missed.

At the Powell River Archives, Teedie Kagume introduced me to her treasures and answered many questions. Moyra Palm of the Powell River Genealogical Society shared her enhanced cemetery records. She also helped with the search for Joe Copeland, as did Jayne Mortenson, a US history buff, but it was Brenda King Finch who found him first.

In Vancouver, Margaret Waddington, the western representative of Canadiana.org (formerly the Canadian Institute for Historical Microreproductions), was particularly helpful. Eagerly, she joined the search for the thirteen people whose names adorn Prideaux Haven. Together, we met with Len McCann of the Vancouver Maritime Museum and Katherine Kalsbeek of UBC Special Collections. From her sickbed, former Special Collections librarian Frances Woodward made suggestions. Through Frances, I met Margaret Hutchins at the BC Archives, all of whose staff were very helpful. We traced the Prideaux Haven names back to 1864 but are still not certain who chose them or why. Tracking down the namesakes is an ongoing project that may require a visit to the offices of the British Admiralty.

The folks at Terracentric Coastal Adventures in Lund were of great assistance. In July 2006, I hitched a ride with them to drop some kayakers off on East Redonda. On the way back, Terracentric's cultural programs coordinator, Erik Blaney, and I looked for Flea Village but did not have enough time to do a thorough search. Erik went back another time and was sure he had found the place, and in August we confirmed it. A group of friends and I hired the Terracentric Zodiac on a perfect summer day. In Homfray Channel, the water turned to glass and reflected the mountains. Maria Christensen Zaikow unerringly navigated to where Bertram Saulter and Frank Pritchard lived on the site of Flea Village. She pointed out the rock on which Phil Lavigne's goat stood, the black cliffs below which the Lindberg farm nestled and the location of her own house in Roscoe Bay.

Later, on my way back from the West Coast, I called in at Seaford on Cortes Island, where Bud Jarvis let me camp in his yard. Once again he told me the Lindberg stories, the Refuge Cove cougar story and others. Then he introduced me to Norm Gibbons and other members of the co-op, who regaled me with more tales of the Refuge Cove area. On the way home, I visited the Campbell River Archives, where Sandra Parrish screened Francis Barrow's video of Phil Lavigne. Even my knee surgery in the Comox Hospital yielded a story. I had heard about film stars anchoring their yachts in Prideaux Haven but hadn't run into anyone who had actually met one. Now I did. Karen Davidson, one of the nursing staff, told me how she had met Bob Hope.

Back at home, many people, especially BC Parks staff, were generous with their time on the phone or by e-mail. Roger Thorne, an award-winning shellfish grower, kindly came to the house for an interview. Rod Tysdale, a retired forester, explained the mysteries of high-leading and other logging lore. Howard White shared his research on factors affecting pre-contact Native populations.

A full list of those interviewed is in the endnotes. Thank you all. I have tried to retell your stories as accurately as possible. Please forgive any omissions. There were also many people to whom I was referred but who I did not have time to phone. My apologies. This book would never have gone to press if I had followed up all the leads.

It's one thing to gather the material, but it's another to put it down in a readable fashion. Thanks to my editor, Audrey McClellan, for making many helpful suggestions that greatly improved the manuscript. Her support was wonderful.

PEOPLE OF DESOLATION SOUND

Those without dates cannot be reliably identified in the BC Archives Vital Events databases.

Name	Birth & death	Location	Pre-emption date	Crown grant date	Lot No.	Buried Cranberry Cemetery *headstone
Arnold, John	1907–1995	Theodosia			L2175	
Berglund, Edward		Thors Cove, Lanc.I	1912	1923	L2313	
Bishop, Mary (McGuffie)	1892–1953	Malaspina Inlet				
Bishop, Peter William	1871–1946	Bishop's Landing	1911	1921	L4201	A1-695*
	1871–1946	Malaspina Inlet	c.1932	Yes	L3785	
Bishop, William Peter	1844–1929	Malaspina Inlet				
Black, George E.	1866–1961	Refuge Cove	n.d.	1913	L2849	
Brister, Mary Gorman		Portage Cove				
Brister, Ross	1902–1972	Portage Cove			L4933	
Chambers, Devina	1871–1931	Okeover				M-215
Chambers, John	1883–1929	Okeover	n.d.	1913	L3911	J-162
Christensen, Bertha (Horner)	1898–1983	Salt Lagoon				
Christensen, Carl	1893–1975	Salt Lagoon	1926	Dis. 1933	L4972	
Christensen, Joe	1927–2006	Salt Lagoon				
Christensen, Maria	1925–	Salt Lagoon				
Copland, Joseph Henry	1844–1936	Portage Cove	1910	1920	L4933	Z-463

Name	Dates	Location				
Cowie, Ernest Walter	1884–1966	Desolation Sound				
Cowie, Ingrid (Andersen)	1914–	Galley Bay				
Crowther, Doris	1887–1967	Penrose Bay				BA-528
Crowther, Nancy	1923–1990	Penrose Bay				BF-252
Crowther, Sidney William J.	1884–1961	Penrose Bay	1927	1942	L4208	BA-57
D'Angio, Katherine	1891–1949	Okeover				
D'Angio, John Sr (Giovanni)	1887–1962	Okeover	1914		L3919	BA-151
D'Angio, John Jr	1921–1995	Okeover				
D'Angio, Raffaelle	1894–1921	Okeover	1914		L3913	T-361
D'Angio, Raffaelle, Jr.	1922–	Okeover	n.d.		L3914	
Danielsson, Ivor	1902–1984	Lloyd Point				
Donley, Robert	1874–1955	Refuge Cove				
Hanson, Amanda	1881–1966	Galley Bay				
Hanson, Axel	1880–1975	Galley Bay	1912	1917	L2839	
Hanson, Axel Ragnar	1899–1974	Galley Bay		1926	L2644	
Hanson, Ed	1908–1963	Okeover				BA-266
Heatley, James Johnstone	1870–1944	Pendrell Sound	1915	Cx	L4180	AF-628
Heatley, Elizabeth	1870–1944	Galley Bay	1932	Cx	L1474	BB-28*
Heatley, Lily	1883–1956	Galley Bay				J-170
	1912–1930	Pendrell Sound				

Name	Birth & death	Location	Pre-emption date	Crown grant date	Lot No.	Buried Cranberry Cemetery *headstone
Hodson, Brooke	1899–1970	Okeover				BB-311
Hope, Doris Rosetta	1895–1981	Refuge Cove				
Hope, Douglas E. (Buster)	1910–1980	Refuge Cove			L4936	
Hope, Norman Edwin	1909–1984	Refuge Cove				
Heatley, Lily	1912–1930	Pendrell Sound				J-170
Jones, Arthur W.	1889–1939	Isabel Bay, Lanc.I	1927	Cx	L4603	
Jones, Helen Y.	1891–1952	Isabel Bay, Lanc.I				
Larson, Edmund	1863–1946	Okeover	1914	Cx	L3767	
Lavigne, Philip	1889–1974	Laura Cove	1908	1930	L4184	A1-713
Lindberg, Eric	1885–1970	Lloyd Point	1915	1925	L3787	
Lindberg, Herman	1873–1960	Pendrell Sound	n.d.	1918	L3697	
McCauley, Joseph Edwin	1882–1954	Refuge Cove				AT-1015*
McGuffie, Margaret	1884–1962	Refuge Cove				AT-1016*
McGuffie, Robert	1935–1999	Grace Harbour				
Mitchell, Chief Joe	1885–1956	Redonda Bay	moved to Stuart Is.			
Olmstead, Gerry (Gerard)	1879–1963	Malaspina Inlet				
Osborn, Francis Preston						

Name	Dates	Location				
Palmer, James Clark	1846–1921	Theodosia	1900	1909	L2175	AP-897
Palmer, Lucy Mildred M.	1898–1983	Tenedos Bay etc.				AA-488*
Palmer, Sarah	1851–1940	Theodosia				
Palmer, Will Cyrus	1884–1966	Tenedos Bay etc.	1902	1909	L1376	AO-888*
Parker, Dan	1898–1986	Malaspina Inlet			L3785	
Parker, Ethel (Bishop)	1926–2003	Malaspina Inlet				
Parker, George Walker	1874–1925	Roffey Is.	n.d.	1919	L4185	
Paul, Elsie (Timothy)	1931–	Redonda Bay				
Pritchard, Francis		Roffey Is.				
Roos, John Oscar	1884–1962	Okeover	1912	1927	L3766	BA-175
Roos, Nunny (Kangas)	1888–1982	Okeover				BA-175
Russell, Lillian	1866–1939	Redonda Bay				
Salo, Vira May (Palmer)	1881–1968	Theodosia				AC-542
Saulter, (Richard) Bertram	1878–1961	Roffey Is.	1915	1919	L4186	
Scott, Ida May	1877–1931	E. Redonda				
Scott, John Bunyan	1856–1938	E. Redonda	1901	None	L5018	J-173
Shuttler, Andrew (Mike)	1858–1931	Melanie Cove	1916	1924	L4354	G-119
Stewart, Archie	1861–1927	Booker Pt.	1907	1914	L3628 L5019	
Thomas, Dorothy	1897–1981	Refuge Cove				
Thomas, Ed	1889–1969	Refuge Cove				BB-3340

Name	Birth & death	Location	Pre-emption date	Crown grant date	Lot No.	Buried Cranberry Cemetery *headstone
Timothy, Jim	1886–1970	Redonda Bay				
Timothy, Molly	1891–1970	Redonda Bay				
Timothy, Willy	1926–1974	Redonda Bay				
Tindall, John Ronald	1907–1954	Refuge Cove			L4936	
Tindall, Margaret Rose	1883–1955	Refuge Cove				
Vaughn, Dewey	1898–1973	Larson's Landing	n.d.	1920	L3767	
Vaughn, Sheridan	1894–1956	Larson's Landing	n.d.	1920	L3767	
Vicary, Syd	1878–1958	Redonda Bay				

PRONUNCIATION GUIDE

Ahpookwum—Ah-*pook*-wum

Arran Rapids—*Air*-ran Rapids

Cheakamus—*Check*-a-moose

Cheen Kwah—*Cheen*-kwah

Chelohsin—Chel-*o*-sin

Cheslakees—Ches-*lak*-ees

Coode Island—Cood Island

Cortes Island—Cor-*tez* Island

Freke Anchorage—Freek Anchorage

Homalco—Ho-*mal*-co

Homfray Channel—*Hom*-fray Channel

Kahkaykay—Kah-*kay*-kay

Klahoose—Kla-*hoos*

Kwakwaka'wakw—Kwack-*wack*-a-wack

Lekwiltok—Leh-*kwil*-tok

Machinay—*Mah*-chin-eye (Vancouver's "Flea Village")

Malaspina Inlet—Mal-a-*speena* Inlet

Mowachaht—*Mow*-a-chat

Nodales Channel—No-*dal*-es Channel

Okeover Arm—*Oak*-oh-ver Arm

Prideaux Haven—*Pri*-doh Haven

Redonda Islands—Re-*don*-da Islands

Roffey Island—*Rof*-ee Island

Sliammon—*Sly*-am-on

Teakerne Arm—*Tea*-kern Arm

Tenedos Bay—*Ten*-e-dos Bay

Theodosia—Theo-*dos*-ya

Thors Cove—pronounce the "h"

Thynne Island—Thin Island

Trevenen Bay—*Trev*-en-en Bay

Toquana—To-*kwa*-na

Tokenatch or Toquenatch—*To*-ke-natch

Tux'wnech—*Tuch*-wen-atch

xenoliths—*zee*-no-liths

Yuculta Rapids—*Yew*-ka-tah

BIBLIOGRAPHY

Andersen, Doris. *Evergreen Islands*. Sidney BC: Gray's Publishing, 1979.

Bancroft, J. Austen. *Geology of the Coast and Islands between the Strait of Georgia and Queen Charlotte Sound, B.C.* Geological Survey of Canada Memoir 23. Ottawa: Geological Survey of Canada, 1913.

Barkhouse, Joyce C. *George Dawson: The Little Giant*. Toronto: Clarke Irwin, 1974.

Blanchet, M. Wylie. *The Curve of Time*. Sidney BC: Gray's, 1977.

Bourne, N., and G.D. Heritage. "Pacific Oyster Breeding in Pendrell Sound, 1974." Technical Report No. 858. Nanaimo BC: Fisheries and Marine Service, 1979.

Bradley, Ken, and Karen Southern. *Powell River's Railway Era*. Victoria: British Columbia Railway Historical Association, 2000.

British Columbia Ministry of Water Land and Air. "Management Plan for Desolation Sound and Copeland Islands Marine Parks and Tux'wench Okeover Arm Provincial Park." November 2003 Draft; www.env.gov.bc.ca/bcparks/explore/parkpgs/okeover.html

Cameron, June. *Destination Cortez Island*. Surrey BC: Heritage, 1999.

Carey, Betty Lowman. *Bijaboji: North to Alaska by Oar*. Madeira Park BC: Harbour Publishing, 2004.

Coffey, Maria. *Sailing Back in Time: A Nostalgic Voyage on Canada's West Coast*. North Vancouver: Whitecap Books, 1996.

Cook, Warren L. *Flood Tide of Empire: Spain and the Pacific Northwest, 1543–1819*. New Haven CT: Yale University Press, 1973.

Cutter, Donald C. *Malaspina & Galiano: Spanish Voyages to the Northwest Coast, 1791 and 1792*. Vancouver: Douglas & McIntyre, 1991.

Daly, Edith Iglauer. "Capi Blanchet," in *Raincoast Chronicles 8*, ed. Howard White. Madeira Park BC: Harbour Publishing, 1983.

Dibbern, George. *Quest*. New York: W.W. Norton, 1941, and London: John Lane, 1941.

Downie, William. *Explorations in Jarvis Inlet, Desolation Sound, B.C., March 19, 1859*. London: Royal Geographical Society, 1861.

Drushka, Ken. *Against Wind and Weather: The History of Towboating in British Columbia*. Vancouver: Douglas & McIntyre, 1981.

———. *Working in the Woods: A History of Logging on the West Coast*. Madeira Park BC: Harbour Publishing, 1992

Duval, Brian, Kalidas Shetty and William H. Thomas. "Phenolic Compounds and Antioxidant Properties in the Snow Alga *Chlamydomonas nivalis* after Exposure to UV Light." *Journal of Applied Phycology*, vol. 11, no. 6 (December 1999), pp. 559–66.

Fisher, Robin. *Vancouver's Voyage: Charting the Northwest Coast*. Vancouver: Douglas & McIntyre, 1992.

Francis, Daniel, ed. *Encyclopedia of British Columbia*. Madeira Park BC: Harbour Publishing, 2000.

Gabrielse, Hubert and C.J. Yorath, eds. *Geology of the Cordilleran Orogen in Canada.* Ottawa: Geological Survey of Canada, 1992.

Gough, Barry M. *The Royal Navy and the Northwest Coast of North America, 1810–1914.* Vancouver: UBC Press, 1971.

———. *Gunboat Frontier: British Maritime Authority and Northwest Coast Indians, 1846–1890.* Vancouver: UBC Press, 1984.

Grundmann, Erika. *Dark Sun: Te Rapunga and the Quest of George Dibbern.* Auckland: David Ling Publishing, 2004.

Hadley, Michael. *God's Little Ships: A History of the Columbia Coast Mission.* Madeira Park BC: Harbour Publishing, 1995.

Higueras, Maria Dolores. *Northwest Coast of America: Iconographic Album of the Malaspina Expedition.* Madrid: Museo Naval, 1991.

Hill, Beth. *Indian Petroglyphs of the Pacific Northwest.* Saanichton BC: Hancock House, 1974.

———. *Upcoast Summers.* Ganges BC: Horsdal & Schubart, 1985.

———. *Seven-Knot Summers.* Victoria: Horsdal & Schubart, 1994.

Homfray, Robert. "A Winter Journey in 1861." *Canadian Frontier,* vol. 1, no. 1 (Summer 1972). Reprinted from *The Province,* December 22, 1894.

Kennedy, Dorothy, and Randy Bouchard. *Sliammon Life, Sliammon Lands.* Vancouver: Talonbooks, 1983.

Kennedy, Liv. *Coastal Villages.* Madeira Park BC: Harbour Publishing. 1991.

Lambert, Barbara Ann. *Chalkdust and Outhouses: West Coast Schools, 1893–1950.* Powell River BC: Barbara Ann Lambert, 2000.

Lange, Owen. *The Wind Came All Ways: A Quest to Understand the Winds, Waves and Weather in the Georgia Basin.* Victoria: Environment Canada, 1998.

Lillard, Charles, with Terry Glavin. *A Voice Great Within Us: The Story of Chinook.* Vancouver: New Star Books, 1998.

Manby, Thomas. *Journal of the Voyages of the HMS Discovery and Chatham.* Fairfield WA: Ye Galleon Press, 1992.

Menzies, Archibald. *Journal of Vancouver's Voyage, April to October, 1792.* Edited, with botanical and ethnological notes, by C.F. Newcombe and a biographical note by J. Forsyth. Victoria: Legislative Assembly, 1923; www.americanjourneys.org

Mobley, Carla. *Mysterious Powell Lake: A Collection of Historical Tales.* Surrey BC: Hancock, 1984.

Morgan, Murray C. *Puget's Sound: A Narrative of Early Tacoma and the Southern Sound.* Seattle: University of Washington Press, 1979; www2.tpl.lib.wa.us/v2/NWRoom/MORGAN/Puget.htm

Mudd-Ruth, Maria. *Rare Bird: Pursuing the Mystery of the Marbled Murrelet.* New York: Rodale, 2005.

Munday, Don. *The Unknown Mountain.* London: Hodder and Stoughton, 1948.

Nicolls, Nan. *North of Anian: The Collected Journals of "Gabrielle III" Cruises in BC Coastal Waters 1978–1989.* Vancouver: Dick Sandwell, 1990.

Quayle, D.B. "Pacific Oyster Culture in British Columbia." *Canadian Bulletin of Fisheries and Aquatic Sciences,* vol. 218 (1988).

Rubin, Dan. *Salt on the Wind: The Sailing Life of Allen and Sharie Farrell.* Victoria: Horsdal & Schubart, 1996.

Rushton, Gerald A. *Whistle Up the Inlet.* Vancouver: J.J. Douglas, 1974.

Sept, J. Duane. *The Beachcomber's Guide to Seashore Life in the Pacific Northwest.* Madeira Park BC: Harbour Publishing, 1999.

Spilsbury, Jim. *Spilsbury's Album: Photographs and Reminiscences of the BC Coast.* Madeira Park BC: Harbour Publishing, 1990.

Thompson, Bill. *Boats, Bucksaws and Blisters: Pioneer Tales of the Powell River Area.* Powell River BC: Powell River Heritage Association, 1990.

———. *Once Upon a Stump: Times and Tales of Powell River Pioneers.* Powell River BC: Powell River Heritage Research Association, 1993.

Twigg, Arthur M. *Union Steamships Remembered, 1920–1958.* Campbell River BC: A.M. Twigg, 1997.

Vancouver, George. *A Voyage of Discovery to the North Pacific Ocean and Round the World, 1791–1795.* 4 vols. Edited by W. Kaye Lamb. London: Hakluyt Society, 1984.

Wainwright, Jack. *Canoe Trips of British Columbia.* Delta BC: Summit, 1994.

Walbran, Capt. John T. *British Columbia Coast Names, 1592–1906.* Vancouver: J.J. Douglas, 1971.

White, Howard and Jim Spilsbury. *Spilsbury's Coast: Pioneer Years in the Wet West.* Madeira Park BC: Harbour Publishing, 1987.

———. *The Accidental Airline: Spilsbury's QCA.* Madeira Park BC: Harbour Publishing, 1988.

White, Stewart Edward. *Skookum Chuk.* Garden City NY: Doubleday, 1925.

Williams, Judith. *Dynamite Stories.* Vancouver: New Star Books, 2003.

———. *Clam Gardens: Aboriginal Mariculture on Canada's West Coast.* Vancouver: New Star Books, 2006.

Williams, Paul. *Apple Bay, or Life on the Planet.* New York: Warner, 1976.

Wolferstan, Bill. *Desolation Sound and the Discovery Islands: Pacific Yachting's Cruising Guide to British Columbia,* vol. 2. North Vancouver: Whitecap Books, 1997.

Yeadon-Jones, Anne and Laurence. *Desolation Sound and the Discovery Islands: A Dreamspeaker Cruising Guide,* vol. 2. Vancouver: Raincoast Books, 2000.

NOTES

1. George Vancouver, *A Voyage of Discovery to the North Pacific Ocean and Round the World, 1791–1795*, ed. W. Kaye Lamb (London: Hakluyt Society, 1984), p. 2:599.

2. Interview with Blake Fougere, Ministry of Forests, April 25, 2006.

3. Maria Mudd Ruth, *Rare Bird: Pursuing the Mystery of the Marbled Murrelet* (New York: Rodale, 2005), p. 267–273.

4. E-mail from Richard Blanchet, January 19, 2007.

5. Edith Iglauer Daly, "Capi Blanchet," in *Raincoast Chronicles 8*, ed. Howard White (Madeira Park BC: Harbour Publishing, 1983).

6. Beth Hill, *Upcoast Summers* (Ganges BC: Horsdal & Schubart, 1985), p. xv.

7. Interview with Murray Mitchell, August 24, 2000.

8. Interview with Chief Joe Mitchell, September 14, 1999.

9. Judith Williams, *Clam Gardens: Aboriginal Mariculture on Canada's West Coast* (Vancouver: New Star Books, 2006), p. 64.

10. Interview with Sue Pielle, September 20, 2000.

11. Dorothy Kennedy and Randy Bouchard, *Sliammon Life, Sliammon Lands* (Vancouver: Talonbooks, 1983), p. 119.

12. Wilson Duff, *The Indian History of BC* (Victoria: Provincial Museum of BC, 1964), p. 91.

13. E-mail from Michelle Washington, January 25, 2007.

14. Charles Lillard with Terry Glavin, *A Voice Great Within Us: The Story of Chinook* (Vancouver: New Star Books, 1998), pp. 44–45.

15. Interviews with Elsie Paul, September 22, 1997, and August 9, 2006.

16. Carla Mobley, *Mysterious Powell Lake: A Collection of Historical Tales* (Surrey BC: Hancock, 1984), p. 28.

17. Interviews with Elsie Paul, September 22, 1997, and August 9, 2006.

18. George Vancouver, *A Voyage of Discovery to the North Pacific Ocean and Round the World, 1791–1795*, 4 vols., ed. W. Kaye Lamb (London: Hakluyt Society, 1984).

19. Thomas Manby, *Journal of the Voyages of the H.M.S. Discovery and Chatham* (Fairfield WA: Ye Galleon Press, 1992).

20. Donald C. Cutter, *Malaspina and Galiano: Spanish Voyages to the Northwest Coast, 1791 and 1792* (Vancouver: Douglas & McIntyre, 1991).

21. Archibald Menzies, *Journal of Vancouver's Voyage, April to October, 1792*, ed., with botanical and ethnological notes, by C.F. Newcombe and a biographical note by J. Forsyth (Victoria: Legislative Assembly, 1923).

22. Maria Dolores Higueras, *Northwest Coast of America: Iconographic Album of the Malaspina Expedition* (Madrid: Museo Naval, 1991), p. 142.

23. Dorothy Kennedy and Randy Bouchard, *Sliammon Life, Sliammon Lands* (Vancouver: Talonbooks, 1983), p. 116.

24. William Downie, *Explorations in Jarvis Inlet, Desolation Sound, BC, March 19, 1859* (London: Royal Geographical Society, 1861).

25. Joyce C. Barkhouse, *George Dawson: The Little Giant* (Toronto: Clarke Irwin, 1974).

26. Robert Homfray, "A Winter Journey in 1861," *Canadian Frontier* vol. 1, no. 1 (Summer 1972), p. 21.

27. Capt. John T. Walbran, *British Columbia Coast Names, 1592–1906* (Vancouver: J.J. Douglas, 1971), p. 384.

28. Patrick Willet Brock, "Dossiers on Ships of the Royal Navy (Pacific Station), 1966," BC Archives MS 224. The *Sutlej* material is in box 2, file 2.

29. The website is ilmbwww.gov.bc.ca/bcnames/

30. There is a photo of the *Kate* on page 18 of "The Humpback Whales of Georgia Strait," *Journal of the Vancouver Aquarium*, vol. 8, 1985.

31. Interview with Ingrid Andersen Cowie, February 12, 1999.

32. Interview with Frank White, June 25, 2006.

33. Ken Drushka, *Against Wind and Weather: The History of Towboating in British Columbia* (Vancouver: Douglas & McIntyre, 1981), p. 44.

34. Ken Drushka, *Working in the Woods: A History of Logging on the West Coast* (Madeira Park BC: Harbour Publishing, 1992). On page 17, Drushka writes that the "first sizeable sawmill on the BC mainland [was] built in 1861."

35. Ibid., p. 17.

36. Bill Thompson, *Boats, Bucksaws and Blisters* (Powell River: Powell River Heritage Research Association, 1990), p. 367.

37. Interview with Maria Christensen Zaikow, June 6, 2006. This is what her father did when he didn't have one of the kids on the other end of the saw.

38. Ibid.

39. Gerald A. Rushton, *Whistle Up the Inlet* (Vancouver: J.J. Douglas, 1974).

40. Interview with Frank White, June 25, 2006.

41. Michael Hadley, *God's Little Ships: A History of the Columbia Coast Mission* (Madeira Park BC: Harbour Publishing, 1995), p. 8.

42. Ibid., p. 24.

43. Interview with Howard White, June 28, 2006.

44. Howard White and Jim Spilsbury, *Spilsbury's Coast: Pioneer Years in the Wet West* (Madeira Park BC: Harbour Publishing, 1987), and Jim Spilsbury, *Spilsbury's Album: Photographs and Reminiscences of the BC Coast* (Madeira Park BC: Harbour Publishing, 1990).

45. Stewart Edward White, *Skookum Chuk* (Garden City NY: Doubleday, 1925), pp 181–212.

46. M. Wylie Blanchet, *The Curve of Time* (Sidney BC: Gray's, 1977), pp. 60–61.

47. The Canadian census of 1911 states that he immigrated in 1884 and became a naturalized citizen in 1910.

48. Interview with Ingrid Andersen Cowie, March 4, 2003.

49. Beth Hill, *Upcoast Summers* (Ganges BC: Horsdal & Schubart, 1985), p. 49.

50. Interview with Maria Christensen Zaikow, August 8, 2006.

51. The movie is now held by the Campbell River Archives.

52. Hill, *Upcoast Summers*, p. 49.

53. Easy to repair, the Easthope engine came in one to four cycles and powered boats all over the coast in the first half of the twentieth century. Its distinctive slow *ka-thunk, ka-thunk* sound was a symbol of its reliability.

54. Bill Wolferstan, *Desolation Sound and the Discovery Islands: Pacific Yachting's Cruising Guide to British Columbia*, Vol. II (North Vancouver: Whitecap Books, 1997), p. 67.

55. Judith Williams, *Dynamite Stories* (Vancouver: New Star Books, 2003), p. 21.

56. Telephone interviews with Bonny McGuffie and Lorraine Jamieson, November 10, 2006.

57. Williams, *Dynamite Stories*, p. 48.

58. Ibid., p. 55.

59. None of these surnames are in the Crown grants registry.

60. Interview with Norm Gibbons, September 3, 2006.

61. Doris Andersen, *Evergreen Islands* (Sidney BC: Gray's Publishing, 1979), pp. 121–22.

62. Ibid., p. 122.

63. Interviews with Maria Christensen Zaikow, March 3 and 21, 2003; June 5, 2003; June 6, 2006; July 26, 2006; and August 8, 2006.

64. Interview with Norm Gibbons, September 3, 2006.

65. Howard White and Jim Spilsbury, *The Accidental Airline: Spilsbury's QCA* (Madeira Park BC: Harbour Publishing, 1988), pp. 43–44.

66. Howard White and Jim Spilsbury, *Spilsbury's Coast: Pioneer Years in the Wet West* (Madeira Park BC: Harbour Publishing, 1987), p. 189.

67. Williams, *Dynamite Stories*, p. 13.

68. Ripple Rock was an undersea mountain that jutted up to within three metres (ten feet) of the surface of Seymour Narrows at low tide. It damaged or sank over a hundred ships and killed more than a hundred people between the mid-1800s and 1958, when it was blown apart by the largest non-nuclear peacetime explosion.

69. Interview with Bud Jarvis, September 3, 2006.

70. Interview with Joyce Parker Mostat, June 21, 2006.

71. Interview with Norm and Denise Gibbons, September 3, 2006.

72. Williams, *Dynamite Stories*, pp. 47–52.

73. Interview with Barb Bloom, July 28, 2006.

74. E-mails from John Dixon, November 12 and 17, 2006.

75. Much of the material in this section is from Thomas Manson's unpublished "History of Redonda Bay 1835–1975." The manuscript is in the BC Archives in Victoria.

76. Andersen, *Evergreen Islands*, pp. 99, 142.

77. E-mail from Betsy Waddington, May 31, 2006.

78. J. Austin Bancroft, *Geology of the Coast and Islands between the Strait of Georgia and Queen Charlotte Sound, BC*, Geological Survey of Canada Memoir 23 (Ottawa: Geological Survey of Canada, 1913).

79. Andersen, *Evergreen Islands*, p. 121. According to MINFILE (http://www.em.gov.bc.ca/Mining/Geolsurv/Minfile/search/), the BC government database that

records all mines and mineral occurrences, there was a limestone quarry on the north end of Redonda that produced 24,126 tonnes of limestone from 1920 to 1924.

80. Andersen, *Evergreen Islands*, p. 124.

81. Ibid., p. 122.

82. Interviews with Elsie Paul, September 22, 1997, and August 9, 2006.

83. Andersen, *Evergreen Islands*, p. 126.

84. Interviews with Maria Christensen Zaikow, March 3 and 21, 2003; June 5, 2003; June 6, 2006; July 26, 2006; and August 8, 2006.

85. The birth of the Dionne quintuplets—Annette, Emilie, Yvonne, Cecile and Marie—was a memorable event for Desolation Sound residents. The five girls were born in Corbeil, Ontario, on May 28, 1934, at a time when multiple births were almost unheard of, and the infants rarely survived. The Dionnes were the only known living quintuplets in the world. The Ontario government passed the Dionne Quintuplets Guardianship Act to protect the girls and "ensure their advancement, education and welfare." Unfortunately, the government took them away from their parents, who had seven other children, and raised them in a special nursery called Quintland, where they were put on display to the paying public through a one-way glass. They became the biggest tourist attraction in the country. Three million people saw them before they were returned to their parents nine years later.

86. Interview with Ingrid Andersen Cowie, March 4, 2003. Ingrid Cowie remembered the one-armed man from the year she taught at the Galley Bay School (1933–34).

87. N. Bourne and G.D. Heritage, "Pacific Oyster Breeding in Pendrell Sound, 1974," Technical Report No. 858 (Nanaimo BC: Fisheries and Marine Service, 1979), pp. 1, 4.

88. Interview with Helen Hanson Anderson, August 5, 1999.

89. Ibid., July 5, 1999.

90. Interview with Rita Heatley Searle, September 16, 2006.

91. *Powell River News*, March 20, 1930.

92. On March 1, 1932, the son of famous aviator Charles Lindbergh was abducted from the Lindberghs' New Jersey home between 9 and 10 p.m. The kidnappers left a ransom note demanding $50,000 (an amount that was later doubled). The abduction caused a media frenzy, which intensified when the murdered child's remains were found on May 12, 1932. Bruno Richard Hauptmann was convicted of the crime and executed in 1936. (It was this crime that caused the US Congress to make kidnapping a federal criminal offence.) Many people I interviewed mentioned this event and used it to date things that happened to them.

93. Interviews with Rita Heatley Searle, September 16, 2006, and January 13, 2007.

94. Howard White and Jim Spilsbury, *Spilsbury's Coast: Pioneer Years in the Wet West* (Madeira Park BC: Harbour Publishing, 1987), p. 51.

95. E-mail from Ron Mangan, October 10, 2006, and article in the *Powell River Town Crier*, September 30, 1991.

96. The property is advertised online at www.niho.com/forsale/detail1.asp?prop=75

97. Interview with Bud Jarvis, September 3, 2006.

98. Interview with Maria Christensen Zaikow, July 28, 2006.

99. Interviews with Ingrid Andersen Cowie, April 25, 2006, and August 8, 2006.

100. M. Wylie Blanchet, *The Curve of Time* (Sidney BC: Gray's, 1977), p. 150.

101. Interview with Maria Christensen Zaikow, June 6, 2006.

102. Don Munday, *The Unknown Mountain* (London: Hodder and Stoughton, 1948), p. 184.

103. Brian Duval, Kalidas Shetty and William H. Thomas, "Phenolic Compounds and Antioxidant Properties in the Snow Alga *Chlamydomonas nivalis* after Exposure to UV Light," *Journal of Applied Phycology*, vol. 11, no. 6 (December 1999), pp. 559–66.

104. The same story appears in Beth Hill's *Seven-Knot Summers* (Victoria: Horsdal & Schubart, 1994), pp. 156–57, but I have written my version as Bud told it to me in September 2006. I have heard him perform the same story several times in the twenty years I have known him.

105. June Cameron, *Destination Cortez Island* (Surrey BC: Heritage House, 1999), p. 180.

106. Telephone interviews with Hans Rosenbloom, October 24, 2006, and January 25, 2007.

107. Telephone interview with Brenda King Finch, August 3, 2006.

108. E-mails from John Dixon, November 12 and 17, 2006.

109. Dorothy Kennedy and Randy Bouchard, *Sliammon Life, Sliammon Lands* (Vancouver: Talonbooks, 1983), p. 157.

110. New Westminster Land District early records up to Lot 2500, seen at BC Archives, August 2006.

111. Ken Drushka, *Working in the Woods: A History of Logging on the West Coast* (Madeira Park BC: Harbour Publishing, 1992), p. 186.

112. Jim Spilsbury, *Spilsbury's Album: Photographs and Reminiscences of the BC Coast* (Madeira Park BC: Harbour Publishing, 1990), p. 49, and Howard White and Jim Spilsbury, *Spilsbury's Coast: Pioneer Years in the Wet West* (Madeira Park BC: Harbour Publishing, 1987), pp. 49–54.

113. Interview with Rod Tysdale, January 5, 2007.

114. Williams, *Dynamite Stories*, p. 12.

115. Telephone interview with Hans Rosenbloom, October 24, 2006.

116. Telephone interview with Gerald Blaney, October 26, 2006.

117. Howard White and Jim Spilsbury, *Spilsbury's Coast: Pioneer Years in the Wet West* (Madeira Park BC: Harbour Publishing, 1987), p. 51.

118. There's a 1918 picture of Copeland with Louis Anderson, Irene Palmer's husband, on page 32 of *Coastal Villages* (Madeira Park BC: Harbour Publishing, 1991).

119. This record is available online through Library and Archives Canada's ArchiviaNet (www.collectionscanada.ca/archivianet/1911/index-e.html). It is in the Census of Canada 1911 database, Reference RG31, Statistics Canada Microfilm Reel Number T-20333, under British Columbia, District 8 (Comox–Atlin), Sub-district 16 (Comox: Malaspina Inlet, Humphrey Channel, Lund, Sliammon). James H. Copland is on line 27 of the second page of pdf files.

120. Telephone interview with Brenda King Finch, August 3, 2006.

121. Interview with Ingrid Andersen Cowie, August 8, 2006.

122. Interview with Bob and Rita De Pape, September 15, 2006.

123. Interview with Elsie Paul, August 9, 2006. Aboriginal children sent to residential school in Sechelt were forbidden to speak their native languages and forced to speak English. They were given a strictly European education and discouraged from learning traditional skills like clam digging.

124. Interviews with Pat Hanson, March 11, 2003, and June 20, 2006.

125. Ed Hanson, interview on tape. His daughter Pat, who has the tape, said this was part of the CBC's *Voice of the Pioneer* series.

126. Interview with Helen Anderson for the "Powell River People" column in the *Powell River News*, August 15, 1999.

127. Ed Hanson, interview on tape., courtesy Pat Hanson

128. Barbara Ann Lambert, *Chalkdust and Outhouses: West Coast Schools, 1893–1950* (Powell River BC: Barbara Ann Lambert, 2000), p. 244.

129. Ibid., p. 35.

130. Interview with Ingrid Andersen Cowie, February 12, 1999.

131. Interview with Ingrid Andersen Cowie, March 4, 2003.

132. Erika Grundmann, *Dark Sun: Te Rapunga and the Quest of George Dibbern* (Auckland: David Ling Publishing, 2004).

133. This is the figure mentioned in Dibbern's October 1938 letter to his daughter Frauke, quoted in Grundmann, *Dark Sun*, p. 488n43. A figure of $548 is quoted in two other books: Dan Rubin, *Salt on the Wind* (Victoria: Horsdal & Schubart, 1996), p. 13, and Maria Coffey, *Sailing Back in Time* (North Vancouver: Whitecap Books, 1996), p. 139. And Grundmann, on page 231 of *Dark Sun*, quotes a letter George sent to his mother-in-law dated October 23, 1938 (the letter to Frauke gives no specific date in October 1938), in which he says he and Eileen bought the property for $600. Dibbern was notoriously cavalier about money, cadging it off everyone and treating Eileen's and Gladys's money as his own. The larger amount may have included an additional parcel of land being considered at that time.

134. Grundmann, *Dark Sun*, photo before p. 225.

135. Interview with Barb Bloom, July 28, 2006.

136. Interview with Joan Treen, October 26, 2006.

137. Paul Williams, *Apple Bay, or Life on the Planet* (New York: Warner, 1976).

138. Interviews with Moyra Palm, March 2003, June 12, 2006, and September 14, 2006.

139. Ken Drushka, *Working in the Woods: A History of Logging on the West Coast* (Madeira Park BC: Harbour Publishing, 1992), p. 17.

140. Interview with Ingrid Andersen Cowie, March 4, 2003.

141. Bessie Banham, "Came to Lund before the turn of the century," *Powell River News*, March 9, 1955.

142. Interview with Eleanor Lusk Anderson, March 13, 2003.

143. Interview with Charlie Fletcher, March 6, 2003.

144. Ken Bradley and Karen Southern, *Powell River's Railway Era* (Victoria: British Columbia Railway Historical Association, 2000), p. 101.

145. Interview with Frank White, June 25, 2006.

146. Bill Thompson, *Boats, Bucksaws and Blisters* (Powell River BC: Powell River Heritage Association, 1990), p. 396.

147. Bill Thompson, *Once Upon a Stump* (Powell River BC: Powell River Heritage Research Association, 1993), p. 47.

148. Interview with Mary Bishop Gussman, July 10, 2006.

149. Interviews with Joyce Parker Mostat, June 21, 2006, and July 12, 2006.

150. Interview with Bud Jarvis, September 2–4, 2006.

151. Telephone interview with Karen Gordon, November 20, 2006.

152. Telephone interview with Wolfgang Goudriaan, October 17, 2006.

153. Interview with Roger Thorne, October 25, 2006.

154. Interviews with Ingrid Andersen Cowie, February 12, 1999; March 4, 2003; April 25, 2006; and August 8, 2006.

155. Mrs. A.W. Jones, Theodosia Arm, British Columbia, correspondence regarding a complaint of ill-treatment of her husband by police at Powell River, National Archives of Canada, volume 323, file no. 1928-1646, finding aid no. 13-2 (former archival reference no. RG13-A-2).

156. Bill Thompson, *Once Upon a Stump* (Powell River BC: Powell River Heritage Research Association, 1993), p. 82.

157. Telephone interview with Derek Poole, October 19, 2006.

158. Interview with Roger Thorne, October 25, 2006.

159. Bill Thompson, *Once Upon a Stump* (Powell River BC: Powell River Heritage Research Association, 1993), pp. 22, 78.

160. Liv Kennedy, *Coastal Villages* (Madeira Park BC: Harbour Publishing, 1991), p. 33.

161. Interview with Sheldon Ahola, August 8, 2006.

162. Thompson, *Once Upon a Stump*, p. 31.

163. Ibid., p. 22.

164. "Ancestor uncle triggers reunion," *Powell River Peak*, July 26, 2006, p. 12. There are two accounts of what happened that terrible day. One is the report of the inquest held in December 1921 (supplied by e-mail, January 17, 2007, by Raffaele's nephew, Frank D'Angio); the other is an interview with John D'Angio that local historian Bill Thompson conducted in November 1990 (Thompson, *Once Upon a Stump*, pp. 21–22). In combining the two accounts, I have given preference to facts reported at the inquest.

165. Thompson, *Once Upon a Stump*, p. 28.

166. Ken Drushka, *Against Wind and Weather: The History of Towboating in British Columbia* (Vancouver: Douglas & McIntyre, 1981), pp. 66–67.

167. Telephone interview with Doris Cummings, granddaughter of John and Devina, September 21, 2006.

168. Barbara Ann Lambert, *Chalkdust and Outhouses: West Coast Schools, 1893–1950* (Powell River BC: Barbara Ann Lambert, 2000), p. 60. It's not clear who owned the lot, and that question cannot be answered until the Land Titles Office makes its historical files freely available to the public.

169. Thompson, *Once Upon a Stump*, p. 30.

170. Interview with Ingrid Andersen Cowie, March 4, 2003.

171. Thompson, *Once Upon a Stump*, p. 278.

172. Bill Thompson, *Boats, Bucksaws and Blisters* (Powell River BC: Powell River Heritage Association, 1990), p. 401.

173. Interview with Irene Rattenbury Apps, June 19, 2006.

174. Thompson, *Boats, Bucksaws and Blisters*, pp. 399–404.

175. Interview with Sheldon Ahola, August 8, 2006.

176. Thompson, *Once Upon a Stump*, p. 28.

177. Interview with John D'Angio, Jr., July 1993.

178. Interview with Mary Boylan, June 9, 1997.

179. Telephone interview with Daniel Hanson, June 20, 2006.

180. Interviews with Pat Hanson, March 11, 2003, and June 20, 2006.

181. Telephone interview with Karen Gordon, November 20, 2006.

182. Interview with Jody Fastabend, October 19, 2006. This lot was originally granted to Alice Violet Bloom and William Bloom (no relation to the Galley Bay Blooms). William may be the "Billy Bloom" whose photograph appears on page 47 of Bill Thompson's *Once Upon a Stump* (Powell River BC: Powell River Heritage Research Association, 1993). The photo was taken in 1938 at the end of one of the spur railroads of the Merrill-Ring logging operation up Theodosia Inlet.

183. Telephone interview with Arlene Carsten, January 24, 2007.

184. See their website at www.bcseakayak.com

185. Telephone interview with Jürgen Köppen, January 24, 2007. His website is at www.cedar-strip.com

186. E-mail from Barbara Plourde, January 24, 2007.

187. Telephone interview with Denise Reinhardt, October 25, 2006.

188. Telephone interview with Jane Cameron, September 11, 2006.

189. D.B. Quayle, "Pacific Oyster Culture in British Columbia," *Canadian Bulletin of Fisheries and Aquatic Science*, 218 (1988), p. 241.

190. Duane Sept, *The Beachcomber's Guide to Seashore Life of the Pacific Northwest* (Madeira Park BC: Harbour Publishing, 1999), p. 71.

191. E-mail from Glen Calvert, October 22, 2006.

192. Interview with Norm and Denise Gibbons, September 3, 2006.

193. E-mail from Susan Canning, October 22, 2006.

194. Bob Paquin, in an interview on January 16, 2007, said the type of scallop grown is a hybrid Japanese scallop, *Patinopecten yessoensis*.

195. Telephone interview with Ray Pillman, January 23, 2007.

196. Interview with Roger Thorne, October 25, 2006.

197. Beth Hill, *Upcoast Summers* (Ganges BC: Horsdal & Schubart, 1985); *Seven-Knot Summers* (Victoria: Horsdal & Schubart, 1994); *Indian Petroglyphs of the Pacific Northwest* (Saanichton BC: Hancock House, 1974).

198. Bill Wolferstan, *Desolation Sound and the Discovery Islands: Pacific Yachting's Cruising Guide to British Columbia*, vol. II (North Vancouver: Whitecap Books, 1997).

199. Anne and Laurence Yeadon-Jones, *Desolation Sound and the Discovery Islands: A Dreamspeaker Cruising Guide*, Vol. 2 (Madeira Park BC: Harbour Publishing, 2006).

200. Interview with Karen Rossman Davidson, around September 29, 2006.

201. Interview with Jock Ferrie, historian for the Royal Vancouver Yacht Club, June 27, 2006.

202. Nan Nicolls, *North of Anian: The Collected Journals of "Gabrielle III" Cruises in BC Coastal Waters 1978–1989* (Vancouver: Dick Sandwell, Publisher, 1990), p. 228.

203. Luke Brocki, "Micro cruisers sail the Sound," *Powell River Peak*, September 13, 2006, p. 26.

204. Interview with Marge McLeod, August 2006.

205. Interview with John Treen, June 2006.

206. A list of the participating cadets was enclosed in a watertight container and placed in a stone cairn erected on top of Kinghorn Island.

207. Paula Brook, "Seaside Sojourn Improves Lake View," *Vancouver Sun*, September 11, 2004, p. D2.

208. Betty Lowman Carey, *Bijaboji: North to Alaska by Oar* (Madeira Park BC: Harbour Publishing, 2004).

209. Telephone interview with Dinty Moore, October 18, 2006.

210. Telephone interview with Garry Hubbard, October 18, 2006.

211. Jack Wainwright, *Canoe Trips of British Columbia* (Delta BC: Summit, 1994), p. 209.

212. Alan Morley, "Prideaux Haven—A Hermit's Paradise," *Vancouver Sun*, May 11, 1966.

213. Telephone interview with Derek Poole, October 19, 2006.

214. Desolation Sound Marine Park Proposal, Victoria B.C.: Parks Branch, Department of Recreation and Conservation, [1973?]

215. Telephone interview with Hugh Ackroyd, BC Parks, October 18, 2006.

216. E-mail from Mel Turner, BC Parks, October 20, 2006.

217. Telephone interview with Derek Poole, October 19, 2006.

218. Interview with Blake Fougere, April 25, 2006.

INDEX

Disabled Sports
  Northwest, 219–220
Discovery, HMS, 28,
  30–31
Discovery Channel, 12
Dixon, John, 77, 116
Dogwood Canoe Club,
  217
dolphins, Pacific white-
  sided, 6
Donley Trading
  Company, 69
Donley, Robert, 69–**70**
Douglas, James, 34–35
douglas fir, 5, 28, 44
Douglass Whaling
  Company, 43
Downie, William, 35
draft dodgers, 111, 120,
  128, 141–142
Dreamspeaker, 212
Durieu System, 24
Dusty, **174**, 175
Dynamite Stories, 77

earthquake, 83
East Redonda Island, 5,
  18, 22, 99–106
Easthope engine, 67, 75,
  136
Easthope, Peck, 67
Edith Island, 228
Edward Point, 38
Elephant, 100
Ellingsen, 84
Ellingsen, Elmer, 137
Elsie mineral claim, 80
Emery, Bill, 103
Eveleigh Island, 23, 38

Farrell, Sharie and Allen,
  140
Ferguson, Ken, 77
Fidler, George and
  Jeannine, 166
Finch, Bill and Brenda,
  124–**127**

fire
  Atwood Bay, 120
  Barrow, 11
  Bishop, 157
  Black Lake, 49
  Chambers, 188–189
  Christensen, 86
  Heatley, 101
  Hope, 76
  Roos, 178, 183
fishing, **17**, 63, 95, **97**,
  179–181, 204
Five BR, 54
Flea Village, 23, **33**, 66
Fletcher, Betty and Bob,
  167
Fletcher, Charlie Fletcher,
  128, 152–153
Fletcher, Fred, **151**, 152
Fletcher, Nellie, **151**, 152
Flume, 90–**93**, 184, 226
Flying Bathtub, 136
Forbes Bay, 101, 107–108,
  117, 120–121, 131
Forward, HMS, 35
Franke, Helmut, 195
Franke, Walter, 167–168
Fraser R. Tannery Ltd.,
  117
Freke Anchorage, 25, 156,
  205
froe, 88
Frolander post office, 146
French, GH, 98

Gabrielle II, 214
Galiano, Dionisio Alcala
  (Capt), 9, 21, 27–31
Galley Bay, **82**–83,
  100–103, 124–125,
  130–**134**–**135**–143.
  See also schools, Galley
  Bay
Gaudet, Judy, 121
Gibbons, Norm and
  Denise, 75–78, 206
Gifford Peninsula, 224
Giroday Sawmills, 83
glaciers, 4–5, 16
Glenhome, 112

goats, 60, 62–63, 90, 92,
  108, 111, 159–160,
  166, 191
Goetz, Dr. Lance, 219
gold, 35–37, 194
Gordon, Karen, 194–195
Gorge Harbour, 137, 204
Gorman, Mary, 124
Goudriaan, Wolfgang and
  Jill, 168
Grace Harbour, 20, 156,
  213
Grappler, HMS, 35
Graveyard (Copplestone)
  Island, 90
Greene, Alan and Heber,
  Rev., 53, 150, 159, 165
Greene, Oscar, 167
Greta, 168
Gussman, Bill, 161
Gussman, Mary Bishop,
  157–158
Gustafson, Frank, 184–
  186
gyppo loggers, 45, 204

Hadley, Constable, 185
Hadley, Michael, 53
Haida First Nation, 20,
  23, 35
handlogging licences, 12,
  44, 150
Hansen, Tiny, 206
Hanson Logging
  Company, 131
Hanson, Amanda, 130–
  132–134, 194
Hanson, Axel, 47, 130–
  132–134
Hanson, Bill, 131–133
Hanson, Corinne, **160**
Hanson, Dot, **160**
Hanson, Daniel, 205
Hanson, Ed, 148, 153,
  160, 194
Hanson, Helen. *See*
  Anderson, Helen
Hanson, Kay, 135
Hanson, Ragnar, 130,
  139, 160–161